Step-By

STEP-PARENTING

Step-By
STEP-PARENTING

JAMES D. ECKLER

BETTERWAY BOOKS
CINCINNATI, OHIO

98   97   96   6   5

Library of Congress Cataloging-in-Publication Data

Eckler, James D.
    Step-by step-parenting : a guide to successful living with a blended
family / James D. Eckler.—2nd ed.
        p.   cm.
    Includes index.
    ISBN 1-55870-294-6
    1. Stepparents—United States—Life skills guides. I. Title.
HQ759.92.E25   1993
306.874—dc20   92-37944
                                                                    CIP

To my family, with love

Contents

CHAPTER 1

The Initial Shock

Surviving the initial shock of the stepfamily can be one of the major steps toward a stepparent's overall survival. A stepparent's entry into a new stepfamily unit may turn out to be one of life's most terrifying experiences. Stepparents everywhere ask the same questions. "Will it ever get any better?" "Am I the only one going through this type of conflict?" While there are no guarantees the situation will improve after the initial shock has subsided, people usually do learn to adjust to their new circumstances.

Statistics tell us that any adult who reads this is a stepparent, is considering the idea, or has a close friend or relative who is a stepparent. If you are not already "one of the above," the odds are you will be sometime during your lifetime.

YOU ARE NOT ALONE

Recent data from the National Center for Health Statistics show a marriage rate of 9.7 per 1,000 and a divorce rate of 4.8 per 1,000; i.e., one of two marriages fails.

Stepfamilies, also referred to as blended families, bi-nuclear families, and reconstituted families, are formed whenever parents remarry. This is a worldwide phenomenon, but it is most common in the United States. Each year approximately 1.5 million people in the United States remarry. Most bring children to the new marriage. 90% of divorced women with children remarry, and studies reveal that more divorced men remarry than divorced women.

Almost 40% of all children born in America today will end up in a stepfamily before they reach the age of 18. There are more than 35 million stepparents in the United States. According to Ann Landers, when a second marriage breaks up it usually is caused by the children.

THE UNEXPECTED

One of the most difficult barriers for the stepparent to overcome is that relationship adjustments have to be made immediately. "Instant parenthood," without the preparation time of a pregnancy. Instead, the step-mother—or stepfather—is greeted by one or all of the following; a rebellious teenage daughter, a defiant ten-year-old son, a spoiled preschooler. Her new husband—or his new wife—expects the new spouse to be a miracle worker who is going to bring instant love and harmony to this new blended family. When this "miracle" does not take place, some second marriages disintegrate very quickly.

DISILLUSIONMENT

Tina Cranford was working on an advertising assignment when she met, and fell in love with Paul Baker. His three children included Angie 5, Tim 7, and Paul, Jr. 11. "I think our first date consisted of lunch and the afternoon in the park," recalled Tina. "Angie was determined to call me by the name of Paul's old girlfriend all afternoon. Well yes, she's only five, but if you think I'm buying that, you're crazy."

It took Tina three years to agree to marriage, mainly because of concern for the children. "I was pretty young then, twenty-four to be exact, to take on those kids. Even though the relationship between their father and me had gone on for three years, the kids were old enough to resent me. The anger and resentment which came from the boys was not all aimed at me, but it was for what had happened to them. Their parents had divorced and their home and stability had been destroyed. They knew what they had lost."

Tina continued, "I always had positive expectations, and tried to create a story-book atmosphere about how nice it was for all of us. But the fact was, it wasn't nice at all for the kids. Their mother had visitation privileges and if she wasn't too busy she would keep her appointments. And their father traveled two days a week for his work and they missed him when he was away. I thought before the marriage how much better it would be for them to be with me instead of the house-keeper, but to them it didn't matter one way or the other."

While a stepmother may see herself entering the home as a Florence Nightingale, to create happiness and a new life for her husband and his children, the children may see a different picture. They see her as a reminder of the family that had been destroyed.

A stepmother brings out the hurt that has been hidden deep within; the death of a mother or the fact that the father does not live with them anymore. The child's hopes have endured that someday the original family would be restored, but the new marriage ended that dream.

No matter what the age of the child, three, thirteen, or thirty, some form of resistance is almost inevitable. It can range from coolness of attitude to vulgarity; from drinking and getting involved with drugs to running away ... even destroying the family auto. Whatever it is, the strains on the new marriage can be so intense only the strong will survive.

THE BARRICADE OF MYTHS

Stepparents entering a new marriage crash immediately into two very tangible myths that will immediately threaten the success of a new stepfamily. A realistic understanding of how these myths can work against a marriage will better prepare the stepparent for the difficult experiences that may lie ahead.

The Wicked Stepmother Myth

People almost instinctively associate the word "stepmother" with the word "wicked." The myth of the wicked stepmother is as old as Cinderella and as threatening as the tale of Snow White. You may recall her stepmother tries to play out the fantasy by poisoning her husband's daughter.

A stepmother from Indiana said, "It's not only your stepchildren who try to convince themselves you're a mean and wicked person, it's their friends and their friends' parents too. One mother said to me, 'So you're Julie's new stepmother!' The tone in her voice was like ice and you'd think I was standing over a batch of witch's brew. I could understand a child's immature way of thinking, but not an adult's."

Literature has given stepfathers equally harsh treatment. Can there have been a more wicked stepfather than the one who treated David Copperfield so badly? Most children grow up aware of these stories. They know what happened to the youngsters involved. Because of this, many children will distrust and even fear stepparents without giving them a chance to show their real love and concern.

It's nearly impossible to build a good relationship when fear poisons its foundation. Many of a child's actions are nothing more than responses to their fears. The stepchild is likely to approach his or her new stepparent with the attitude, "I'm gonna get you before you get me." Of course this is simply a defense developed by the child to protect against the "expected."

A loving stepchild-to-stepparent relationship takes a long time to develop. Some children never do learn that their stepparent is really very much like their natural parent. Many times the battle is over before they learn that truth. The marriage is destroyed and the stepparent is gone. He or she never had a chance.

The Myth of Instant Love

Some starry-eyed romanticists may disagree, but there is no such thing as love at first sight. A person may be overwhelmingly attracted to another, but real love develops only as the relationship matures. The myth of instant love places unreal expectations on all members of the stepfamily.

Twenty-seven-year-old Jessica has never been married. She is now planning to enter into a stepfamily with fiance Scott and his two teenage daughters. Scott has told her he loves her very much, which is true. However, he has also told her how excited his girls are to have her as their new stepmother. His dreams are one big happy family and he's trying to convince Jessica how nice it all is going to be.

Jessica enters the family with mixed feelings. Having heard about the children, she cannot help but wonder how they will get along. Scott is not helping matters by making promises which are beyond his ability to keep.

The children also are expected to be waiting at the chapel with open arms. Instead, they see the upcoming marriage as presenting them with another adult with whom they must share their dad. And they realize any hopes of a reconciliation for the original family have been dashed. An adult cannot expect a child to be optimistic and loving when the child sees her world ending.

Love cannot be forced. If stepfamily members are pressured to "instantly love" the new mother or father, they miss the opportunity to relax, to see if they can develop a more relaxed liking for one another. Experts agree that it takes from three to five years for the new family members to work through the obstacles they are likely to face in developing good and positive feelings. These barriers must come down before a loving relationship can be created.

THE HONEYMOON SURPRISE

The reservations were made and the plans completed. "The night before the wedding, Betty's three-year-old daughter came down with strep throat," Jim said. "Betty's mother laid a guilt trip on us when she said, 'a sick child needs to be with its mother.' What else could I do but say that we'd take our honeymoon another time?"

Jim's story is not all that unusual for a stepparent. The conditions surrounding a second marriage are much different from a traditional first marriage and honeymoon. Now, in addition to the bride and groom to consider, there are two, three ... maybe even more.

Ellen's honeymoon plans were shattered when Timothy showed up. "My aunt was going to keep Timothy, Sid's six-year-old. Instead, she was hospitalized the morning of our wedding and it was too late to make other arrangements." Ellen complained, "We had no other choice but to take him along. Can you imagine the embarrassment when the three of us checked into the honeymoon suite of the hotel?"

In groups where this topic has been discussed the question most often asked was, "How did you stand it?" A twenty-two-year-old, married for the first time said it all. "Grit your teeth and bear it." Those who experienced it were apt to say, "What's the alternative? You either go and take the kid along or postpone the honeymoon with the possibility of it being cancelled altogether." Even if a third party is forced to come along, make the adjustments and get the best out of it.

An understanding attitude at such an important time will help lay a strong foundation for the marriage. The spouse is likely to be just as upset about the situation. In addition, he or she is carrying the guilt that the trip was ruined because of his or her child. A display of support at a time like this will let your mate know you'll be there when the going gets rough. If you refuse to cooperate and understand during one crisis, your spouse will wonder how you will react to the next one.

"Being a stepparent you have to learn to make the best of it a lot of time," said Sharon. "But it's worth it later. It took us six years and now we feel that we've finally made it."

LACK OF PRIVACY

Then come the frequent invasions of privacy. Even if the stepchildren show up only on visits, these visits can easily come at the wrong time. One couple planned for a pre-vacation. They wanted some restful time alone before his boys arrived for the summer. "Just a few days before leaving, the bad news came that one of the boys, the only one of the four I can't stand," said the stepmother, "would get out of school ahead of the others. Bob said, 'Let's take him with us, he'll be so lonely sitting around the house all by himself.' I was furious but finally gave in. There's no way to explain what our pre-vacation turned into. I would not do it again."

"When we married," said Donna (who had married a widower about a year after his wife's death) "we had the youngest son, Gregory, in bed with us for the first six months. He couldn't sleep. He thought monsters were invading his room. The next oldest, James, wandered through the house in his sleep. And the girl, who was ten, had to wear protective pads to bed because of frequent wetting. And, wouldn't you know it, as soon as she stopped wetting the bed, her monthly cycle started."

BEYOND THE BEDROOM

The deprivation of privacy for the stepparent extends beyond the bedroom. Most men and women gradually become accustomed to parental inconveniences, but the impact on freedom of movement begins instantly for the couple with children; for example, when a spontaneous decision to go out forces them to begin an urgent search for a sitter.

"I didn't realize how nice it was," recalled Jackie. "On the spur of the moment we could change our plans and go out for a meal or movie instead of staying in. Now it's a major ordeal trying to locate someone at the last minute. It wasn't like that before we married. Ken's housekeeper was always willing to stay over with the kids. Her services were terminated the day after the wedding. Ken said we wouldn't need her now that I was here and we could use the money."

Jackie shares this particular problem with many other stepparents. Her uncomfortable circumstances are not all the fault of the children.

Her husband has dumped responsibility on her and has failed to assume his share of the load. Her frustration at the inconvenience and unfairness causes resentment to build up against the stepchildren. All she understands is that it wasn't like this before.

Toddlers also can create havoc with a stepparent's privacy by destroying personal items. As a toddler moves into the family's territory, shelves, tables, and other reachable surfaces must be cleared of all adult possessions. "I never had to move these things for my nieces and nephews, but now it's either keep them out of reach or have them destroyed."

Relaxed phone conversations become a thing of the past. Four-year-olds seem to interrupt constantly when a parent is speaking on the phone. The "instant" parent is not as used to these persistent intrusions (as a biological parent would be), and when this happens there is a higher degree of annoyance.

Men seem to be most offended by the noise that inevitably accompanies whatever is going on in the child's world and often have little patience in dealing with it. The biological parent tends to be more tolerant of the constant (and often noisy) presence of young people.

FINANCIALLY SPEAKING

Waking up one morning to find that you now are partially responsible for the finances of a multi-person household can be devastating, particularly to a formerly single person. In most cases the remarried divorced person has just experienced a costly divorce, and it's likely some of the charges have not yet been paid. Property settlements never seem fair, and it usually looks as though the other party "won." Whatever the outcome, the cost of starting over and supporting children already in the family can be intimidating.

"For the past six years I've worked hard and enjoyed the freedom of being self-supporting," explained Doris. "The little reward I allow myself is my lunch hour shopping in the nearby shops. Shortly after Gene and I married he asked if I would pick up a back-to-school outfit for his twelve-year-old daughter. I gave many excuses but none seem to satisfy him so I finally gave in. When I handed him the package he said thanks and that was it. Never once did he offer to reimburse my expense for the outfit, I was expected to enjoy buying for his little girl, who by the way, hates me and I don't feel much better about her. Should I be thrilled for that?"

Money tends to be a touchy subject in any marriage. One member will always spend too much on his or her favorite pastime, the groceries will be too expensive, or the kids' clothes will cost more than the budget allows. A traditional family is accustomed to coping with these routine occurrences. The instant parent is not, and these natural and recurring events may strike him or her as catastrophic developments.

"I can't get over how much money she spends on her boys," replied Greg. "Before we married she seemed so conservative. The clothes she bought for herself were nice, but not the expensive line. There were times she'd buy clothes for me and I was always pleased at how little they cost. This was one of the traits which attracted me to her. I'm conservative too. But then came the boys. She will stop nothing short of famous brand clothes. A pair of shorts for her eight-year-old cost more than I spend on a pair of slacks for work."

Some stepmothers are women who have never experienced the joys of mothering. They dream that some day they will have children of their own, but frequently the financial pressures typical of most stepfamilies force those dreams to be postponed, even sacrificed altogether. If the couple does decide to have a child, financial pressures can force a young mother back to work sooner than she would prefer.

And so she loses the important nurturing time with her infant.

STEP-PARENTING IS AGELESS

In the traditional family a couple knows at what age they no longer will consider parenthood. This is not the case in the stepfamily.

A college professor vividly described the apprehension his four-year-old stepson aroused. "Me being fifty-five and never until now having had any experience of fatherhood, natural, step, or foster," he shuddered. "The astonishingly skillful construction of instant havoc where I was used to tidiness and order. There is also the deranged creativity. He makes sugar by mixing salt, cigarette ash, and plain spit. Children will find anything they want to find, and getting up in the middle of the night, I have found his small naked body darting from some forbidden corner back to bed."

I'M THE SAME AGE AS HIS DAUGHTER!

"You might at least have had the courtesy to discuss it with me. I'm not a child you know!" The initial shock is not always felt most by the stepparent. With older men often marrying younger women in a second marriage, many stepmothers are quite close in age to their stepchildren. Usually the man and his bride-to-be have discussed the age difference. Often, however, the children have not been informed. In some cases the children have not even been told who their stepmother will be.

Ben is 54 and in great shape for his age. He works out regularly and plays tennis three times a week. His two daughters, Karen 24 and Susan 22, are married and have families of their own. His son Jeff is engaged and a junior in college. Ben's divorce from Celeste came as no surprise. For the last few years the two were never seen together publicly except for formal dinners. Finally, after thirty-two years, the marriage ended. Six months later Ben married the secretary, age 26, of one of his tennis buddies. His children did not object to his happiness, but the new wife's young age made it difficult for them to develop a good relationship with her.

When parents, for whatever reasons, do not discuss the new marriage with their children they add more stress to what is already a difficult relationship-building environment. Advance notice of his or her age will help prepare the children. It won't guarantee their early approval, but it will help ease early tensions.

PUBLIC REJECTION

The young wife/stepmother has more on her plate than coping with the children. She also will be the victim of the kinds of public accusations that abound when a woman marries a man who was married previously. If her husband is divorced, her friends, co-workers, and society in general will turn their backs on her—no matter what the circumstances of his divorce.

One husband said, "My first marriage lasted nineteen years. Our first separation came shortly after the birth of our third child, but for financial reasons we were forced back together. After nine more years of fighting, the last two years under professional counseling, we finally decided to hang it up. The woman I started dating and eventually married nine months later, was practically run out of our small community by her 'former' friends. They were holding her totally responsible for breaking up my marriage." He commented later, "some of those old friends have finally seen the happiness she's brought into my life and they have come forward to apologize. The apologies were appreciated, but it would have been a much easier beginning if we had not been forced to live under false implications."

The new wife's role in a second marriage seems to be almost a no-win situation. If her husband is divorced she gets blamed for breaking up the marriage. If he is a widower, the second wife is seen as an inferior successor to the saint whose shoes she is trying to fill.

YOU CAN'T TELL

Second wives (often in vain) will try to defend their new role by attempting to explain the circumstances of their husband's first marriage. But who listens after the divorce? People say, "She's only trying to cover up for what she's done." And the children are not willing to admit their parents had serious problems. The stepmother's defense falls on deaf ears. "Why do you kids hate me? You know how your parents fought before the divorce, and I had nothing to do with that."

Rather than try to fight this kind of unfair treatment, keeping quiet is usually the best approach. Let the success of the new marriage speak for itself. A rebellious teenager might come around when he or she sees their father's happiness. Tina said, "I knew my mom and dad weren't going to make it, but I just didn't want to admit it was over. Even after the divorce I hoped that someday they would get back together. I made my new stepmother miserable while she was trying to make my dad and me happy. I finally told her I knew it wasn't her fault and I apologized for my actions."

IT'S NOT ALL BAD

Insurance specialist Lori Peterson was 29 when she met Tim Brooks, a widower with two daughters ages six and nine. They married a year after they met. "Our first meeting was a blind date set up by a co-worker of mine, who knew Tim before his first wife's death," recalled Lori. The first evening together was more than either of us expected, and before the night was over Tim asked me out for another date. He asked if I would mind his bringing the girls along, which I didn't. They picked me up and we went to the movie 'BLACK BEAUTY,' and the two girls made sure they sat between us the whole evening. It was one well-planned evening by two suspicious little girls."

However, the girls developed an instant friendship for Lori and encouraged the romance. "When Tim would pick me up for dates the girls would send little notes, asking how I was doing or inquiring about Sam, my new little kitten. After that first night at the movies they both were friendly toward me. They didn't seem to mind when their father held my hand and they would even giggle when they saw him sneak a kiss. I was wondering if it would continue after the wedding, but now two years later it hasn't changed."

CONCLUSION

Newly-married stepparents who have no biological children will suffer initially because of that inexperience. They probably have lived in childless circles where people have white rugs, keep glass objects on low shelves, and never walk into the bathroom to find an unflushed toilet. These parents are at a disadvantage because they don't know what constitutes normal child behavior. Because of this unfamiliarity, an "instant" parent also runs the risk of being too critical or too obliging.

The initial shock for a newcomer to parenthood may be horrendous, but when there is patience and a determination to make the relationships work, success is possible.

CHAPTER 2

Off to a Good Start

Once the gun has sounded and the race has begun it's how the participants choose to run their race that's important. If the runners watch their
step and pace themselves according to their own physical fitness, odds
are that they will at least be around to cross the finish line. But if they
choose to run ahead of the pack and burn themselves out early, more
than likely they will not be able to complete the race. A runner's preparation and early conduct will usually dictate his performance.

One stepmother said, "Becoming part of a stepfamily is like entering a long distance marathon that's well under way and you have to
run extra hard just to catch the pack." The family is already adjusted
and setting their own pace. you're the outsider who has to catch up and
try to fit in."

A person looking on might wonder why anyone would ever take
on such a task, but the stepparent must realize once these words are
spoken—"I now pronounce you husband and wife"—the race is on.

A good start requires that you understand the challenge, learn the
course, plan the strategy, and prepare yourself.

UNDERSTANDING THE CHALLENGE

Begin by learning as much as possible about the rules and the other
participants. You don't want to get ready for a 100-meter dash when
you are going to be running a marathon. Many stepparents admit afterwards that they were completely unprepared for their encounter
with their blended family.

DEFINING THE ROLE

The word "step" derives from an old English term meaning "bereaved"
or "deprived." In earlier times, when a man or woman remarried following the death of a spouse, the stepparent was considered a replacement parent; someone who "stepped in" to rescue the bereaved family.
Today, the marriage is more likely to be ended by divorce than by
death, and the new marriage partner is seen merely as another adult in

the home. The stepparent now is someone added to the family rather than a needed replacement.

Two terms used frequently throughout the book are; "traditional family" and "stepfamily." The traditional family includes a husband and wife and a child or children who are their biological offspring. The stepfamily is a family where includes at least one spouse who is a stepparent. Some stepfamilies will have children from more than one previous marriage living under the same roof. In some cases, stepchildren do not live in the household but visit from time to time.

There is no blood tie between a stepparent and a stepchild, and there is no feeling of family that binds aunts, uncles, cousins, etc. together—whether or not they like each other. The stepparent does not inherit a parent's legal rights over a stepchild.

The stepfamily begins at the wedding. While a young bride-to-be may be eagerly awaiting the wedding ceremony to be concluded, when she says "I do," she instantly becomes the stepmother to her husband's children. A new marriage is difficult enough without an instant family. The adjustment period so desperately needed by a husband and wife can be seriously hindered by a child's interference.

The challenge, as mate and stepparent, is to merge the fragments from two traditional families, which have already begun their separate life-styles, into a new and harmonious unit—the stepfamily.

LEARNING THE COURSE

One must study every detail of the "course" as quickly as possible, in order to feel comfortable in this new environment. Professional race car drivers will take time to practice with their cars to familiarize themselves with the course. Some will even walk over specific areas so they can discover any hazards which might not be visible from inside the car. Even after the practice time and the course familiarization, outside interference can change the conditions of the course dramatically. A sudden drop in temperature, moisture on the surface, or an extremely warm race day, can make it feel like a different track. No matter how anxious the drivers may be to compete, they negotiate the first few laps cautiously.

This analogy may be a bit strained, but it will give you a sense of how difficult it can be to "compete" successfully as a new stepparent. You can think you know your new spouse's children well before the marriage, but outside interference from in-laws, grandparents, and the absent biological parent can turn a normally sweet and agreeable youngster into a rebellious stepchild.

TAKING A GOOD LOOK AT THE KIDS

The age of the children is an important factor to consider in the creation of a new stepfamily. The general belief is that younger children will have less trouble adapting to changes in their lives than older children do. A three-year-old who lives four days a week with one parent and three days with the other will accept another change as part of his or her normal lifestyle. Where older children are already established in their relationships and daily living routines, change is more difficult.

Since the younger child typically adapts to a new situation and new stepparent more easily, he or she is less apt to create stress in the new stepfamily. Older children may not dislike or hate the new stepparent, they simply do not like their new arrangement. It is easier for them to get angry with a stranger—the new stepparent—than to direct their anger at the biological parent.

The ages, mannerisms, and accustomed lifestyles of the children should be considered by the stepparent before the marriage, but often that is not the case.

Following the death of his wife, William turned to his two teenage sons for companionship. The evening meal became a routine that all three enjoyed. The food was prepared by the housekeeper before she went home, and during the meal William and his sons would share their experiences of the day. Afterwards, the chores of cleaning the table and washing the dishes were alternated in mature fashion.

Abandoned by her first husband, Brenda did not handle her responsibilities very well. All of the household obligations fell on her shoulders; finances, house care, overseeing the daily routines of her two young daughters (ages seven and five)—plus working a job away from the home. A neighbor took care of the girls until Brenda returned home, and sometimes she would have the evening meal on the stove. Because Brenda was too tired to exercise any control over them, the girls spent their evenings doing as they pleased. Brenda would collapse in front of the television set until bedtime.

When William and Brenda married, he expected life to go on as before. Brenda's girls anticipated the same discipline-free life-style they had enjoyed before. Neither family fragment was entirely right or wrong, but it was soon clear they would not be able to coexist within the same household. William's boys thought the girls were lazy and disrespectful. The girls blamed William for being mean and much too demanding.

To go through the combining process, families must take steps to blend their various lifestyles as harmoniously as possible. The key word is *compromise*. To reduce friction, parents should plan events with the needs and interests of all individuals in mind. It does not necessarily mean to give in, but each side must make concessions.

WHERE TO LIVE

When her marriage dissolved, Linda gained custody of the children and the house. Following his divorce (a different marriage break-up)

Carl moved into a furnished, one bedroom apartment. When Carl and Linda decided to marry, it made sense for Carl to move into Linda's large home. At least it seemed right at the time.

"I felt like I was trespassing on someone else's property," recalled Carl. "I slept in Linda's bed, I rested on Linda's sofa, and I tried not to interfere with Linda's children. When my kids came for their weekend visit, I would ask them to be especially careful since all of this was Linda's. It wasn't until we packed up and moved into a different residence that I felt relaxed in our home."

There are good arguments against moving in this situation. Changing schools will only make it harder on the children. The family would be better off financially staying put rather than incurring the expense of moving. And if the children can stay close to their biological father it would be better for them. One course of action would be for the new stepfamily to move into a neutral area. Sometimes, to cut down on the disruption, a relocation in the same neighborhood might be the answer. And sometimes it might not.

Mark said, "I agreed to stay in the same neighborhood that was home for my new wife and her children. Before I knew it, my stepchildren's father began dropping by uninvited. I would even find him there with the kids when I returned from work. The only way we were going to make it was to leave the area. I now drive a little farther to and from work, but at least I know who isn't going to be there when I get home."

Of course finances are important in deciding where to live and relocating is expensive. If you own your home, however, you have an investment you should (at least) recover when the house is sold. If your present living situation is really unpleasant for one reason or another, this "money in the bank" could make a move more attainable, the temporary disruption more tolerable.

THE FINANCIAL PICTURE

Being aware of a new spouse's finances will not make the bills go away, but it will lessen the shock. Money (or lack of same) has the potential to create stress in any household, but it can be even more critical for the stepfamily home. It is not uncommon for one spouse to be financially obligated to more than one home. For example, the man in the home continues to be accountable for child support, and in many circumstances alimony. "Half of Adam's income goes into alimony and child support," says Helen, Adam's second wife. "It's not easy for those payments to come out every month." A new wife may be forced to work in order to meet the financial obligations of the combined family. Or the husband may need to assume some of the financial support for his new stepchildren. "Can we afford a baby of our own on our budget?" is a question that often arises.

Each stepfamily is different. Mike, father of three kids, divorced his wife to marry Felicia, mother of two. Their solution was for Mike to "help out" in the finances of the new home rather than being the main source of income. That was fine for Felicia, who did not marry Mike for financial dependency. She said, "I could never respect Mike the way I do if he didn't live up to his responsibilities.

The spouse who is the natural always has to be sensitive to the needs of the stepparent. Chuck said, "When I married Dorene, mother of two girls, I anticipated the child support payments to help on the family expenses. I did not think it should be mine to spend freely, but I thought the kids were part of the family and their income should be included. Dorene expected the money to go into a separate bank account for the kids later. She said it's the kids' money and I had no right to it. I finally put my foot down when it came time to buy school clothes and she expected me to pay for them."

Couples can maintain separate bank accounts successfully, especially when there are two households to consider. A good understanding of each spouse's obligations will be helpful, including the expenses of his or her children and each partner's personal expenses. With this understanding, each spouse will contribute a specified amount into the overall operation of the new household.

PLANNING THE STRATEGY

Now it's time for planning. A person may be getting ready for the wedding, in the first months of the marriage, or celebrating a wedding anniversary, but it never is too late to plan. The phrase, "Today is the first day of the rest of your life," fits the situation perfectly.

BUILDING RELATIONSHIPS

A new stepfamily creates the need for new relationships. A union has already been joined between the husband and wife, its foundation having been started on the first date. But the kids are a different matter. In most cases they were involved very little during the courtship. Then, after the wedding, the stepparent begins his or her invasion of the child's "sacred ground."

Whenever a death or divorce occurs a new closeness develops between the child and its remaining parent. The younger child tends to cling more, with the fear that "Someday mommy's going to leave me too." The older child and teenager form new bonds with the parent based more on friendship. Whatever situations develop, the stepparent is seen as posing a threat to those existing relationships.

HONESTY IS A MUST

The challenging task facing stepparents is to build new relationships without disrupting the existing ones. Many stepparents approach their assignment determined to make it. "I've got to make those kids like me!" This attitude induces some stepparents to try anything. But a relationship erected on what the child perceives as insincerity, as forced friendliness, will soon crumble.

"Bob is wonderful with my two boys," replied Joanna. "Their real father never took time to throw the ball or play in the yard. But every evening when Bob comes, he always spends a little time with them."

Don't start something you can't finish. Bob is forty-two and never had time to play ball with his son. And the chance of this attention to his stepchildren continuing after the wedding is slim. Three months into the marriage and Bob is never seen in the yard except to mow the lawn. Joanna is humiliated, and refuses to talk about it with friends. The boys feel that Bob used them to get to their mother. If Bob is going to develop positive relationships in his stepfamily, he must first tear down the negative one he has built with his stepsons and repair the damage he has caused with his wife.

"When we dated, Glenn always brought little gifts for the girls," said Carol. "Even the first weeks into our marriage he'd stop on his way home and pick up treats. I told him he was spoiling them, but he said he was afraid they wouldn't like him if he didn't bring them something. Love can't be bought and some day the buying will stop. The kids are only enjoying the gifts they are given and they are not learning love."

A stepparent's efforts to be accepted are often ruined when the child finds out that he or she can't deliver. It doesn't take kids very long to see when a person's word is not very good. Respect cannot just be promised. It must be earned.

BE CONSISTENT

Parental consistency is a requirement in every home, especially in a stepfamily's home. Stepchildren have just been through a catastrophic event in their lives. One parent has been removed by either death or divorce and—usually not too many months later—another parent has entered their lives. The child's security system has been badly shaken and the remaining parent's remarriage should serve as a foundation for rebuilding that security. Unfortunately, that is not always the case.

Alex, divorced and the father of two teenage sons who live with him, leaves home at 6:45 a.m., moments before the alarm sounds to wake the boys. Jackie, his new wife should leave home no later than 7:15 a.m. in order to be at work on time. By her departure time the boys should be out of bed and preparing for school. Instead, she usually ends up fighting to get them moving. Because of the morning hassle Jackie often is late to work.

"Tomorrow morning you boys are on your own. You'll need to get up by yourself because I'm going on to work even if you are still asleep." Next morning the alarm sounds and then it's shut off. Jackie soon realizes the boys have gone back to sleep. Into their room she screams, "I told you boys that you would have to get yourselves up and I meant it. Now get up!"

Jackie had good intentions but her behavior was not consistent with what she said. Even though parents and stepparents mean well, giving in under a little pressure only reveals weakness. It will contribute nothing toward the building of solid relationships. Kids are inclined to test their new stepparent's limits but they are just looking for someone they can trust.

"When Ann's seventeen-year-old son came in one hour after curfew I warned him that the next time it happened he wouldn't get in," said Hank. "The very next evening at ten minutes past midnight I secured the lock. An hour later I heard him yelling and pounding on the door, but this time I meant business. I went to the window and told him either to sleep in his car or under the stars."

It's not so much what we say as the action that supports our words. Bill finished by saying, "You see, I love my stepson and I wanted him to love me. If I expected our relationship to go anywhere I had to start it in the right direction. We're more than stepdad and stepson now, we're good friends." There's no guarantee that all relationships will end as solid as Bill's and his stepson's, but they have a chance to succeed only if a good effort is made.

AVOID PLAYING FAVORITES

The stepfamily unit can be made up of a variety of parts. One or both spouses can be a stepparent and the children may or may not live in the home. But when children from both spouses live under the same roof, which often happens, there are many opportunities for inconsistent parental behavior. It's natural for biological parents to be more lenient with their offspring and to expect more from their spouse's child. Don't anticipate much respect from the stepchild if this happens. If a clean room is expected from a teenage stepson, it also should be demanded from a teenage daughter.

"Dad, why does she let Sharon drive her car but won't let me?" If there are two qualified teenage drivers in the home, treat them equally. Parents tend to trust the biological child they have raised more than someone else's child they barely know. Sometimes, to be fair and to nurture a beginning relationship, it becomes necessary to take a chance.

In other situations, trying to avoid "wicked stepmother" accusations, stepparents will favor the stepchild. This is unfair to their own children, who need the parent as an ally in what they may perceive as hostile territory.

Whichever the situation, it's better to be realistic with the stepchild. "I do care more for my child because I have known him longer, just as you have a close and loving relationship with your own brother and sister and parent. In time, I hope we will grow closer as we get to know one another." People in stepfamilies do not have to love one another equally. They should, however, be fair to one another.

RESPECT

The United States was founded on the premise of equality for all. Foreigners continue to come to its shores with the hope of becoming part of the great democracy. Yet. in millions of microcosms of American society — blended family households — there are situations where equality does not exist. If only one person in a relationship is granted respect, there is no equality. If adults want and sometimes demand respect from children, they must return that respect in kind.

Timothy, eleven, has just moved in with his father and new stepmother, and has done so with the deepest desire to please his dad. The stepmother began with a long list of expectations for him; He must be a straight "A" student, play tennis and little league ball, master his piano lessons to perfection, keep his room spotless, and show nothing less than impeccable manners at all times. Timothy is considered an excellent student, but his father can't understand his continuous nightmares and the serious twitch which irritates his stepmother.

Timothy's dad has told him over and over how proud he is that he's doing so well and that he doesn't expect perfection. But his stepmother tells him in private that if he doesn't do all of those things he is letting his father down. The relentless pressure applied by the stepmother is a profound display of disrespect for Timothy as a person. He is being used to enhance her own prestige instead of accepting him as a stepson. Timothy is entitled to her respect as well as his father's. It is absolutely wrong for her to make unreasonable demands of him to satisfy her own cruel needs.

Daniel, ten, was visiting his father for the weekend. The family went for an outing at the amusement park and Daniel wanted one more ride on the roller coaster. His stepsisters, Cindy, nine and Ellen, seven, wanted to go to the Arcade. The group started immediately in that direction while Daniel continued to beg. His stepmother crossly refused and said, "We are tired of riding and we're going to play Arcade." When Daniel got excited he would begin to stutter, and the more he begged, the more difficult his speech became. Finally, his stepmother looked at the girls and began to mock him. Cindy and Ellen burst into laughter and joined the mocking. Daniel closed his mouth and bit his lip to keep from crying.

Humiliation by a stepparent for any reason shows an intense lack of respect. Daniel's stuttering revealed he had a problem. Mockery only tears him down in front of his stepsisters. Whether it be the natural parent or stepparent, the goal of parenting is to raise children to be happy productive adults. Respect for the child means he must be looked upon as a human being with the same rights as an adult. (It does not mean, however, a child has the same right to do as adults do.)

Each person in a family unit—infant, preschooler, young child, teenager, or adult—has a different role and should be respected for it. For good relations to flourish in the stepfamily unit, there should be mutual respect between and among all family members.

SELF PREPARATION

Getting into shape for the challenge ahead is the most difficult step for the stepparent. Everything happens instantly in the stepfamily, and there is no time to prepare. Men and women jump into marriage completely unaware of what is involved in stepparenthood. "Not only was I unprepared," said Brenda. "If I had known it was like this I probably wouldn't have done it."

John visited the sports center to watch his first boxing event. When one of the boxers failed to show John volunteered. He was unprepared, inexperienced, out of shape, and looked like a fool in the ring. Everything was new to him. The first punch almost knocked him out and he doesn't know if he should quit or get up and try again. When he stands, the only thing he has learned is to protect the area he was hit the first time. Unexpectedly, he's hit again from another angle.

This will sound absurd to many. If you're a stepparent, however, it sounds familiar. Most stepparents learn that the only meaningful preparation they can make is accomplished during the actual event — the hopeful coming together of a stepfamily.

ONE STEP AT A TIME

A stepparent always has the feeling of being on probation. There's a sense of comparison, competition, resentment, and even jealousy, and a feeling of continual jousting with the ghost of the saint who lived there before.

Start slowly! Remember you're a "step" parent. Build relationships in steps. You want the family's respect, and you want to become part of their family unit. Don't begin by taking over. Even if there is great need for a manager, move with caution. Let the young people show "you" the way. No one's going to say that changes can't be made later, but for now learn from them.

Great strides can be made in a relationship by simply asking for their assistance. The children already have a preconceived (probably largely negative) idea of who you are, and the best way to tear down that barrier is by being humble. "Susan, I'm new at this and I would sure appreciate your help." Susan just learned that her opinion is respected by you and that no changes will be made without considering her needs and interests.

There still may be hostility. If there is, give it time to abate. The stepfamily might never develop into an ideal situation, but with time most family members will adjust to one another. Most stepchildren are feeling the same pressures as the new stepparent. Stay cool.

And don't overdo it. Many stepparents try too hard to win a child's affection, feeling a compulsion to be better than the natural parent. When this happens the child's responses reflect suspicion, hesitance, and even withdrawal. The kids pick up the sense that the stepparent is "not real." More than likely they're right. A person who overreacts to a situation will some day revert back to his or her natural self, creating another change for the stepfamily to endure.

Go easy on your predecessor. The natural parent might not have been a good mother, but the child doesn't want, or need, to be reminded of it. The child usually will defend the natural parent no matter how badly he or she was treated, and negative comments only bring dissension into the home. Don't say or do things that only agitate others and do nothing to promote family harmony.

Maintain a neutral posture in discussions about the former mate. Time will come when the stepchild wants to talk about his or her absent parent. This may be a game a wise child wants to play, or it might be an honest attempt at conversation. Remember that what is said could be used against you. If the child wants to confide in you about a problem or disagreement, listen, but don't take sides. A child's opinion and attitude can change very quickly. If you sided with her when she complained about her parent, now you're the rotten person who has a grudge against the wonderful mom.

Try to relate to the child's disappointments, his or her feelings of abandonment, and the mixed feelings of being pushed and pulled in different directions at the same time. Not until you feel their pain can you begin to build a relationship based on trust and understanding.

CONCLUSION

Stepfamilies are rapidly becoming an American majority in our nation, but the members of this majority still feel so alone. No matter what the experts say, it is not a traditional family and the complexities of these new relationships cannot be handled as if it were. The difficulties are tremendous, and how stepparents approach their task will have a great deal to do with their outcome. A good start will not guarantee a "winning" blended family, but it will greatly improve the chances for success.

CHAPTER 3

Surviving the Weekend

The weekend can bring both pleasure and pain to the stepfamily home. While the natural parent waits with anticipation of a son or daughter's arrival, the stepparent may look forward to the same arrival with feelings ranging from fear to bitterness. The visiting child will cause drastic change in the ongoing family structure, demand the full attention of his or her natural parent, and may even arouse feelings of jealousy on the part of the stepparent (who continues to entertain visions of the honeymoon privacy and exclusivity).

Establishing a workable three-way parent, child, and stepparent relationship can be very difficult. However, as one stepmother put it, "It's simple. If I don't work to make it three-way, I'll be the one left out."

Courts are granting more fathers custody of their children today, but the majority of weekend stepparents are stepmothers. If she's willing, the stepmother can assume a variety of roles during the visit. When several children come at one time and compete for their father's time, she can be helpful in planning an activity for some of the children, and allow her spouse time with the child who might be in greatest need of attention. The child not immediately involved with Daddy may balk, but will be consoled when he or she gets to be the focus of the parent's concentration.

Consistency of visitation is another important factor. A child who visits on a regular basis can be absorbed into the family's regular routines more comfortably than a youngster who visits sporadically, coming only on holidays and summer vacations. For the occasional visitor, major adjustments need to be made by everyone. The stepparent can be helpful by quietly stepping back and letting the parent spend quality time alone with the child. The regular visitor needs certain times alone with the parent, but here that special attention is not as critical a need.

MAKE THEM FEEL AT HOME

Even though children do not spend all their time with the family, they are *not* guests. They are members of the household. A separate room should be set aside for them if at all possible. If not, a dresser, closet, alcove, or some particular area should be designated as permanently belonging to that child. He or she needs somewhere to park belongings and know they will be there for the next visit. Children will not feel a part of the family if there is no place for them.

Encourage the children to meet friends in the neighborhood. Visiting children, especially those old enough to plan their own time with friends, may feel awkward in the noncustodial home if they do not have friends close by. A wise stepparent might make arrangements during the week for a youngster to stop by on the weekend. A word of caution though; some youngsters may see this as your way of getting them out of the house. Done with the right attitude, however, most children will appreciate the gesture. Having a neighborhood friend to be with would provide a change of pace and take some pressure off the family.

It might be helpful to encourage the visiting child to invite a friend from home for the weekend. This not only puts the child at ease but also confers legitimacy on the new home. Don't be too upset if the offer is refused. The child may be ashamed of his or her situation, or the youngster might not want to share the limited time available.

The visit not only affects the life of the visiting child, it also interrupts the lives of the children living in the home. Both sets of children anticipate the weekend with some uncertainty. The live-in children will have their lives disrupted by having to share time, space, and attention, and they too must be reassured of their value and worth in the family.

Experts agree that most weekend stepchildren are confused about the rules of their new home. Visiting children cannot be expected to conform to the rules if they do not know what they are. On a summer visit to her father's, Leigh, age twelve, was caught running through the house. "I told her how much I loved her and enjoyed having her in our home, but running inside the house was prohibited. She pouted for awhile and then came out with a big smile."

Mike's three children, Cindy seventeen, Nick fourteen, and Susan eight, live with their mother. Lori has custody of her two active, preschool boys. Since Lori's ex-husband had visitation rights every other weekend, same as Mike, it seemed like a good idea to have all the children one weekend and no kids the next. "It sounded great," said Lori. "But what a price to pay for that weekend alone, five kids in a two bedroom, one bath apartment."

You never knew what to expect. If Cindy and her mother had quarreled during the week (which they usually did), she would take it out on Mike and me and ruin the whole weekend. You couldn't plan ahead because you didn't know if one or all three were coming. Since Mike moved out, the kids had become spoiled by their mother and no one enjoyed being around them. They argued among themselves, then spent the remainder of the time pouting or criticizing one another." Lori finished by saying, "Everything I tried went wrong. His kids resented me and my boys because we were with their father all of the time, and I couldn't help that. It didn't get better until we finally sat down with all five and made some basic rules, a clear definition of what wasn't allowed. The most difficult was when Mike told his kids he wanted them to visit, but only if they could behave in a pleasant manner. Cindy didn't show up for a month, but now that she's back it's altogether better.

Following are some basic guidelines which can be helpful for the weekend stepparent:

FOCUS ON THE MAIN RESPONSIBILITY

Sometimes it's easy to get priorities turned around. Often it happens unintentionally. A second wife must appreciate that no matter how much her husband loves her, he still has his children to consider. She could demand that she be the constant focus of all his attention, but for the sake of the marriage she should try to understand that he's with her all week, but with his kids only on weekends.

A wife's goal is to succeed in her marriage more than as a step-mother. She may think that her husband's children have little effect on her marriage, but she's wrong. His children have a lot to do with his feelings and they play a big part in the relationship between him and his wife. Gil explained, "When my kids come for the weekend they can't do anything right. She won't even try to be civil to them, she just criticizes them to me the whole time. Then on Sunday night after they've gone home, she comes around putting her arms around me. I don't want anything to do with her then. If she can't be decent to my kids, then she's not much of a wife."

The weekend's petty annoyances will seem more severe to a step-mother than to her husband. Even if the kids do upset him, he's going to pamper them to make their time more enjoyable. It may be uncomfortable, but good communications and a little understanding will go a long way toward easing the frustrations.

YOU'RE NOT THEIR MOTHER

Some stepmothers are driven to try to assume a role that really isn't theirs. It may be because they never have had the privilege of mothering a child and this will be their closest opportunity. Others feel the need to compete with the first wife, trying always to be better. Most second wives are merely seeking their husband's approval. "If I can only win his children's love."

If the natural mother has died, the stepmother might be able to fill some of the emptiness, but if she's still living, it is best not to upset the child by trying, in effect, to replace the mother. Very little can be gained with a momentary "victory" over the natural mother. A boy's love may be borrowed, but he still will be going home on Sunday, and he'll spend the whole next week in turmoil and frustration.

Carolyn played Santa every weekend her stepson came to visit; shopping, ball games, amusement park visits, and new toys ... a little boy's dream. He says he does not love his real mother anymore and hates to go home. But that mother is still a big part of him and now he's confused by his feelings.

A thirteen-year-old girl sums it up, "I really like my new stepmother except when she tries to act like my mom, I'd rather have her as a friend." It's better said, "I'm your father's new wife. You're not my kids, but I hope that some day you'll grow to respect and love me for what I am."

LET HIM SET THE STANDARD

Since he's the child's father let him set the conditions. At first it might be difficult to accept, but it's a very practical way of handling a potentially touchy situation. The husband may want his wife to take an active role with his kids, or he may not want her to be as involved a stepmother as she'd like. There are many reasons which might validate a father's behavior in setting the rules for his new wife and his children. In his first marriage, how the children were disciplined always caused arguments. Now he feels the decisions are his alone to make.

Also, guilt from the divorce and the feeling of abandoning his kids might influence his conduct. He only sees his children on visits and he wants the freedom to express his love towards them without interference.

Frequently, remarks made with good intentions can be taken as personal attacks. "I work for county services," said Mona, "and I'm aware of a problem at the school where my husband's daughter attends. I suggested a change of school, and I know the move would be for the best. My husband resented my advice and construed it as insinuating that he was a poor father."

Experts only say, "Consider his feelings." Pauline said, "I'm ashamed of the way I feel about his kids. If I could only see my children as little as he sees his I couldn't stand it. Yet when his kids come to our house I resent both them and the way he acts around them."

A second wife must learn that if she moves too fast and begins giving orders, a father—her husband—can become hurt and angry. She should remember his importance to her, and not complicate things further.

CONCENTRATE ON THE RELATIONSHIP

Weekend stepparents face the same false assumption as a live-in stepparent. A person cannot automatically love another person simply because that person is related to someone they do love. Evelyn said, "I met every other weekend, for two years, with dreadful anticipation.

The kids were out of control and complained the entire two days. When they left I felt relieved and guilty that I had never learned to love them." She finally confessed her feelings to her husband by saying, "I hope you don't hate me, but I just can't love your kids." He responded, "You didn't marry my kids, you married me."

Developing a love relationship takes time, and "weekend only" relationships make it even more difficult. Something started on one weekend can be forgotten and the excitement can be lost, because of the days between visits.

It is not essential that you love your stepchildren, but you must respect them and show concern for their welfare. Show kindness to the children, but don't try to force a response. Don't hold back feelings, good or bad, from the kids. Honesty is always the best and kids are first to recognize phoniness. Time can work both ways. Don't push, but don't let them step on you either.

"Jeff is my fourteen-year-old stepson," recalled Wanda. "When I married his father and Jeff began his visits I told myself that I had to, somehow, learn to love this kid. I pushed to the limit, but got nowhere. I was ashamed, but didn't want my husband to know my real feelings. Then one day it happened, I just gave up and started over. First I resolved the idea that I had to love Jeff. It sounded cold, but it was a fact I had to accept. Next, I went to work on my marriage. It had suffered for some time as I wrestled with my feelings. As for Jeff, I became the congenial weekend host. He would take me for what I was, and I did the same for him. Two years later, to my shock, Jeff asked his father if he could live with us. His only explanation was, 'I just like it here.'"

In trying too hard, stepparents often run the risk of driving the child away. Jeff recognized security in the home with his father and stepmother. Their marriage was good and he knew he could live in their environment. Wanda said, "I still don't have the love for him that I have for my kids, but we have a great relationship."

WALKING ON THIN ICE

Some stepparents wonder what's going to shatter first, them or the thin ice on which they're walking. "It's either the kids, their mother, or my husband, that I have to be careful around," said one distraught stepmother. "I never know whom I'm going to offend next."

Sara is a social worker for the state of Florida. Upon entering her home one Friday evening she discovered her visiting fifteen-year-old stepdaughter lounging on the sofa reading a book. Sara, just making conversation and not really interested in the book, asked what she was reading. To her surprise, the book was definitely not suitable for a fifteen-year-old and she reprimanded her stepdaughter for choosing it. With disappointment in her voice the girl said, "But my mom said it was okay." Sara knew she had just self-destructed by inadvertently cutting down the girl's mother.

At the same time, children can also turn into watch dogs. "My thirteen-year-old stepson is always trying to put me down. He doesn't like the meals I prepare, he complains about my two girls, and he's persistently trying to catch me at something. I discovered recently that he was deliberately leaving things out in his room hoping that I would remove them."

Whenever a child tries to trap a stepparent or makes a mistake intentionally, there is little a stepparent can do except play it straight. Don't get caught in one of their traps and don't play their game by trying to get even. Going to the spouse is usually fruitless because he or she will not want to believe their child would do such a thing? Time and patience can help, but in times like these stepparenting can be very lonely.

Stress is also produced as a result of trying too hard. "Every hint my stepdaughter would drop, I would try my best to fulfill it. My husband had more foresight when he said, 'just forget it.'" A stepparent's uncertain condition places him or her in a chronically fearful state, afraid the relationship they hope to achieve will never be accomplished. Happiness can never be found when a person lives in constant fear.

DON'T GET STEPPED ON

A husband needs support and understanding when it comes to his children, but that does not mean a new wife should be treated as a slave or doormat. She is a member of the family and has every right to demand and expect certain behavior. If she does not get involved in family matters, however, her "rewards" will be slim. "Ann refused to correct my children when they visited," said Edward. "I told her countless times to get onto them when they misbehaved. The kids would have obeyed and learned to respect her. Now they feel that she really doesn't want a relationship with them." If a wife refuses to take part in the control of the children, she should also hold her tongue when it comes to criticizing them to their father.

Sharon married a divorced attorney, the father of two sons who visit on alternating weekends. At a Saturday evening cookout she fixed them hamburgers and hot dogs. The boys rudely demanded steaks. Sharon replied, "When you're buying the groceries around here we'll eat steak."

Ann still couldn't bring herself to correct Edward's kids, and Sharon said, "It took me quite sometime before I could make myself do it, but when I learned it was such a relief." Most stepmothers are afraid of being rejected by the kids, or disapproved of by their husbands. Since the stepmother is also the father's wife, she should not have to tolerate disobedience. If his children will not do as they ask, take it up with him. "I'll not permit her laziness when I need her help with the dishes."

Compromises are frequently needed for the sake of the marriage. A person might overlook some bothersome situations but insist on other changes. Whatever compromise is worked out must be between stepparent and spouse, not stepparent and stepchild. It's not good for a child to feel he or she has a bargaining chip which can be used in the marriage relationship. Conflict of any kind will always put the natural parent in an uncomfortable situation. Ask yourself this important question: "Is my way of doing things important enough to jeopardize the relationship with my mate?"

BE FAIR TO THE VISITOR

The weekend stepmother will have a greater tendency to treat acts of misbehavior unfairly. The same act committed by one of her children might be looked upon as mischievous and handled routinely, but if the stepchild does it it may be looked upon as a major offense deserving strong disciplinary action.

"We are fortunate to have a separate bedroom for Adam," explained Julie. Pete and Julie have been married two years, and Timothy, Julie's four-year-old lives with them. Adam, Pete's thirteen-year-old son, only visits on alternating weekends. According to Julie, "I complained incessantly about Adam's untidiness and I always compared his and Timothy's room. Then one day Pete knocked me right off my soap box when he said, 'No wonder Timothy's room is so neat, you're always in there doing something, cleaning or straightening things up.' I was so resentful of Adam's presence that I wanted to strike out at him for anything. His room would look just as good if I spent equal time cleaning it."

Stepparents (especially stepmothers) feel rejection, and sometimes they try to retaliate by looking for faults in the children. They want to put down the kids in the eyes of their parent and other people. You serve yourself better by taking a good look at your overall situation, not just the weekend intrusion or the inconvenience. It's particularly important not to look for something — some imaginary problem — that's not there.

THE EXCEPTIONAL PROBLEMS

Not all weekend dilemmas can be worked out harmoniously. Some problems will demand more time and attention than others. Some problems may not have satisfactory solutions. You might just not want to make the effort it would take to get along with the stepchildren. "I've changed my mind, it's me or the kids." What can a husband do? Phyllis said, "It's simply too good without the kids to want them around."

Some stepparents pretend to love the kids to gain control over mates. Jack is divorced and the father of three children who live with their mother. Martha, his new wife, admitted "I pretended to care for the kids and I schemed until one-by-one they came to live with us." After all of her manipulation she came out on top, at least temporarily. Martha triumphed over the ex-wife, diminished her husband, and convinced the children that neither parent cared for them as much as she did. But how long will these "pretend" relationships last.

Fathers can also be guilty of destroying good intentions. Faye, a second wife married Andrew, father of ten-year-old Stephanie. Faye said, "When I married Andrew I was expecting weekend visits, holidays, and special occasions with Stephanie. I wanted everything possible to make us a family, even if it was only part-time. After returned presents from birthdays and Christmas and futile attempts at persuading Andrew to resume his visitation rights, I finally realized he simply didn't care. Stephanie had been a burden on him after the divorce and he was content to forget her now."

When a father develops this type of attitude, it not only is terribly unfair to the child and he is cheating himself of the joy he could be sharing with her. But the stepmother, limited to what her husband will permit, finds her hands are pretty much tied.

The role of part-time stepparent may change to full-time stepparent. Even if one parent has custody, after a child reaches a certain age, he or she may choose for themselves to live with the other parent. Each state has laws which determine the age at which a child can make such decisions.

For Marge Jackson, after six months of marriage, her husband's fourteen-year-old son moved in. "I was not ready for it then and now three years later I anxiously wait for the day he'll move out. My oldest child was eight and I was not prepared for this teenager. At first I tried to cope with it for my husband's sake, but now it's merely survival."

Raising children is stressful in itself. It is especially traumatic being a stepparent to a child you do not want. It's difficult to overcome and some admit they never do. One stepmother summed it up when she said, "I'll never accept him, but I won't risk losing my marriage either."

A GOOD LOOK

A stepparent may feel there are conflicting standards to live by. One day it's time to stand up for your rights, but on another day you compromise and give in a little. No wife, husband, stepmother, or stepfather should ever surrender his or her rights in a relationship, but recognize that sometimes it is not your rights for which you fighting, it's their pride.

Problems can arise in the husband and wife relationship when the wife's wants and needs come into conflict with the wants and needs of her husband's children and she is determined to get her way. But don't fight over his children except when they become an obstacle to the marriage. Discuss how the conflict is effecting the marriage, but don't attack him about his kids. Keep his wants and needs in mind also, and choose your words carefully.

CONCLUSION

One of the principal goals of marriage is a happy home. Try to create ways to maintain smooth relationships between and among the natural parent, the stepparent, and the children. Don't be jealous of the time the natural parent spends with his or her kids. Private moments are important to a parent and child who see one another only occasionally. If those private moments are not shared over the weekend, both parent and child will feel an emptiness during the week.

When the husband and wife have a strong relationship, any problems that may develop with the children don't seem as unmanageable.

CHAPTER 4

The Games Stepchildren Play

At one time or another, all children will play psychological games to test a parent's limitations, manipulating them to get what they want. The innocent, inexperienced stepparent is even more vulnerable, challenged by a barrage of schemes and tactics from the first day of their arrival into the new family.

The stepparent may one day discover that he or she stands alone, pitted against other family members by a stepchild's cunning ploy or maneuver. And where the stepfamily consists of more than one stepchild, the "game" becomes even more complex. The children may choose to attack together, making it two or three against one, or each may devise his or her own plan. That actually creates an even more difficult predicament, never knowing from which direction or from what child the assault will come.

The stepparent will seldom feel victorious when pitted against another family member. "It's like playing against a stacked deck," said one stepmother. "When it's you and the natural parent, no one wins. If a miracle happens and you catch the kid at his or her own game, you still lose. You might have won the skirmish, but it did little for the overall relationship." These games are serious and their often lasting effects may jeopardize the couple's marriage.

The best defense is stay alert at all times and proceed with caution. Learn to recognize the snares quickly. By side stepping a trap, you may foil the plan completely or at least postpone its impact for a while.

STEPPARENT VS. THE NATURAL PARENT

"Dad, did you know that Ellen had me ride home from school with Mike today?" The stepchild is shrewd, little ten-year-old Sara. Mike is the sixteen-year-old neighbor, in whom Dad has little trust, and Ellen is the young stepmother. Ellen has done nothing wrong, but her conniving stepdaughter is taking advantage of her father's distrust of Mike. An unexpected crisis at Ellen's office caused her to delay picking Sara up from school. Innocently—with good intentions—to keep her from waiting alone on the school grounds, Ellen asked Mike for the favor.

Games which are intended to hurt the stepparent are often based on deceit, a lie, or, in Ellen's case, a half truth. Since all the facts were not reported, Dad had to form his opinion on the information he was given. His first instinct was to believe his young wife had acted erroneously and had used poor judgment in asking Mike to bring the girl home. He did not know, and did not consider, that Mike's mother was waiting at home for Sara, and it was much safer for her there than waiting in an empty school yard.

The defense against a half-truth or lie is a simple, clear explanation without argument. A child's schemes may sometimes be brought to light when a parent learns the side of the story which was not told originally. *Do not attack the child.* When this happens, the parent is likely to side with a son or daughter and refuse to hear the true facts.

"Why doesn't he like me?" It takes a child a very short time to figure out what really gets to his parents. A mother wants to believe more than anything that the new husband she has chosen cares for them and has their best interest at heart. A clever youngster can play with this emotion and win, as mother tries to over-compensate for any losses her child has endured. It can also cause serious rifts in the husband-wife relationship, sometimes with a lasting effect on the marriage.

The counteraction again is honesty. A child's behavior can make them unlikable, especially to a stepparent who has enjoyed being part of a well-mannered family. But a straight-forward answer, explaining what mannerisms are the most upsetting, can often lead to an agreement that will produce harmony in the home. A vengeful retaliation can only make an already complex situation more difficult. Few natural parents will let someone, even a spouse, verbally attack his or her own child.

No parent wants to think his or her child is being treated unfairly. A child will rarely, if ever, voice a plea in front of the stepparent. It's more effective when the stepparent cannot defend herself. The natural parent's typical response to an allegation from the child will be to over-react; granting special favors and allowances, and more or less placing the unaware stepparent on probation. A wise parent will first confront the stepparent about the accusation and deal with it accordingly. But few parents will act wisely when they think their children have been wronged.

Fairness with all children at all times should be the standard for the stepfamily home. When it's consistent neither parent is likely to fall for underhanded schemes.

STEPPARENTS VS. ABSENT PARENT

Stepparents always feel compelled to compare themselves to the absent parent, either to prove their worthiness to the new spouse or to show the children how much better parents they can be. Children quickly sense the competition and use it to their benefit.

"Mom lets me do it." Few stepparents will have a close enough relationship with the ex-spouse to feel comfortable contacting them to find out for sure. Further questioning usually results in more serious confrontations causing the natural parent to get involved. He or she generally sides with the child, if only to make the conditions more pleasant (especially if a weekend visit is involved). The trapped step-parent may get the violent reaction from the natural mother when she finds out what her child was allowed to do. Most assuredly the child did not tell how the stepparent was tricked.

"My new wife Cindy wanted to make it the best possible summer for my fourteen-year-old daughter," said Martin. The two went shop-ping for swim wear and my daughter picked a very skimpy bikini for the beach. She told Cindy her mom wouldn't mind since she had one like it at home. At the end of the summer when my daughter returned home her mother quickly telephoned her disapproval. Cindy tried to defend herself but my ex-wife would not listen."

Whenever there is a question about behavior or clothing it's best to define the rules of the home. Whether mom allows it or not, it's not allowed here. The child may not appreciate your stand, but you'll know you did the right thing.

"At home, Mom yells at me for no reason. Don't you think that's terrible?" Some children misbehave to get attention, while others only want sympathy. A stepchild might be unaware of what he or she is doing in making accusations, or they may be intentionally plotting to put a stepparent into a bad situation. "Mom, do you want to know what Dad's new wife said about you?"

Do not take what the child says as being completely accurate. Keep your reactions low-key. Let the child know that he or she is loved and that you would do nothing intentionally to cause bad feel-ings. And never encourage a youngster by speaking negatively of the absent parent. A child could believe that he or she is earning approval by agreeing with you.

Children learn early to use the guilt feelings of parents and the competition of steprelatives to get what they want. "Dad's going to buy me a new three-wheeler for Christmas." When parents live apart, kids instinctively know they can increase their personal wealth when Mom, Dad, stepparents, and step-grandparents rival for the title of "best." The game produces only one winner, the child.

The best response is to acknowledge how nice the gift will be. "That's wonderful. I'd like to see it when you get it." The child has been informed that you are wise to his game and frustrates his efforts to create gift-giving competition. The statement should not be made as a put-down to the child, but a message that you have no intention to bet-ter the gift.

When the child sees that you are not going to play the game he might ask for a similar gift. Don't be afraid to say "no." Don't accuse the other person of trying to buy the child's love, even if it may be the motive behind the gift. Let the subject drop.

"I want to go live with my daddy." Demands by a child to live with the other parent may be concealing other messages or it might be an attempt to escape a coming punishment. Whatever the motive, he or she is questioning who is in control. Usually the parent is more affected by this blackmail than the stepparent. Most stepparents would simply say, "Good riddance." But when the mother believes her husband is too harsh with his punishment or the father thinks his new wife is overbearing, the threat could have serious consequence within the marriage.

The best answer is a direct one. "No, you may not go live with your father until you're older. If you still choose to then I will not stop you." Then search for the real problem. Don't try to reason with the child by asking what made him say it. Draw the youngster out, show genuine interest and patience. Most children will open up. Just don't panic by giving in or retaliating with threats of your own.

The child may be genuine about his desire to move. He misses the absent parent or feels sorry that he's all alone. Assure the youngster you do understand. Sympathize with his perfectly normal feelings. Sometimes a quick phone call to the absent parent may provide reassurance. Children can understand more than we think. Explain why custody was granted and at what age he can make the move if that is still what he wants.

STEPPARENT VS. STEPCHILD

While dissension games are initiated by the stepchild, most of them will pit the stepparent against another family member and will not involve the child in the mainstream of conflict. However, there are situations that will lead the stepparent and stepchild into a direct confrontation.

"You're not my real mother." If it's not spoken verbally the child has communicated the message to the stepparent through looks or actions which have said the same thing. The child is aggressively attempting to test the stepparent's authority in the new home. If he or she backs down or shows signs of weakness, the child will take control. Once established, that is a difficult condition to change.

Let the child know early that he or she must obey you and your rules. "You're right. I'm not your real mother and no one will change that. But when you are in our house and with me, you'll do as I say." Authority is established and the child can now relax. If the natural parent living in the home fails to support the stepparent, the child will feel free to challenge every decision the stepparent makes. This not only harms the marriage relationship, but also creates feelings of insecurity in the child.

"If you cared for me you'd let me do it." Children are aware of a stepparent's need for love and acceptance in the new relationships, and realize instantly what bargaining chips they hold. "He wants to make a good impression on my mom and to do that I've got to like him." The initial urge is to give in at least one time, but don't bargain with the child. Tell her your feelings and you don't think it's fair that you should be forced to put your love to a test. Let her know that love is not bought or sold, but that it comes as a result of an honest, trusting relationship.

STEPPARENTS VS. THEIR OWN CHILDREN

The games stepchildren play are motivated not only by a desire for material gain, but also to degrade the stepparent. "Your mom told me that she couldn't trust you with the car." Anything disruptive will suffice. Children sometimes believe that if they can only rid the home of its intruders, the stepparent and his or her children, things will get back to normal. Their lifestyle will never be the same as before, but children do not always understand this as quickly as adults.

Once the lie or accusation has been uncovered go immediately to its source. Confront the guilty stepchild and then clearly define the house rules. "Even though I am the stepparent here, I will not tolerate such behavior." Handle each situation individually, explaining to the youngster your rules concerning car use. Talk only to the stepchild involved, not with or in front of other children.

It's important to seek out the motive behind the stepchild's behavior. A young child may believe that if the stepparent were to leave, the natural mother or father would return. This would be a good time for the natural parent to explain that the absent parent will not be living in the home again.

Stepchildren want to be loved too. "I heard Sandy say a bad word at school today. What are you going to do about it?" Find out if Sandy really did use unacceptable language and tell her how you feel about it. Then tell her how you feel about her and that there is no need to compete for your love. Explain that you do love your natural child more because she has been with you since birth. But tell her that, in time, you expect to love her too.

Experts agree that there are so many things which can motivate a child's actions that a person cannot be quite sure what is responsible at any given moment. But understanding that it is a child doing childish things will help the stepparent. Always be an adult in your reactions, and don't retaliate by humiliating the youngster when she is only trying to earn your love.

STEPPARENT VS. GRANDPARENTS

Grandparents are not members of the immediate family, but they are influential parties nonetheless. "I don't have to obey you while grandma's here." The child may or may not speak these words, but his actions will speak for him. Eugene said, "Her boys are perfect gentlemen until their grandparents come to visit, then it's bedlam until they leave. I won't correct the boys in front of their grandparents because they get upset and the boys know it."

Stepparents will generally back off when the in-laws visit because they want to make a good impression. It's difficult to get someone to earn someone's friendship when you are spanking their grandchild. But the child should never feel he has the upper hand. Upsetting Grandma would be unfortunate, but order in the home must be maintained.

CONCLUSION

Stepparenting will always be a serious responsibility, never something to be taken lightly. Kids are always going to put stepparents to the test. They often will try to humiliate them and put them at a disadvantage. But be consistent and hang in there. If the home and stepfamily stay together, everybody wins.

CHAPTER 5

Background Differences

Knowing that the stepfamily is a unit merged from elements of other families helps a person understand there *will be* conflicts in the new home. It also is important to note there is a big difference in knowing that and understanding the *source* of the conflict. If a person understands that, he or she often can control the situation before it gets out of hand. Unlike the first, most couples uniting in a second marriage arrive at the altar from completely different backgrounds. In the first marriage the couple probably came from families of more or less the same financial status, attended the same school or college, and were brought up in the same faith.

Couples of second marriages meet through every possible circumstance, and often have little awareness of each other's backgrounds. "We work at the same office day-in and day-out, I see how Charles handles himself, and I know we'll be compatible." What a person does at the office offers few clues as to how he or she will react in a marriage.

In a recent conversation, Diane admitted, "The biggest obstacle in my marriage to Charles is our background differences. What we believe in, who we want as friends, our different interests. You don't think much about it when you're dating, and then all at once there's this big barrier." Children do not necessarily add to the problem, but they are more lives affected by the dilemmas background and attitude problems can create.

Secretaries marry bosses and doctors marry nurses, but while that may give the new wives more or less equal financial status with their successful husbands, it cannot give them similar backgrounds. Financially they may be compatible, but educationally, even culturally, they might be miles apart.

Ethnic boundaries no longer exist for many Americans, and interracial marriages have become accepted in many communities. However, such differences between the marriage partners lie at the heart of many problems in new blended families. After the marriage, their love may be strong and enduring enough to enable them to work through problems created by background differences.

But what about the children? They're not in love. They have just emerged from a broken home which has devastated their lives. The new marriage has ended any chance for reconciliation and they are not excited about solving any problems. In the creation of a new stepfamily, there are more lives involved than just two adults getting married. "I don't care how much you love him," fifteen-year-old Janet argued with her mother, "he's no good for us."

Many divorced parents see the importance of remaining in the same neighborhood, or as close as possible, so children can make the adjustments from the broken home gradually. These adjustments are made all the more difficult if the second marriage forces them into completely different surroundings.

With background differences as the root cause of so many stepfamily problems, I saw the need to divide this chapter into three specific categories: *Reactions from the child, Identifying the problem, and Solutions.* Since no two blended families will encounter the same situations it would be impossible to give an example to every crisis. However, there should be enough broadly-applicable material here to assist families in their search for family harmony and a successful marriage. Being prepared won't solve or alleviate all problems, but it can help a parent neutralize a major crisis.

REACTIONS FROM THE CHILD

Hostility

Alex screamed, "I don't care what you say, I don't want to live in the same house with that woman!" A timid boy, eleven-year-old Alex had never been a child to display anger. His flare-ups were wholly unexpected, and devastating to a surprised father and very unsuspecting stepmother.

Hostility can be expressed in both words and actions. When a child is unable to absorb his pain, the normal response is to lash out. When this has little effect on the situation, his next step would be to add action to the outburst.

Slamming the door behind him, Chet yelled, "I can't see why you did this to us." Exhibition of hostility is usually a release from built up energy brought on by the situation. Another child might act in a completely opposite way; not speaking, ignoring all family members, and refusing to cooperate. Whatever the response, it usually will be unrelated to the child's normal behavior and not directed toward any particular family member.

Resentment

"You may think this marriage was made in heaven, but wait until he's had a few weeks with us." Though reactions seem similar, resentment more of a "get even" effect. It often is brought on when a child has had to sacrifice something or has been placed in a uncomfortable situation. Unlike hostility, resentment usually will be directed toward a specific individual—often the remaining natural parent.

Peer pressure is one of the major challenges facing young people today. A child might easily become embarrassed about his or her new environment and retaliate at home. An unkind word spoken by a friend or classmate can easily destroy a child's self-confidence.

Children forced out of their secure surroundings want to retaliate. They are not mad at the world, just upset with their new situation. Anger at the absent parent, even if he or she was responsible for the break-up, can now be redirected to the other parent who has stuck by them through it all. The child has a new crisis now and doesn't like it.

Frustration

"I really want this to work out for you, but the more I try to make do with the change, the more frustrated I become." No matter what the circumstances and no matter how hard they may try, some children do not cope well with change ... but neither do some adults. Frustration in children will be expressed in a variety of ways. One child might respond with tenseness. Another will show symptoms of depression. Still others will become hyperactive. Some children's behavior may manifest signs of all three of these conditions. Sound frustrating? It is, especially to a new blended family already coping with a number of adjustments.

IDENTIFYING THE PROBLEM

Financial Differences

"I'm sorry we can't afford it." Diana said to her twelve-year-old son, who wanted a new tennis racket. Financial concerns affect virtually every family, both traditional and stepfamilies. Whenever a child has been raised in one financial environment it's difficult to change to another, especially downward, even if this has not been caused by the breaking up of a family.

In a traditional home, the customary decline in living standards is not usually by choice. A mother or father out of work—or some other misfortune—often will pull the family together. It would not be uncommon for a child to pick up part-time work to help through a crisis. Or if one parent has to work extra hours to supplement the income, the children often will do more around the home to lighten that parent's burden.

"If you hadn't married Clint we wouldn't be like this!" Linda blurted out in despair. "I don't care how much he can do for us," Tom cried, "or how nice this house is, I liked it better before." Changes in financial status can be for the better or the worse. When single parents remarry to improve their financial status (it does happen), some children see this as positive. To others it can be devastating. Children will often base their security in friendships, classmates, and a familiar neighborhood, with its ball field and playground. When a youngster is taken away from all of this, he or she is thrust into a whole new world. The new environment may offer more financially, but it's not the same.

Educational and Professional Differences

Educational and professional differences often coexist with financial differences. "But he's so stupid," Joy shouted in disgust. As was stated earlier, peer pressures have a great influence in the lives of children. A step down from the status of the absent parent in lifestyle, profession, or education level, remarked on by a negative comment at school, could cause trouble within the new blended family.

Ethnic Differences

"Don't you love us anymore? What will our friends think?" A recent census revealed there were 956,000 interracial married couples in the nation. 219,000, a little more than 22 percent, were unions between Blacks and Caucasians. The majority involved white and other races; Asians, American Indians, and Eskimos. Some of these marriages joined Blacks with mates who were not Caucasian. From 1980 to 1988, the number of interracial marriages climbed 46.8 percent, according to the U.S. Census Bureau.

The report does not disclose how many of these unions were second marriages and if so how many children were involved. It does reveal, however, that ethnic boundaries are being crossed. "I can't believe you're going out with her," protested thirteen-year-old Tammy. Many interracial relationship conflicts will surface before the marriage. It's likely others will develop after the marriage. A wise couple will deal with each problem as it occurs, not take the "we'll straighten everything out after we are married" approach.

To a secure couple in love, racial differences are not important. "I love him so much, and he's so good to me. I don't care if he's black, green, or yellow." To the child it can be an emotionally charged development, and a big problem after the marriage.

Special Interest Differences

Adults develop all sorts of special interests; sports, hobbies, handyman, crafts, hunting, and fishing are just a few examples. These influence the child as he or she grows up. Such interests might seem of no concern during the courtship, but they could evolve into very real problems in the new home. "He can't do anything," complained seven-year-old Steven to his mother. Though it might seem insignificant to her, it can have a great impact on a child.

Because he always worked while he was growing up, Steven's new stepfather never had an opportunity to play sports. It didn't matter to him who won the Super Bowl or the World Series. On the other hand,

Steven's father played college ball and now coaches a high school football team. Sports are important to Stephen. A wise man once said, "When we cease to dream we die." Children raised in the home with a sports-minded parent often dream of becoming big league stars one day. There's nothing wrong with dreaming. Without it, and the hard work talented athletes endure to fulfill their dreams, we would not have the Olympic medalists and other gifted athletes we enjoy and admire today.

"I don't see what he gets out of playing ball all the time," complained the new stepfather. "It wouldn't hurt him to work a little more around the house." When a child loses support and encouragement from his family, the dream begins to fade—and with it the child's spirit.

"Why won't you get out there and play ball like other boys." The reverse situation also develops. An over-zealous sports minded stepfather also can have an adverse effect on the child's self-confidence and interests. Not all children are cut out to be ballplayers. When this occurs, the child feels additional pressure. With the pressure comes additional conflict in the home.

SOLUTIONS

It would be impossible to give examples of all of the conflicts that could develop in a new blended family, and equally difficult to propose problem solutions that would work in each case. What might succeed in one home could fail completely in another. There are some solutions that will work in most situations, but sometimes two or three will have to be utilized simultaneously to obtain the desired result.

Understanding

With tension (latent if not obvious) already high in the blended family, a poor reaction often can turn a manageable situation into a major problem. "I don't care what you think, I love Ted and that's good enough for me!" It's fine that Mom loves Ted, but how she shares her feelings with a struggling teenage daughter affects the home environment. Tempers flare and conflicts snowball.

A wise parent and stepparent should begin by first analyzing how their new union will affect the children. What they see as possible future difficulties should not stop the marriage or break up the relationship, but it should help them prepare them for what is ahead.

Try to see the situation from the child's viewpoint. Be understanding without saying, "I understand." If you have not grown up in a broken home, had your parent marry someone with a complete different background, been forced to move to unfamiliar surroundings, and been ridiculed at school by classmates, don't say "I understand." You don't. Children don't want to hear lies.

Be truthful. "Linda, I don't understand what you're going through, but I want to help." Or, "I know this is putting you in a difficult position." This is not saying, "I understand everything, but it's telling the child, "I'm here for you." Those are some of the most reassuring words they can hear. A child can feel destroyed by his or her agony, to the point that she feels deserted. Knowing a parent is still there for her is very important.

"It's not so bad. You'll see." Whatever the predicament, don't make light of it. Children don't see this kind of situation with any kind of perspective. They only see the chaos their life is in right now.

Understanding is not a corrective action. It's an attitude. Acknowledging someone else's pain will not take it away, but it does let that individual know he or she has a confidant; someone to lean on and talk with, who support them without criticism.

Here is a note written at a high school graduation, two years after Donna's marriage to Clarence, an interracial union. "Mom, when you married Clarence, I thought my world ended. The kids at school ridiculed me so much I didn't want to wake up in the mornings. I didn't think you loved me anymore, and I never felt so alone. Thanks for seeing me through my crisis."

Working Together

Children need help in passing through the various phases in their struggle back to normal happy lives. One of the phases is the grave "feeling of abandonment" brought on by the absent parent's departure. Children often will compete for attention or added affection from the remaining parent. When a mother or father remarries, the child feels he or she has lost the only remaining parent. There is no longer an ally in the home for them. "Ted and I have nothing in common, but Mom loves him."

In general, children do not want conflicts in the home any more than adults do. Most of their offensive actions are nothing more than their acting out the frustration brought on by their new position forced upon them. Working together with the child reassures her she is still wanted and is an important member of the new family. "Ellen, I know Ted is not like your father, but I do love him. If you'll work with us we'll do everything to make it pleasant for you."

Making the Offer

How parents handle the crisis usually dictates its outcome. "It doesn't matter what you want. You're doing it our way." Tim is six-years-old. He doesn't like his new stepfather, hates his new home, and wants to live with his father. Mom realizes Tim is only six and not ready to choose for himself. She also knows the courts have given her custody, so—from her adult standpoint—it really doesn't matter that Tim is not happy with his situation. But a little diplomacy will go a long way toward helping him adjust.

The same approach will work with an older child. Depending on age, he or she may be able to make some decisions, and typically will at least make an effort to work through the crisis.

"If you'll work with us." Children want to blame someone for their unhappiness. Your offer to work through the crisis with them has the effect of throwing a bucket of water onto a raging fire. It may not put it out completely, but it is a step in the right direction. From this point on, if the child completely refuses to cooperate, the problem becomes pretty much his alone. There are no guarantees of success even if he agrees to work at it, but an honest effort at cooperation can solve many problems.

Don't Sacrifice Authority

Many parents try too hard to make the child happy. Parents and children agreeing to work together does make the family a team, not just individuals pulling away from each other, but every team needs a captain. There must be someone to make the final decision. Working together offers the child a chance for input and a chance to voice his or her disagreements, but it doesn't give the child final decision-making authority. A parent who grants that right to a child has lost more than his authority. He has lost the child's respect.

Ask for Help

Working together is also asking the child for his or her help. It's not good to have all the answers. An over-zealous father building a doghouse with his son can be a prime example. If the man does all the work—selects his tools, cuts the wood and hammers the nails without any assistance from the boy—it's not long before the child loses interest and starts to wander around the yard looking for something else to do.

A wise parent will ask for help. "Will you hold this for me while I cut the board?" or "Will you hammer the nail in here?" Include the child and he'll work all day.

"Allen, I know Ted's not athletic. He may not feel comfortable in the yard tossing the football like your father. But, if you'll work with us, I believe he'll be very supportive." Allen may discover qualities in Ted that were not part of his father's make-up. This is not putting one man in competition with another, or degrading an absent father; it's just helping a child build a relationship with a new stepparent.

Communication

Communicate with the child. Many times when a parent remarries the lines of communication between parent and child have been broken. The child believes the parent has betrayed him by remarrying and may believe he too, like his natural parent, will be replaced. This is only a misunderstanding, but without proper communication from the parent children are left to believe what they want.

We Won't Go Back

Leaving children in the dark to believe what they want can also open the door for more serious problems. With background differences causing major problems in many blended families, it is not surprising children sometimes reason the way they do. When children live with the suspicion that if they cause enough disturbance, Mom might decide to go back with Dad, there will be no end to the problems they might create.

When parents fail to draw definite boundaries adolescents easily become confused and frustrated. Even though it should be understood that the marriage signifies the divorce is final and there will be no reconciliation, some children refuse to give up. Emphasizing background differences can be used as a tough offense. "She'll see the light one day and we'll go back."

A simple definitive statement can clear the air. "Joy, I wish that our home would be united. I know that you and many others wonder why I married Ted, but that's between him and me. We are going to make it. No matter how much you disagree there will be no going back."

Minimize the Differences

"Just because Cliff didn't play high school or college sports doesn't mean he won't be an excellent resource on your science project." Children, like adults, often become so absorbed with their current predicament they refuse to see any advantages. "Did I tell you Sharon took clothes design in college?" Or, "Did you know Mark rebuilt the engine in his pickup truck?"

Don't overstate the new stepparent's virtues or use his or her accomplishments as a way to put down the absent parent. Children have heard enough back-biting. Just stimulate the child's awareness of the possibilities. Point out positive characteristics. Remember, the child will not be looking for them by himself.

Don't Make False Promises

"I know you'll love Brian." Or, "Give it a little time, you and Donna will become very close." There are no guarantees a child will ever love his stepfather or develop a close relationship with a stepmother. The more a child is backed into a corner, the more likely he or she will become defensive. False promises only harm the relationship between parent and child. In most cases it's not the person that the child dislikes, it's the background differences.

It's Only Temporary

"I know my marriage to Darin has upset you very much. I wanted you to be happy, but it doesn't look very promising. I hope you will understand. I'll not always have you with me and Darin is the man I want to be with." It's good to let the child know the facts. His or her situation is temporary. One day an older child will move out on his or her own. The younger child, at the age set by the state's laws, also can choose with which parent he or she wishes to live.

When a child realizes that his or her predicament is only temporary she often is more willing to cooperate. "Mom, I never looked at it that way before. I'll do what I can to help." When the initial pressure is removed the tension also eases in the home. The child then sees that his or her situation is not so bad after all. Advising the child of this is not an answer to everything, but it does create a diversion and gives the blended family more time to create a workable environment.

A Reminder

"He's not like Dad, and I hate his house." "She can't do anything, why did you marry her?" The list of unpleasant remarks is seemingly endless. Broken homes are created by overwhelming problems, but the home did not break up overnight. Most families have gone through months, even years, of turmoil before divorce becomes their only escape. When the child is so absorbed in her current misery, she often forgets how bad things were before.

The screaming, the fighting, the abuse, and the sleepless nights may all be forgotten because of her more recent dissatisfaction. "Helen, you know how it was before your father left. You told me how you would hide in the closet when he came home. A reminder will at least cause the child to compare her new situation with the pain and misery she left behind. Being in a home with a loving parent and caring stepparent, trying to build a successful new life, is much better than the years of misery … no matter what problems exist.

CONCLUSION

Couples from various backgrounds are forming new blended families every day. Some of them will make it, others will fail. What happens depends upon the family. Those who just drift, thinking everything will be all right, probably will fail. Those who work at it, constantly trying new ways to improve relationships, are likely to succeed.

Gene, 32, is a black man. Darlene, his new wife, is white and 30, with two sons ages seven and nine. To the community this was an unacceptable union. Because of harassment, Darlene finally gave up her good law office job and took one in the city office that paid less. Three years later Darlene admits, "I never thought it would have been so difficult for the boys. The outside pressure was tremendous. Gene and I could handle it, but it hurts when you see your kids going through so much for something you've done. If Gene and I had known how hard it was going to be, we both would have probably said let's forget it. But we were so determined this time that we never stopped trying."

Gene and Darlene are both involved in the Band Boosters organization and other activities at the boys' school. They attribute the family's success to their involvement in the boys' lives. A co-worker of Gene says, "I don't think I would have had the stamina, but those two showed that it can be done."

CHAPTER 6

Understanding the Stepchild

Five-year-old Kevin sat at the breakfast table eating while his stepdad drank coffee and read the morning paper. Kevin began to tap his foot against his chair. "Stop that," the annoyed stepfather said. Keven stopped for a while, but soon started again. "Kevin, did you hear me? I said to stop." The tapping stopped for a short time and then started again. Raging, the stepfather slammed down the paper and grabbed the boy by the arm yelling, "I said to stop! Why do you constantly try to annoy me? Can't you just sit and eat quietly?"

Loud noises, annoying habits, and nervous twitches are among the many things which frustrate parents, especially instant stepparents. Kevin can't answer because he doesn't know why he does those things. But there is a reason somewhere, and there are ways to handle the situation without causing more tension in an already fragile stepfamily.

The stepfamily is not the traditional family, but it is a family unit with a husband, wife, and children. They just are not all blood related. Goals for the stepfamily should be virtually identical to those of the traditional family; to establish lasting relationships, to raise happy and contented children, and to live happily together. Since these goals were not attained in the first marriage, stepfamily couples should be more determined than "first marrieds" to succeed in their second marriage.

Children will play a major part in the success or failure of the new family unit. If the kids and stepmom get along, dad will be happy. Or, if the stepfather can tolerate the children's behavior, he is not likely to leave.

To function well with children and to understand their behavior, at the same time stimulating them to grow in a useful, cooperative way, a person must know something of the psychological mechanisms involved. All human behavior has a purpose and represents movement toward a certain goal. Sometimes a parent may know the purpose behind a child's action, but other times she may not. To the instant stepparent it can seem overwhelming. "I didn't know raising kids was so complicated!" If the stepparent wishes to someday have a good relationship with the child, a good understanding of the child and what motivates his or her activity is essential.

Before a child's direction can be modified there must also be a knowledge of what makes him move. A child can be forced to behave differently, but unless what motivates the action is changed he will revert to his original behavior.

Occasionally, information pertaining to the behavior can be uncovered by examining the outcome the child obtains. In Kevin's case his stepfather became harassed by the tapping sound. Yelling at Kevin and grabbing his arm made Kevin the victor in that situation. Kevin may not have been aware that he wanted to irritate his stepfather, yet he had an unconscious desire to do so. On the other hand, it's possible he knew exactly what he was doing.

If stepparents could see the situation through the eyes of the stepchild they would better understand the child's actions.

A CHILD'S LOSS

In humans, and especially in children, there is a need to try to make sense out of what has happened and why it has happened. The stepfamily has been formed because of the loss of a parent, either by death or divorce. Children will go to all extremes to examine the events which led up to the loss in order to prevent further losses. "What's wrong with me?" or "What did I do?" are questions they ask themselves repeatedly.

An impatient stepparent may refuse to see why the child is taking her loss so seriously. In death, the reasoning is, time should have healed the wounds. For divorce, the span between the divorce and remarriage should have served as a sufficient period of adjustment. One teenage girl said, "I thought I had gotten over the divorce and the loss of my father's presence until the day my mom remarried. I didn't realize until then that my dad would never be coming back."

Whatever has occurred, life must go on. Rules should not be changed to accommodate a child's sadness. But, the stepparent should be conscious of the fact that the child has suffered a loss in her life and is now being forced to accept a significantly different lifestyle.

THE CHILD'S GUILT

Many children assume they were in some way responsible for the loss they incurred. "I was so bad or unlovable that my own parent wouldn't stay with me." The child may soon begin to act out his or her understanding of how he or she was bad. Some children will withdraw from affection and caring, "How could anyone love me when my own father didn't?" and they will refuse to trust anyone.

If a child attributes the loss to "wrong" feelings, he may never allow those feelings again or he may avoid feelings altogether. "I don't care what happens and you can't make me." To an adult this may sound foolish, but a child can believe that his bad thoughts and feelings toward a parent caused the divorce or death.

Children who do attribute the loss of a parent to wrong thinking may become so uncertain that their ability to think correctly is impeded. They could have trouble in school, problems making decisions, or even difficulty trusting themselves. Search out the unwarranted guilt the child is living with, and try to help him back to a normal way of life.

DISORGANIZATION

Jeff is normally a good student, but his grades are slipping. He doesn't have the drive to settle down and get into his work. He rarely knows where to begin reading when called on in class, and in discussions around the table Jeff seems to be miles away. Grieving takes a lot of work. So much that there is little energy left for living.

Children in such a disorganized state will respond very little to accusations of laziness and daydreaming. Try to give them time to discuss their loss. Grieving children also will have trouble following simple instructions, sometimes irritating a stepparent who is accustomed to obedience. Sent into the next room to retrieve three items, the child may return with one, or call out, "What did you say?"

Simply because a child displays these symptoms does not guarantee grieving is the cause. But something is on his mind that should not be there. The quicker help is made available to him, the better for both child and parents.

THE DESIRE TO BELONG

The strongest motivation is the desire to belong. A child's security or lack of it depends upon his or her feeling of acceptance within the group or family. From infancy, the child worked to establish his place in the home. The divorce destroyed that work and whatever he rebuilt after the divorce was damaged at the time of the remarriage. A new family is now formed with a new parent he knows little about and new brothers and sisters with whom he never has had to contend before. Mom's words are little comfort when she says, "We're a family now and everything is going to be all right."

Everything's not all right, at least not for the child. Children are expert observers, but they can be very poor judges. A child often draws wrong conclusions. A caring stepfather may be misconstrued as only trying to win mom's approval. Or a childless stepmother can be accused of trying to steal the child's love from the natural mother. With parent and stepparent trying hard to build a new family and give everyone a sense of belonging, the child can be working against himself.

Not all bad feelings are triggered by anger and resentment. They may be a child's misinterpretation of comments or events, in his or her overanxious desire to belong.

UNDERSTANDING THE WEEKEND VISITOR

All during the week people look forward to the weekend; two glorious days of relaxation and recreation. School children know it's a time away from teachers and homework. But what about the weekend stepchild? She is forced to change her normal routine, to "invade" a crowded house or apartment, and be expected to overflow with excitement about being there. In many cases the child would rather skip the visit, but mom can be so glad to get her out of the house she is not given a choice.

The constant change of routine can make it difficult for the child. It's changing first on a Friday, then changing back Sunday evening. Younger children can have feeding habits disrupted, toilet training hindered, and their learning process slowed because of the added confusion. The weekend visit for the older child or adolescent may come into conflict with other planned activities, like a party or a ball game.

Before judging a child's actions and reactions, try to search out and appreciate the real cause. A little understanding might be the right foundation for the beginning of a strong relationship.

SIGNS OF IMMATURITY

A child's common reaction to trauma, or to any situation that disrupts the usual pattern of satisfaction,is for him or her to fall back to an earlier level of development in hope of regaining the contentment previously enjoyed. Or the child may cease to advance beyond the current developmental level to avoid taking on the additional responsibilities that accompany higher levels of maturation.

Some children may revert to stages of infancy, with thumb sucking and the use of baby talk. Or a fully toilet-trained child may start having accidents again or ask the parent for assistance when using the bathroom. School age children will sometimes fake an illness to avoid the pressure of school, trying to stay home to be pampered. Others may respond to their new environment with whining and complaining about their chores. Even in children who used to work well with others, the desire for individual attention takes precedence.

Developmental regression and stagnation tend to be temporary setbacks that should clear up within a few weeks or months. When they persist, other factors usually can be found. The natural parent may be overindulging the child in some way, trying to compensate for any loss. When this situation develops and the parents become aware of what is happening, it probably is time for a husband and wife strategy session.

AFFECTED SELF-ESTEEM

Losing a parent, for any reason, and joining another family delivers a powerful blow to a child's developing sense of trust and self-esteem. If the child has had the satisfaction of developing and experiencing a secure feeling of self-worth and a sense of self-control, he is likely to be a more competent, trusting, and confident person. The longer this foundation has been established, the more apt he is to expect himself to be able to meet life's challenges, and the more trust he puts into others to help him. A child without a good base is more vulnerable and apt to have problems in adjusting.

Alan is fourteen years old and for the past two years he has done odd jobs to earn extra spending money. Alan's father worked with him in the beginning, helping him with the jobs and teaching him to manage his money effectively. Alan's teachers recognized his drive for success and commented about his high level of self-esteem. But during Alan's ninth year of school his parents divorced and Alan's father moved away.

No one anticipated Alan's reaction. His grades plummeted, his outgoing personality turned to shyness, and his self-control vanished. His mother tried to maintain the household, but she lacked the leadership needed for a stable home life.

When a child suddenly loses a parent, the foundation of his self-esteem is challenged. His trust in the consistency of the parent's availability for support, protection, and comfort is eroded. And he may be afraid to restructure his confidence, especially if the remaining parent shows signs of weakness or vulnerability.

Developing stepfamily relationships will be impeded because of the child's fears that all relationships will end in failure. A child who has never had a stable and secure relationship with a natural parent will be even more untrusting. The child might have been told repeatedly that he doesn't measure up. His self-image is that of one who is unlovable and unwanted. When adversity comes he expects others to reject him and be hostile rather than helpful.

A strong sense of shame also follows the child's loss, making her feel unloved and unworthy. Karen's mother left with her boss, abandoning Karen and her father. "Was I so unlovable that my own mother couldn't stand to be around me?" Instead of confidence in one's self and an increased feeling of self-esteem, the child feels publicly exposed and disgraced.

Self-esteem so disrupted will not immediately repair itself when there is a new marriage, but the speed and degree of recovery depends upon the child. He or she can either erect a new foundation or reestablish the old one founded in the absent parent. The older child might find it less complicated to build that foundation within himself, no longer needing another person.

FEARS OF ABANDONMENT

The perception of children of divorce is that the parent abandoned them. Even with reassurance that they will always be loved, the child tends to hold onto the idea, "What's going to happen next?" The stable world has ended and there's no guarantee that what happened won't happen again.

Children tend to generalize from past experiences and may come to view all human relationships as potentially unstable. If the custodial parent was instrumental in the absent parent's departure, what's to keep that from happening to the new stepparent. "He may not be around too long."

Younger children speculate that they too might be subject to ejection from the home for some misbehavior. For example, a mother might have initiated the divorce because of certain unacceptable activities on the part of the father. But the child sees only that her dad was forced to leave because he, the child, was bad and wonders what's to stop mother from doing the same thing again.

Stepparents cannot do much to alleviate it, but they need to understand the confusion about the absent parent which children bring into the new family. Does he still love me? Will he visit or is he gone forever? These children often will ask similar questions of the custodial parent. It's not unusual for the child to ask for reassurance many times during the day.

It is hard to live with the fear of abandonment. Some children will try to decrease their feeling of pending desertion by provoking punishment from the remaining parent. They are willing to suffer pain for the assurance that the parent is still very much there. What better way to know of a parent's existence than to be hit or slapped by them?

Many of the childish fears will diminish with time. A wise stepparent will watch for these and other signs and try to understand the child's inner feelings. Before a good relationship can be established, the true source of the behavior must be uncovered.

FRUSTRATIONS

At the parent's wedding the child, with virtually no voice in the situation, becomes a stepchild. The ceremony makes the mother or father someone else's new spouse, but it makes the child part of a family he knows little about. He is scared, curious, and jealous, but—in spite of these conflicting feelings—expected to be happy.

Few adults can endure the pain of death or divorce calmly. No child can. The confusion and fright cut deeply and the scars remain forever. "I've got so many grandparents now I can't keep up with them all," said seven-year-old Samantha. Children of stepfamilies have two parents, two stepparents, and four sets of grandparents, all competing for the child's love and attention.

Grandparents in particular are offended if they are not invited to every recital and school function. And it's too much for the youngster to choose one person over another. When quarreling parties are placed in one auditorium, the child fears public embarrassment from a noisy stepfamily argument. "Why can't I just love them all the same?"

"He doesn't act like a normal child." Stepparents are too quick to label the new arrival in the home. A stepmother's opinion of a normal child derives from the completely subjective theory that her kids are normal and all others are abnormal.

WHAT FORMS A LIFE?

The child is introduced to society through the experiences of the parents. He will form views and opinions that reflect his family's outlook on various subjects. He absorbs their values, beliefs, and convictions and tries to fit within the family pattern, or the standard set by the parents. His concept of material advantages also reflects the economic examples of his mother and father. And if his parents look down on people, the child may take the same approach and seek superiority in racial and ethnically-mixed social circles.

"He acts just like his mother." Stepparents are quick to criticize by comparing the child to the absent parent. He may not act exactly like his mother, but he is a mixture of many things provided from his first family. If the parents were warm, friendly, and cooperative, the same relationships are apt to develop between family members. But if they were hostile and competed for dominance, the same style is likely to develop in the child. Simply because the child has become a stepchild overnight does not mean he is able to wipe out all those years of personal development and immediately become a different person.

The stepparent must understand there are reasons behind a child's behavior, be it good or bad. If the child is young enough when he joins the reconstructed family, he or she may assume some of the stepparent's traits pretty quickly. But a weekend visitor of any age will rarely adapt any stepparent's characteristics unless there is a very close relationship between the two and the child tries to emulate the adult.

PRECONCEIVED IDEAS

Stepparents need to remember that Cinderella is the stepchild everyone knows. Little children delight in the excitement and suspense, believe in the magic, and rejoice at the victorious ending. Sadly, they remember for the rest of their lives that stepmothers are bad and stepchildren are good. No matter how good their intentions might be, they have a very hard time lightening the stepmother's black image. Cinderella's miserable experiences take young readers to the very center of their sensitivities.

Children also are aware of the adult usage of the term "stepchild."

A slum or ghetto area is now called, "The stepchild of the city." If you want to indicate neglect, say stepchild, and everyone will understand the definition. Children come to their new family with these ideas tucked away. It's not that they intend to cause problems, but they are afraid to reach out for fear of being hurt further.

PLACING THE BLAME

Long before the final decision for divorce, children are exposed to the question, "Who's at fault?" In the weeks and months of fighting parents are constantly blaming each other for difficulties incurred in the marriage. Although no fault divorce laws prevail in many areas, strong opinions still exist. And where couples extend disagreements over custody, alimony, and child support, lawyers usually can be depended on to intensify the problems.

Children tend to think in the most simple terms, and the younger they are, the less likely they are to accept and understand the language of joint difficulties. The parent who initiated the divorce is the more likely candidate for blame even if he or she is the one who received custody. The reproach is brought into the stepfamily by the child and is transferred to the logical scapegoat, the stepparent. "If you'd have left my mother alone she would have gone back to my dad!"

Sheena said, "It didn't matter who I married, my daughter condemned him." It's easier for a child to blame a stepparent rather than hold a grudge against a loving parent. From the child's standpoint, they only know what they had and now it's gone. Someone has to be at fault.

GUILT OVER DISLOYALTY

Many children of divorce live with some conflict of disloyalty. They are brought up with a deep sense of commitment to family members, especially to parents, and are taught from birth to love and respect them. When the divorce happens children are forced to make decisions and take actions that reveal, without question, where their loyalties lie.

Some children side with the parent with whom they are living in order to avoid alienating that parent. But at the same time they feel guilty for disloyalty to the absent parent. The stepfamily only makes the situation more complex. There is not only a third party, the stepparent, to contend with, but a whole new family. The confusing time of divorce has passed and the restless period between marriages is over, but the child still lives in fear of disloyalty to the absent parent if he or she expresses pleasure in the new home.

The absent parent is the key ingredient, but few parents—even for the sake of their children—are willing to help them adjust to their new environment. A wise and compassionate stepparent will not force the child, but will try to understand why the child is hesitant to reach out and help her through the difficult time. Fear of losing a loved one's love is more than a child can bear to think about.

ADJUSTING

The adjustment period is always difficult for a newly married couple, and children only make it more complicated. "How come it's taking him so long to adjust?" John was thirteen and his sister, Ellen, was eleven when their parents divorced. Ellen's grades dropped drastically, and three months later her mother was called in for private consultation. Ellen, usually an outgoing student, became quiet and withdrawn and would spend endless hours in her room alone. John's grades also plummeted. His friendly demeanor changed to rudeness overnight, and soon his friends began excluding him from their plans.

Six months later John has not changed, and is satisfied with his new label—a loner. On the other hand, Ellen became her old self. Her grades were up to normal and she was excited about her mother's new boyfriend. By the end of the year the mother remarried. Ellen went on as usual, but John, never recovered from the original upset, had even more trouble accepting his new situation.

Same divorce, same second marriage, but two different reactions. In the beginning Ellen, since she was the younger of the two, was expected to be more upset over the circumstances than John. However, a puzzling pattern has been uncovered in divorces involving children. Boys take the failure harder than girls, take longer to adjust, and exhibit more disruptive behavior. "Boys are simply more vulnerable to stress of any kind than girls," says Dr. Jerome Kagan, professor of psychology at Harvard University and a specialist in early childhood development.

The findings conflict with the macho behavior men expect from boys and will confuse and frustrate many an anxious stepfather.

LOSS OF RESPONSIBILITY

When parents divorce, the work of the home must go on. A mother or father left alone to run the household soon discovers it's more than one person can do. Wise parents will delegate certain chores to the children in order to lighten their load and to ensure everything gets done. Where the mother is alone, the son will often take on the responsibilities abandoned by the father, and try to be the man around the house. If the father is the custodial parent, the children will take over the household roles vacated by the mother.

Most children enjoy the added responsibility and they adapt to their obligations and accept their new lifestyle. However, the single parent doesn't see things the same way. He or she is depressed and missing adult companionship, and sees remarriage is the only solution. But the kids who worked so hard to make life pleasant for the parent are not ready to surrender the duties they have assumed and enjoyed. The son is no longer needed to be the man around the house after the second marriage. And the teenage daughter who tried to fill mom's shoes, cooking and taking care of the younger children, finds herself replaced by a stepmother. Filling those roles may have been tough, but they did it for the parent and they feel pretty good about themselves.

Stepparents need to understand what motivates children's behavior, good or bad. Negative reaction may not be the result of hatred or personal differences; it might just be caused by confusion over the new situation in which they find themselves. Help bring the child back to a normal, happy life where he or she can continue to grow and develop as a person. Whether you are a stepmother or stepfather, your spouse needs your help in this situation.

CHAPTER 7

Building Strong Relationships

The success and future of the stepfamily hinges upon the ability of its members to develop lasting, positive relationships with each other. Creating a good relationship between stepparent and stepchild is extremely difficult because of the many barriers to be overcome. However, this relationship carries great importance because of its overall influence on the bond between husband and wife.

"My daughter was better off when it was just the two of us, "said Karla. "I thought when I married Phil everything would be better for her." Second marriages occur for a variety of reasons. But, whatever the reason, a parent does not want to discover her child's welfare has deteriorated due to the marriage. A poor relationship between a child and its stepparent does not make for a good home life.

"If you don't care about my kids, then I don't think you care much about me!" Very few parents can relax and enjoy a new marriage when they know their children are unhappy. The stepparent should not be expected to be a miracle worker (some kids can't be satisfied, no matter how hard the stepparent tries), but for the benefit of the home and marriage, he should make an honest effort.

Researchers agree that stepfathers are more likely to establish and maintain good relationships with stepchildren than stepmothers. The probable cause for this conclusion is the fact that stepmothers spend more time with the stepchildren, allowing time for disharmony to develop.

IT'S NOT AN EASY TASK

Good relationships do not happen by accident. They come as a result of perseverance, self-sacrifice, and hard work. The main objective for a stepparent and stepchild should be friendship, not a master-slave relationship; a friendship based on equality, caring, common interests, and respect. You cannot buy a child's friendship by making him or her feel indebted to you. "Look what I've given up so you could live with us." Or, "See how much it cost for you to live like this and you don't appreciate it."

Friendship is earned by being a friend. It requires understanding, mutual love, spending quality time together, and simply liking the child. "There is a magic that rests in the relationship between a child and a warm, sensitive, knowledgeable adult," said Edward Zigler, Professor of Psychology at Yale University. "It is in the fullness of that relationship that we see the child's path to growth and development."

The relationship is hindered from the beginning because there has been no basis for love between the stepparent and stepchild. The stepparent comes to the family jealous of the spouse's love for his or her child and also frightened of the extra responsibility. On the other hand, the child has preconceived fears of the stepparent and is afraid to reach out. According to T.S. Eliot, "The major cause of anxiety and depression in this century is our inability to love or be loved." You do not walk into another person's life and secure an instant love for them. Yet the stepparent and stepchild are thrust into a family situation without preparation, sometimes with nothing more than an introduction.

INGREDIENTS FOR SUCCESS

Three key ingredients are necessary for building positive relationships: unconditional love, caring, and cherishing. It's difficult to master these elements in step-relations because no blood ties exist between adult and child.

Unconditional Love

Unconditional love means no "ifs." It's described as loving the child apart from what he or she does or does not do. Not, "I'll love you if you'll do this for me." But, "I'll love you no matter what you do." A positive relationship cannot exist when one party feels he or she is unworthy of love and must earn it from the other.

Unconditional love includes accepting a child's right to be different and to hold different views and opinions. Learn to understand the child's moods and emotions, and stand beside him when he is in trouble. A natural parent who has nurtured the child from birth feels a closeness to the child and will more easily display unconditional love. But the stepparent wonders "How else can I feel? I only became his stepmother two weeks ago!"

Children need to sense a dependable source of security in their rapidly changing world. At no time should withdrawal of love or rejection be used as punishment for misbehavior. The child should always feel secure in a parent or stepparent's basic love and acceptance. In a close, unconditional love relationship both parties are more free to be themselves and to act spontaneously without fear of being rejected by the other. Weaknesses are accepted, not exploited.

The opposite of unconditional is conditional which is the foundation for most of the love in current society. A love based totally on merit, "If you love me you'll ..." When a child discovers that love was acquired by merit it senses that someday, for some reason, that love will be withdrawn.

Caring

Caring means to have a deep interest in everything about the other person. Be concerned for his or her thoughts, feelings, and what happens to them in general. It's placing the child's welfare on, at least, an equal footing with your own. Where this type of atmosphere exists, the child begins to think differently about himself, "If someone cares so much for me, maybe I should care more about myself."

When a stepparent displays care and concern, a stepchild struggling with life's unpleasantries can be encouraged to pick himself up and make the best of his circumstances. Also, the child who learns that a stepparent has his welfare at heart, is more likely to accept the rules and regulations set up in the new home.

Cherishing

Cherishing is loving and appreciating the child for the unique qualities that make him what he is, not what he has accomplished or what you would like him to be. Simple statements such as "You're really special to me," or "You are an important person," can do wonders for a child who is searching for identity and security after the collapse of his home. Many stepparents find this hard to do since they too are struggling in a new situation.

Unconditional love, caring, and cherishing are all necessary, but they can seem impossible challenges to the stepparent. Caring for another person does not happen instantly. Nor can a person be concerned about another's thoughts and feelings until they know and understand them. Some step-relationships take years before they reach stability.

TIME IS IMPORTANT

"I'm too busy now, you'll have to wait until later." Children hear this from parents and stepparents daily. These words are spoken not only because there is no love yet in the relationship, but also because parents do not have the commitment to spend time with the children. Good relationships take time; time to learn about the child, who he is, and what he likes and dislikes. In return, the child needs to discover who the stepparent is.

QUALITY TIME

There is a definite distinction between merely allowing a child in your presence and giving him quality time alone. The new stepfamily may consist of his, mine, and our kids and it's difficult to give evenly to all.

But, the child didn't ask to be put into the situation. For the greatest family harmony, give each child the same amount of time each week and explain the reasons for doing so. The biological child may get offended when forced to share her parent with a step-sibling, but she must understand it's for the good of the overall family.

Set aside from one half to two hours every week for each child. This quality time should not be canceled except for very unusual circumstances. Establish certain goals for this time. Both parties should try to think of activities which they enjoy and can share. This is not the time for lecturing or criticizing, or for trying to persuade the child to do something. Initiate the conversation so the child will become relaxed and feel that he or she is really wanted. One stepfather said, "I didn't think I could possibly enjoy spending any time alone with my stepson until we tried it. Now we both look forward to Saturday mornings, just the two of us."

Quality time allows the child to become an active part of an adult's life.

BUILD A COMFORTING RELATIONSHIP

Every person gets frightened or has feelings of insecurity at one time or another. When this happens, that person—child or adult—needs comfort, some consoling when she is down. The stepchild has just been through one of life's most devastating storms; loss of a parent through death or divorce. The circumstances of both can result in serious damage to the child's security system. When a child's pain cannot be shared with another, it becomes a cancer, always eating away at him.

Children whose emotional needs are not attended to may turn to drugs, violence, or other forms of self-destructive behavior. At this time a wise stepparent will move in and become the anchor the child so desperately needs. This is a time for consoling and soothing, not a time to criticize or give advice.

WAYS TO EXPRESS COMFORT

Stay calm. The last thing an upset child needs in a time of crisis is someone excited. Create an atmosphere of safety and optimism. "The greatest gift my mother gave me was optimism," Brett said. "No matter how bad today is, tomorrow was going to be better."

Show compassion. Seeing things from the child's perspective makes things more understandable. "I'm sorry you've been through so much." A little sympathy or compassion at the right time can go a long way in a new relationship.

Listen carefully. Some children will not want to talk about their problems and hurts, but others will. Whichever the case, encourage the children to open up. "A problem shared is on its way to being resolved." Try to hear what the child is really saying. Children will sometimes conceal their actual hurt until they know the listener can be trusted. Never do anything to cause doubt in a child's mind.

Show love. A hurting child often will come down too hard on himself. Assure him that no matter what he thinks, you are standing by him. "I love you no matter what happened."

Respond in time of need. Children will not always give clear signals indicating the kind of help they need, or how much. Some will accept only so much help, fearing being too vulnerable. The signals may be vague, so a stepparent must be sensitive to certain signs; unexplained silence, irritability, withdrawal, drinking, or even overeating. Respond with love.

Be there. Sometimes comfort is given just by being there. A stepchild is more apt to appreciate a stepparent's presence than his advice. And a hurting stepchild may interpret good intentions as prying into private affairs. Often, after quiet consolation, there will be time for talk later.

Their problems are not unique. Children, like adults, tend to think no one else has problems like theirs. Few problems exist today that haven't been researched and described in books or articles. Find a book on the particular subject and let the child see for herself the views and opinions others have on "her" situation. A wise stepparent might relate a similar experience from her own life and how it affected her. Don't talk down to the child, and don't make up a story merely to soothe her hurt. It can only hurt the relationship when the child thinks the adult is making light of a very real problem in her life.

When a child needs a shoulder to lean on, give him exactly that; don't shame or find fault, be careful not to minimize the problem, and don't threaten punishment.

PUT TRUST IN THE RELATIONSHIP

Politicians capitalize on the public's need for trust when they pledge, "I am a man you can depend upon." People look for leaders who are honest, straightforward, and truthful; someone who has their best interest at heart. A stepchild is looking for the same traits in stepparents.

The stepchild's home has been destroyed and he or she is searching for someone who can be a foundation for their renewed stability. Because of the child's immature thinking, the custodial parent may not always have the child's trust. "You made my daddy go away and I don't want to stay with you." The parent may have initiated the divorce for good reasons, but those reasons tend to be complicated and not easy to use in convincing a hurting child. All she knows is her dad was forced to leave and mom brought home another man whom she wants to take her dad's place.

An alert stepparent should step in when he sees the child begin to reject the custodial parent. To a hurting child, the stepparent may be the least of two evils. With her existing feelings as they are toward her mother, there is no one else to trust. The stepparent is selected only on the premise that he has done nothing thus far to hurt the child or to cause her *not* to trust. The opportunities may be slim, but if the step-parent ignores them, the child likely will place her trust in someone outside the home; a friend, relative, or someone not as qualified as the stepparent. If this occurs it may be difficult for the stepparent to gain that trust later.

HONESTY AND RELIABILITY

Trust is based on two principles, honesty and reliability. No matter what their age, people want honest answers to questions. When a person tells a child that something won't hurt and it does, the child has been deceived. Adults try to shield children from impending hurt by saying, "Everything's going to be all right." When the child comes face-to-face with divorce or death, they soon learn everything is not all right. The "trustability" of that person, even with its good inten-tions, has been damaged in the eyes of the child. A child may not un-derstand all things, but her level of understanding improves when she is given honest answers.

Nobody's perfect, yet adults try to give that impression to chil-dren. When parents and stepparents refuse to admit their faults and failures, they are teaching the children in their care not to own up to their own shortcomings.

Stepparents feel the need to exaggerate and boast on issues, but they are still forms of deception. "Christy, I'm sorry I didn't pick that up for you today. I was too busy." Admit that you forgot. A stepchild will be much more open to sharing her thoughts and weaknesses when she learns that adults make mistakes too.

Don't make promises that can't be kept. It's so important to step-parents to win a child's love and attention they will sometimes promise too much. An unkept promise only comes back to haunt the relation-ship. Rather than promising quickly now and reneging later, it's better to say, "I can't say for sure, but I'll do my best to get it." A child will not be inclined to argue with a person's best.

Children want adults to be themselves. Don't hide behind a façade, but be genuine in all actions. If you're having a bad day, admit it. When the children upset you, confront them with true feelings. Or if it's an answer you're not sure of, be honest. Stepparents who confess their inadequacies advance in credi-bility in the eyes of a child.

Trust also is built on reliability. Stepparents need to be consistent day after day. Do not fluctuate from cheerful, loving, and appreciative one day to angry, reclusive, and sad the next. "One thing I can say for my stepmom," said Trish, "if she says she'll be here, I can depend on it."

The child is trying to rebuild. Help her with the foundation.

THE RELATIONSHIP NEEDS AFFECTION

Many stepparents come into their new role with a sincere desire to show love to the stepchild. But after months, sometimes years, there still are no signs of love in the relationship. Some people are embarrassed to tell other family members, especially stepfamily members they love or care for them. "We just never did that in our home," recalled Ted. "Now it's difficult for me to say those words to my stepson."

Affection means expressing feelings of love, either verbally, or by positive facial expressions—such as a smile—or by touch. Some people signify love and concern less directly, with hard work, self-sacrifice, or by giving gifts. Such efforts are fine, but they lack the warmth and impact of a direct statement or physical gesture. Allen said, with tears in his eyes, "I know my dad worked hard to provide things our family needed, but never once did he ever put his arm around me or my brother and tell us how much he loved us." There should never be any doubt in a child's mind about your love for him.

Affection tells the child not only that you love her, but you like her as well. "If Paul could only see what he's doing to Ellen," said Margaret. I know he loves my daughter. When we go out he buys for her just as he does for his kids, and he makes sure she has everything she needs. But he's never told her of his love. After two years Ellen tends to avoid him when he's home and Paul can't understand her distant behavior.

Affection given and received contributes in a number of ways to the harmony of a household. For example, a child who experiences affection will also be more likely to accept discipline.

Stepchildren also need the closeness of a touch. They have just lost the closeness from one parent and part of the physical affection they used to enjoy is now missing. The need to be touched, caressed, and cuddled is as basic as the need for food. Expressions of affection should vary with the age of the child. Some children will respond best to a joyful hug while others prefer a more restrained pat on the arm or shoulder.

Where expressions of physical affection do not come easily, put them into practice gradually. Be creative. A simple note left on a child's dresser saying, "I'm glad to be your stepmom, and I hope we can become closer." The signal says you're interested in building a relationship, but how closely and quickly you will leave up to the child.

Smile and joke with each other Often. Develop a warm family feeling in the home. Praise more than criticize. Tell the children you are learning to love them by sharing confidences and mutual expressions of tenderness. Give them loving greetings and goodbyes. Don't send out conflicting messages by saying I love you, then pulling away when they get too close.

GIVE THEM THEIR DUE RESPECT

Respect is a two way street. Children are criticized and sometimes punished for acts of disrespect toward a parent or stepparent. Yet, adults scream at their children and step-children in a manner they would never use with a friend or neighbor.

To respect someone is to hold in high regard the worth of that person. Don't embarrass the child by being critical in front of his or her friends. And don't publicly discuss things that were shared in private. When this happens the relationship is shattered.

Adults are prone to ask children's opinions on a subject, but really not be interested in their views. Consider their answers seriously. Don't ask to merely be nice and then ignore their response. It's insincere and the child will soon see through the pretense. "Why ask? You don't really care."

Respect a child's opinion even when it is different from yours. "I disagree with you on that, but let's look at it again." Most stepparents are not willing to spend time to help the child, to treat him as an adult. It's easier being a dictator.

Respect a child's personal belongings and toys. Don't throw things away without first consulting the child. If the room is not kept clean you may warn him or her by saying, "I've asked you before to clean your room and you haven't done it. If it has not been cleaned by tomorrow I'm going to clean and I may throw away something you want to keep." The warning is clear that important things might be missing after the cleaning.

SETTING A GOOD EXAMPLE

The child needs a stepparent for many reasons. In families where the mother is custodial parent, the child has not had a proper example for a father for some time. The natural father may be coming on weekends, but he has a different role now. He's still the child's father, but he is not the mother's husband. She will not greet him at the door with a loving kiss nor will he bring her gifts on special days. Instead, he'll wait outside for her to bring the children to him.

More fathers are gaining custody today than ever before. And when the father is the custodial parent, the mother is no longer the lady of the house. The kids will still love their biological parent, but the stepparent will set the example.

TAKE TIME TO EXPLAIN

Children need examples and sometimes explanations of what's being done. They often have no idea why adults do some things. Children are more likely to pay attention to what's being done if they know the motivation behind the project. "I think it's important to be helpful when a neighbor is sick," says a mother leaving the house with a large cooking pot. "That's why I'm taking him the soup."

Or, "If we work together we can make our community a better place to live in." The child better understands the reasoning and can relate the activities to his or her own behavior.

Children also need to see examples of people who experience some of the same challenges in life they encounter. Stepchildren are struggling and it is common for them to believe no one else has problems like theirs. They will be more apt to identify with a person's behavior if they see him or her trying to cope in ways similar to their own, or in ways they can adapt.

A father figure going out to clean the garage might say, "This place is a mess and I don't know where to begin. I think I'll start in one corner and see how much I can get done in an hour." The child learns that all work might not get done at once, but he or she will learn to do a little at a time. The example demonstrates a way of coping with what may look like an insurmountable challenge by taking it on one step at a time.

DISPLAY POSITIVE REACTIONS

Make important activities seem appealing. Children are more inclined to imitate behavior that earns positive rewards. If dad cleans the bathroom and stepmom rewards him with a big hug and a kiss, Johnny is likely to follow in his dad's helpful footsteps; much more so than if stepmom complained about how poorly the job was done. Parents should clarify the benefits. "I feel much better in my room now that I've cleaned it and rearranged the furniture."

When Karen and Ted married, his two girls were eager to help with the house work. "Now", says Karen resentfully, "You have to threaten them just to clean their room." Ted's first wife, now deceased, was the ideal housewife. Her relaxed attitude about cleaning let her enjoy having the girls help. But Karen is a career woman who complains constantly when it comes to house work. Same house and mostly the same work load, yet the attitude toward the job has had a negative influence on the girls.

SET A GOOD STANDARD

Adults need to set the standard. Modeling is an effective way of modifying some traits that may cause children problems. Instead of being quick to find fault, adults should demonstrate the positive qualities they want the children to develop. For example, when a child wants things his or her way all the time, show how to resolve conflict. "You know I really like to eat lunch out on Fridays, but today I'll fix lunch at home since Grandma's coming to visit. It makes her happy to eat in our home."

Children who lack an adult role model, male or female, forfeit their opportunity to learn how to treat others. On birthdays and special occasions include the children in the buying of gifts for the spouse. What better way for a young boy to learn how to treat a wife in his own marriage. A wife may honor a special occasion by serving her husband's favorite meal. Explain to the children why it's significant.

Any positive results of such behavior examples may not be recognized in the children until years later, when they find themselves in similar situations. Then they will tend to handle their problems and relationships in the manner shown by their adult role models. Needless to say, negative behavior examples will result in negative outcomes.

A REAL FAMILY SPIRIT

The stepchild has not always been part of the current family situation. Not too long ago he or she was part of a traditional family, with two biological parents and living in a different household. After the divorce or death, the child became part of a single parent home, learning new experiences and usually taking on additional responsibilities. When the natural parent remarried, he or she became an instant stepchild with even more changes. If the child feels uncomfortable in the new surroundings, the process of building a relationship between stepchild and stepparent will be severely handicapped.

Family spirit can be the vaccine—the miracle drug—that enables families to overcome the inevitable conflicts and tensions which plague them. Family spirit develops only when family members identify with each other and with the family as a whole. "But he's not our dad, how can we be a family?" Or, "You're not my mother and I won't listen to you." A close stepfamily will not happen accidentally. The parents must promote it by stressing mutual acceptance, enjoyment, support, and consideration.

Three components are essential in the development of a pleasant, warm family atmosphere: shared activities, a sense of kinship, and family values. Where families spend a considerable amount of time together in common interests they will develop a sense of bonding together. For young children, have game time for a half-hour after dinner. Let family members take turns selecting their favorite game, with a different game each evening. Family meal times which stress mutual sharing of experiences and enjoyment are also important. And include all family members in decisions which pertain to the whole family, such as vacations, major purchases, or weekend trips.

DECISION MAKING, A GROWING TOOL

Children can learn by participating in major decisions. Buying a family auto can be used as a tool to bring the family together *and* to teach decision making. What does the family prefer, two door or four door? What make and model is best for the whole family? Teenagers can shop the want ads and investigate prospective dealers, taking some of the legwork out of the process. When all members, including stepchildren, are involved, the family becomes more united.

DISCOVERING KINSHIP

"I don't want to go see his parents, I don't know them!" On the wedding day, the parents of the bride and groom also had some changes to experience. Not only are they welcoming a new daughter or son-in-law, they are becoming instant step-grandparents to the new in-law's children. There are also step-aunts and step-uncles the children know nothing about.

Try to change that as quickly as possible. Bring the children closer to their extended family. Plan activities which will include the relatives and the stepchildren. Encourage interaction, to start building strong family ties.

Don't be discouraged if things don't come together all at once. Sometimes adolescents will resent being forced into such situations. A little giving goes a long way. Younger children are more apt to feel included when they get to play with other youngsters. Family history and ancestors should not be a main topic of conversation at first. Later, when the relationship matures, the stepchild will want to know more about his or her step-heritage.

Feeling part of the family quickly is extremely important to the new stepchild, as it minimizes feelings of alienation and loneliness.

FAMILY VALUES

A family always should maintain certain goals and values. These create a family image which each member can draw upon to affirm his or her personal worth and identity. And it also serves as a foundation for individual pride. Adults should teach children values that promote good family feeling, sharing, friendliness, and loyalty.

THE HOME SHOULD BE AN ENJOYABLE PLACE TO LIVE

Some homes reflect coolness, while others present a warm, loving atmosphere. Enjoyment and satisfaction determine the climate in the home. Material wealth does not guarantee happiness. There are truly some things money can't buy.

A home designed for enjoyment sets its values on happy, giving, and cooperative children; not on their being better than everyone else, the smartest in the class, or the most popular. Experts agree that children who are pushed to succeed live under extreme, unwarranted pressure. Families need to consider, "Are we living to work and achieve, or are we working and achieving in order to live and enjoy ourselves?"

Benefits of an enjoyable home range from pleasure, fun, relaxation, and closeness. An atmosphere such as this allows all members, including stepchildren, more freedom to grow and to develop the positive, integral relationships needed for the home.

Couples should begin immediately to set the pattern for the home by building a sturdy husband and wife relationship. Be a good example by not arguing in front of the children and discourage quarreling between other family members. Couples should agree to disagree without fighting, be slow to criticize, and quick to praise. Be friendly with one another and welcome the children's friends into the home.

"Sharon, it's a real joy to be part of the family with you and your father. I'm nervous about being a stepmother to a teenage daughter, but I want our home to be one of warmth and joy. I have a lot to learn and I'd appreciate your help."

There are no guarantees to stepparenting, but a good relationship between stepparent and stepchild will determine how both will spend the next few years of their lives. The outcome will depend mostly on the effort the stepparent makes to build a positive relationship.

CHAPTER 8

Communication:
the Stepparent's Dilemma

Communication is described as the means by which relating takes place. Everything a person does in relation to another is sent as some form of message. There is no way a person cannot communicate, even when he does not wish to or is unaware that he is doing so; gestures, rolling the eyes, shrugging the shoulders, the tone of voice, slamming something shut, turning the back, or even silence. The way a person turns away or toward another, the raising of an eyebrow, a half smile, the manner in which someone gets up or sits down. All are messages of some type.

The stepfamily is a tangled web of communication difficulties; stepparent and stepchild, stepparent and spouse (stepchild's parent), stepparent and absent parent, parent and absent parent, parent and child, child and absent parent, as well as the extended family of aunts, uncles, cousins, and grandparents. If there is a problem in any one of these relationships, the whole household feels the negative effects.

Verbal communication can be painful for some people. Ted is talkative and Audrea is the quiet one. During an argument recently, which seemed all one-sided since Ted was doing all the talking, he lashed out suddenly and said, "Why don't you say something instead of just sitting there?" Audrea replied, "Why should I? You seem to have said it all and I can't convince you differently." Since it has all been said, or so it seems, the silent one seethes inwardly and feels inadequate to voice her opinion. Fear can turn to apathy and work against a relationship. "Why bother to work it out?"

The passive partner might try to sit out the trouble by eating, sleeping, drinking, shopping, withdrawing — doing anything to become detached from the issue. This person must be helped to feel again; one cannot recognize love and affection if he or she doesn't also recognize hostility and anger.

DECIDE ON REAL COMMUNICATION

"No one ever listens to me!" Whether husband, wife, or child, people owe it to themselves and to other members of their stepfamily to develop the art of communicating. Communication cannot occur if only one person responds. Listening is essential. For example, if the person refuses to answer the telephone, the message cannot get through. Also, a constant busy signal will cause the caller to give up and decide to use some other method. A letter or note is a form of communication, but it is a poor substitute for a face-to-face conversation.

The words, "I just can't get that man to listen to me" and "I'm trying so hard to fit into this family!" might be voiced by a frustrated stepmother who is trying to communicate a problem to her husband, and a stepdaughter who is striving for acceptance.

The statements have to be understood against the background of the past. Greg, divorced from Jackie, is remarried and has custody of their teenage son. Whenever Jackie calls to speak with her son, she and Greg end up in a verbal battle. "Why can't you treat me decently," says Jackie. "You have our son." Jackie has resolved the conflict of the past and is ready to establish a good relationship with her ex-husband. She has "forgotten" the battle of the property settlement and how she tried to have Greg incarcerated. Communication is a process of complicated relating, a pattern of behavior, and responding to what each has experienced over a period of time.

LEARN TO LISTEN

Research reveals that certain skills are necessary for effective listening; undivided attention, encouraged conversation, asking the right questions, sorting out the real message, and empathy.

Undivided Attention

Undivided attention means uninterrupted time with another person. Adults should devote certain time—every day if possible—to listening to family members. For those who can't set a regular time, at least touch base with each other before leaving home. "I hope you have a good day." Or, "I'll be thinking of you when you take that test." Words of encouragement go a long way in a relationship. Being precise, even if it's brief, tells the person you are thinking about him and what he is facing. "I know you're going to have a busy day today. Good luck."

At a convenient time in the evening (maybe during the meal or shortly after), before the family has dispersed, talk and listen to one another. Talk about work, school, problems around the house, office problems, frustrations, or general happenings of the day. Take turns and open up honestly. A new stepchild might have mixed feelings. "I want to be part of this family, but I'm not ready to open myself up to them." Don't push anyone, but encourage the process.

Listen to everything; not only the words, but the in-depth meanings. There might be a signal of serious need which should be heard. Listening requires each party to give of himself and to be willing to receive the other person's innermost messages.

Encourage Conversation

Use your body to show a child you are listening and hearing what is being said. Use good eye contact. Let the child know he or she has your complete attention. If there is something else happening at the same time, either disregard it or let the child know that your full attention cannot be given now.

Body posture and distance can confirm to the child the quality of the reception she is getting. An upright seated posture with the upper body leaning slightly forward is a good indication you are interested in what's being said. Slouching in the chair tells her you don't think the message is important. Folded arms and tightly crossed legs indicate a defensive attitude. Studies reveal most people are comfortable about two or three feet apart. A shy person may require more.

Facial expressions can be used to encourage the child. Respond to the topic of conversation. If alertness is shown the child will be more willing to talk. Billy is trying to show his stepdad the work he did at school. "I don't know why I bother; you'd rather be watching the news." If you can't listen to the child at that moment, say so, and have him wait until later. The conversation is only delayed, not broken. The child is assured what he has to say is important and you will get back with him.

Like adults, most children want to talk. They just aren't sure anyone is listening. If the door is opened and interest expressed, they will take it from there. "Tell me, John, how was your day at school today." Once the child has begun, the listener needs only short responses to keep the conversation going. Maintain eye contact, smile or nod, and a simple, "I see," or "Yes" says to the child "I'm following you. Do not take over the conversation, change the subject, or interrupt the child's thought pattern.

A stepparent's golden opportunity for a relationship is to express concern about a child's experiences of the day. The interaction at the first such meeting generally will determine the outcome. A warm welcome might include cookies or a light snack that will not spoil an appetite for the evening meal. Respond to excitement with excitement and interest, to sadness or upset with concern.

Asking the Right Questions

Confusion, anxiety, and frustration often cause youngsters to misread their own behavior. The right questions at the right time will keep the communications lines open. "How do you feel about it now?" This helps the child take a good look at his own reaction to the problem and sort out how he feels about it. A parent or stepparent should not condone or condemn the child for his stand. You just want to help him put into focus the feelings inherent in the experience.

Sometimes adults are too quick to rush in with solutions and not give the child a chance to work through his or her own dilemma. The question, "What does it mean to you?" unlocks and says to the child, "I want to help, but I don't want to push."

The Real Messages

Lack of background knowledge on other family members can hinder communication. The courtship provided necessary information about the new spouse, but told little about the children. What upsets them? What turns them off? Or, what encourages them? When a person is unaware of another person's temperament it's easy to misinterpret a statement or gesture.

Communication problems also occur when a message has two separate meanings or can be misinterpreted, or when a recipient's feelings cause him or her to hear the wrong message or only part of it. The part that was missed could change the whole meaning. Both parties can improve their messages and listening skills by double-checking what is said. "Is this what you're telling me?"

The more two people argue, the more likely they will misunderstand each other. "I've explained to my wife," says Phil, "I really don't mean the things I say when we quarrel, but when my back's against the wall, I fight." Communication is one way of showing respect. The words used, the tone of voice, and when a statement is made, are all signals to the other person.

When one person tries a little harder to understand the other, it sends back the unspoken message, I really do care. "Donna, are you saying you're moving back to your mother's because she needs you or because you don't like the arrangements here?" Once the real motive is uncovered the stepparent can work to remedy the situation. A little giving from each side often leads to a better home life.

Empathy

A friend once said, "Don't tell someone you know how they feel if you haven't been through the identical crisis." Children want honesty. A stepparent whose parents have never separated or divorced cannot say,"I know how you feel." If the stepparent has not had a parent die she cannot say, "I know what you're going through."

Though a person may not have experienced the same grief, empathy allows them to be honestly sympathetic. Empathy requires people to change their way of looking at things so they can better understand the child's feelings and views. The first step is trying to see the situation through the eyes of the child. "I have never experienced what you're going through, but I can see it would be difficult to cope with." The child hears, "I'm trying to help. Help me to help you."

Empathy also allows the stepparent to see behind a child's defenses and to better understand the real meaning of her difficult behavior. Marlene said, "I tried every way I knew to reach out to my new stepdaughter, but her attacks were merciless. I finally discovered that before her parent's divorce she had been very dependent upon her mother, and it was her mother who ran off with another man. She subconsciously was trying to get back at her mother by attacking me."

Children tend to take punishment and criticism better after they have been given a clear understanding of their point of view. Fewer problems are likely to emerge once the child feels, "Well, it must not be all bad. My parents understand."

While empathy is important in strengthening the relationships between stepparent and stepchild, it should not be confused with sympathy. Sympathy is feeling sorry for someone; empathy is trying to feel the way the other person feels.

THE DOS AND DON'TS OF COMMUNICATION

"It never fails," says Charlene, "If I talk to the kids, they shut up." If nagging and trying too hard are your usual approaches, children will tend to clam up. Keep the lines open, and don't be too aggressive.

If the stepmother is waiting at the door for her stepdaughter, expecting to hear everything that happened at the school dance, the girl will likely plead headache or tiredness and leave her stepmother standing there. She may want to be alone with her romantic thoughts. But the next morning, a more patient and relaxed parent or stepparent will, more than likely, hear talk of the dance all day long.

"I'd like to talk with my new stepmom, but I want to do it on my terms." Kids sometimes put stepparents into a no-win situation. When there's too much interest, it's interfering. If there's not enough interest, they don't care.

Carl, father of two teenage girls, is married to Nora in his second marriage. Carl said, "We've been married four years and I couldn't understand why the girls shied away from Nora. She is younger than their mother which should give them more in common. Every time we go shopping Nora buys for them, but they still refuse to get close to her. About six months ago I noticed a big change. The girls were finally reaching out to her as never before. When I asked Nora what happened she said 'I finally gave up trying to get them to like me. And I decided if they wanted a relationship that I was willing.' It's so good to hear the three of them getting along so well."

When Nora stopped pushing, the girls relaxed. Stepchildren feel they have been through enough. "I didn't choose for Dad to leave." Or, "It's not my fault we're in this mess." When the pressure's off the kids can make their own decision to talk or not.

Wait to hear the whole message. "My folks want to listen," said Kyle, "but before I finish they begin to preach. A friend I know experimented with drugs, and I wanted to know how I could help him. My folks got on the stand about drug abuse, teenage suicide, and sex, before I could convince them it wasn't me I was talking about. I was sorry I'd asked them."

Many adults live in constant fear of the possible influence of drug and alcohol on their children. Any sign of interest will throw them into an immediate panic. But, even if the child is guilty, a parent or stepparent can be of little help if the lines of communication have been destroyed. Always let them know the house rules on the issue, but keep them assured of your love and concern.

SAY WHAT YOU MEAN

Correct phraseology is important in communication. Say what you mean without attacking. Pick the words carefully; "I feel..." rather than, "You are..." or "You always..." Telling a stepdaughter, "I believe your outfit would look more attractive with the blue sweater. Have you considered it?" is much better than saying, "The colors you're wearing do not go together." You have disapproved of her decision, but you have not condemned it or her. Concern has been expressed since some thought went into the suggestion. More important, the child has been given the opportunity to reject the suggestion.

YELLING IS NOT COMMUNICATION

Everyone's aware of the parent shopping, with two or three kids, who shouts, "If you don't quit that right now, I'm going to clobber you." Occasionally the mother may follow through with the threat, but more often than not the threat is an empty one and the kids know it. They continue to wreak havoc in the store, leaving the staff and other customers muttering to themselves.

Parents should be fair, non-nagging, and consistent caretakers, not authority figures given to shouting empty threats. Yelling is unconscious competition with other voices. When one person turns up the volume, others in the conversation follow suit. If the sound on the television is high, people in the same room speak more loudly to be heard. Proper communication can only be achieved with calm voices and mutual respect.

IF YOU KNOW IT, DON'T FLAUNT IT

An enthusiastic stepparent can offend other family members by being too eager to prove how wise he or she really is. "Your hair would look better if you wore it down." Or, every place the family visits, he has been there before and wants to give his expertise in a guided tour.

The spouse with no children of his own has the urge to prove how good a stepfather he can be. Those who have children want to flaunt their experience. There is a time to display knowledge and a time to keep your mouth shut. William said about his stepfather, "I know I'm not perfect, but neither is he."

GIVE THEM CREDIT

Most kids want to be older than their actual age. A child who is eight and a half will tell you he is eight and a half, not eight. Teenagers feel they have "arrived" when they reach the magical age of thirteen. Children do enjoy talking to adults, but only if they are treated as equals, not talked down to or patronized. This attitude often is expressed in a slightly raised voice. "Well honey, what can I do for you?" A child who is striving for maturity immediately becomes defensive.

Don't always play the role of "Supermom" of "Superdad." Children will feel closer to an adult who allows them to see the real person; fallible, an occasional bad mood, admitting to mistakes, and being human.

THINK TWICE BEFORE GIVING AN ANSWER

Few people who ask for an opinion really want it. Many counselors support the view that when people ask for advice, they just want support for a decision they already have made. A young girl asking her stepmother, "What do you think I should do about this boy?" may not really want advice. Her response to the stepmother's answer — no matter how good and sincere that answer was—might be, "Quit trying to run my life. I should have known you wouldn't like him."

Answering the question with a question may encourage her to think for herself. "I don't know much about the boy. Where does he live?" Don't back out of the communication. Remember that she came for help, a good sign. And don't take an immediately negative position, by saying something like "I don't know. What are his bad points?" This tells the girl you assume he is not good for her and shuts down any more communication.

Let her talk freely about what she sees as his good points and she will begin to see for herself what some of his not so good characteristics might be. "Well, he's nice, but he does do things that annoy me." Or, "I think he's cute, but he does have poor manners." When you don't condemn, she will respect your honesty—even if she does not agree right away.

TALK WITH CHILDREN

Talking with children is different from talking with adults. A childless stepparent may know facts and figures which would fascinate another adult, but be of little value in talking with a child. It does not matter how many children in the world are starving; just that there are some is important.

The ability to talk with children is just as important as listening. When a child stops listening before the talking stops, a lengthy direction can end up a half completed project. Make it brief. Explain, then let the child respond to the explanation. Feed him a little, get a response, and feed him a little more. Take as much time as you need, but keep the information in segments that take no longer than thirty seconds.

Keep it simple. Young children especially should be spoken to with simple words in short, to the point sentences. Stepparents may become frustrated by dialogues with children, but they should learn from them. "What are you doing?" "Nothing." "What would you like to do today?" "Play." The child wants to talk and get it over with so he can go do what he would like to do.

Speak slowly and exaggerate your intonation. If the child does not understand, quickly rephrase the message even more simply.

TAKE A GOOD LOOK

Proceed with caution in areas where there may be strong differences of opinion. Stay on neutral ground. A stepparent who is quick to agree with a child's bad remarks about a friend might be forced to eat those words later. It's strange how quickly a girl or boy will forget quarrels with their friends and how long they remember the negative remarks made by a stepparent, even if those remarks only substantiated the child's claim. Hear the bad news and forget it. A day or two later it probably will not matter at all.

Both stepsiblings and biological siblings will have their rivalries. Let them air their disagreements, but try to keep them under control. After tempers have cooled down, you can analyze their differences. Usually current and potential trouble spots can be minimized, if not eliminated altogether.

The way family members communicate sets the tone of the home environment; creative and happy or hurtful and frustrating, a place for growth or a place for neglect. The home is where family members test the waters. "If my own family can't understand me, what can I expect from the rest of the world?"

Without communication there can be no meaningful relationships in the home.

CHAPTER 9

Help, I'm a Stepmother

A stepmother's cry for help often falls on deaf ears, as friends and co-workers are quick to criticize. "You made your bed, now lie in it." When a person thinks of the many negative statements associated with the word *stepmother*, it makes them wonder why anyone would want to be one. Wicked, intruder, home wrecker, part-time mother, daddy's *new* wife; all these and more are used to describe the role of the stepmother.

When a woman marries a struggling widower, the public and his children see her as falling far short of the saint whose place she is taking. If she marries a divorced man, someone who tried everything to hold his marriage together, she is looked upon as the destroyer of a happy home. Whichever the situation, the new stepmother becomes the "bad guy".

Not only is she looked down on, but the expectations imposed on her seem endless; be a good replacement, a problem solver, get along with the kids' father, greet their mother with a smile, be the family bookkeeper, and help with the bills left over from his first marriage. Learn to receive a little and give a lot.

The stepmother's role sounds terrible. However, when you talk with one she'll say, "Oh, everything's fine." Or, "It's working out great." No one wants to admit she is having a hard time meeting her new responsibilities. And when everyone else conceals their problems, it makes a stepmother feel she is the only one having a hard time. A private talk usually reveals the alarming truth.

One of the purposes of this book is to inform the hurting stepparent he or she is not alone. While being aware of this may not solve any problems, it can be comforting to know that many others across the nation are going through similar conflicts and discouragements. Though lonely feelings still exist, statistics show that the stepparenting phenomenon is growing rapidly and awareness of the inherent problems in these new relationships is more evident.

Next time you attend a high school or college graduation, look around. Not all events are important enough to draw both divorced parents, but the diploma represents a major milestone in a child's life. Both parents feel they have had equal responsibility for the achievement and want to be present for the important affair. Observe the "two" couples centered around the graduate, holding his diploma tightly and anxiously waiting for the uncomfortable situation to end.

There is the innocent small talk, the glances measuring each other's appearance, and frozen smiles on every face, the natural parents not wanting the stepparent to feel out of place. The diploma represents a highlight achievement for the child and both sets of parents are happy for the occasion. But the one who is least involved—who knows the least about the child—is the father's new wife, the stepmother.

CONFLICTS

The most common statement both stepmothers and stepfathers make is, "I just didn't expect it to be like this." All newly-married couples fantasize that their marriage is different than all others; free of conflict, and a marriage made in heaven. "We love each other so much that our love can overcome anything."

Such expectations are rarely realized by the newly-married parents in a stepfamily because of the multiplied problems which beset the second marriage. If the children had been promised a beautiful life after the marriage, they likely will be disillusioned very quickly—even though the new situation is far superior to the life they had before. Their problems and perceptions only add to the stepmother's frustrations, as she wonders, "What will it take to make these kids happy?" I know life now is better than what they had, but they just don't appreciate it."

Today's laws are giving more fathers custody of their children than ever before, but most children will remain with the natural mother. The stepmother may be confused by this; she has the name, but the job of mothering remains with the woman who lives with her stepchildren. She has similar feelings for the kids, but few opportunities to help them.

The stepmother's role is not that of a functional mother, except for the weekend and vacation visits. Even then, however, she is more hostess than mother. The most she can hope for is to earn their love and respect on a part-time basis, and be satisfied to know that her contribution will have some influence on the children's lives. It seems a small pleasure, but a little is better than nothing at all.

All conflicts must be dealt with on an individual basis. Whether the difficulty involves a problem child, a rude neighbor, too much responsibility, or an awkward position in some relationship, it is easier to address each one as it develops rather than trying to cope with everything at once. Stepparents who give up prematurely are guilty of seeing only the overall picture—all their problems at the same time—and don't like what they see. Conflicts are a part of life. Instead of wasting valuable time trying to think up ways to elude conflicts altogether, they should be trying to figure out ways to deal with them.

THE STEPMOTHER AND HER STEPCHILDREN

Children and their new stepmother often develop close personal relationships. But getting to that point can be a rough trip, sometimes seemingly impossible to travel. Rachel said, "His older daughter will have nothing to do with me, but the younger child has responded because of his need for a mother figure." A close friend recalled, "My son moved in with us three years ago and still refuses to reach out to my wife. He's afraid if he responds to her that his mother will be offended. Our home has become a lonely hotel room for my son and it continues to frustrate my wife."

PROMISES, EXPECTATIONS, AND JEALOUSIES

Often, because of unrealistic promises made by the father, stepmothers walk into all kinds of unexpected surprises. "The kids need a mother and I'm sure they're going to love you." No matter what the kids are like, he can't be sure they will respond that way. The new stepmother is foolish to believe him.

A thirteen-year-old girl had been close to her mother. When the mother died, all of her dependence was transferred to her father. When he announced his decision to marry she was shocked and felt betrayed. Almost a year later she still is unable to accept her new stepmother. She resists any change the stepmother tries to make in the home and avoids any advice given to her in love.

In a single parent home the child will frequently slip into a substitute role for the remaining parent. A father will discover his daughter taking on the household duties; cooking, cleaning, and spending a great deal of time with the parent as they comfort each other. When this occurs the child is likely to resent any adult who shows up to take her place.

"I learned early that my relationship with Joan would lead to serious repercussions," recalled Adam. "Once we decided on marriage Joan began to do more and more around my apartment. When my two girls would come to visit on weekends they felt I didn't need their help anymore. Up to this point the girls had always enjoyed Joan's company and the four of us would spend a lot of time together. Now the girls resent Joan and the changes she's made. They complain after every visit about something she has done wrong."

Jealousy of the absent parent's time is the issue with weekend visitors. It's not so much the children dislike or disapprove of their new stepmother but that they resent her time with their father.

One disillusioned stepmother remarked, "I had great plans for my new marriage and I was especially excited about the weekends his children would come to visit. I imagined me with the girl and him in the yard playing with his son. Then we'd all go out for a meal or movie together. Instead, the girl hated me and absolutely would not leave her father's side. His son, being two years older, at least acknowledged my presence, but that was it. The first evening was a catastrophe and I soon surrendered my dreams and decided to stay out of their way when they're here. Eleven days out of fourteen my husband and I have a lovely relationship, our only arguments having to do with the kids. I love my husband and learned to live with my situation."

A wise observer once said, "A stepmother's true love stands the test by recognizing the importance of a mother's love and lets that love grow unhindered by any feelings of rivalry." It's unfortunate that most goodwill gestures made for a stepchild are not primarily for the child, but reflect the stepmother's desire to replace her husband's first wife.

CONFLICTING NEEDS

Trouble comes when a stepmother's needs and the children's needs are not compatible. A young woman marries a divorcee whose three small children live with the ex-spouse. The new wife insists on trying to please them to the point that they are upset and so is their mother. The stepmother then tries to overcome the turmoil she has started but she is still driven to reach for the children's love. She is not setting out to hurt anyone, but she is blinded by the force of her own desire. When her needs become her first priority, she is unable to control herself or to make rational decisions.

Stepmothers should realize children sometimes will take advantage of their situation. "If I can't get what I want at home, I'll throw stepmom a little attention and get anything I want." To the kids she merely represents a good time. And the kids may not be the only ones taking advantage. Her husband might be as well. His motives are no more influenced by the children's best interests than his new wife's are. The divorce has left him bitter and he dreams of retribution. He encourages his new wife to avenge his hurt without having to admit it —even to himself. He supports her, but does not look like the guilty one.

"I think it's wonderful how Ellen is doing for the kids." All the attention appears respectable to husband, children, family, and friends. None of the actual intent shows, and no one would suspect the charming stepmother has only her own happiness in mind. Her selfish incentive—an all-out drive for the children's love.

Heed this warning. That behavior will collapse one day. The stepchild may be convinced he has received all the stepmother has promised—two homes with love, and two mothers who care—and then find he has none. Because her affectionate seduction has been motivated only by a desire to meet her own needs, she may abandon him now that she believes she has his love.

Such a self-centered woman can seriously damage a child's inner security. If her intent is to stand between the child and its father, this too can affect the relationship. The child needs to know both his mother and father love him. The divorce was a separation of parents, not a break between parent and child.

A sincere, loving stepmother will have one objective: a stable marriage and family. She should take a serious look at what she is, wife to her husband, and allow him a continuing, unhindered relationship with his children. She also has to keep in mind what she is not— the children's mother. But she can be a loyal friend, caring more for their welfare than her own selfish objectives.

With all the frustrations and expectations involved in a stepmother-stepchild relationship, the stepmother must remain tolerant and understanding, even when she is treated unfairly. Realize that the kids are going through a major upheaval in their lives and the adjustments they have to make to their new life style are not easy ones. The father has a new bride with whom he can enjoy love and affection, erasing the hurt and heartache of his first marriage, but the child needs time and opportunity to catch up.

Most children will respond positively when they realize what is expected of them and that the outcome of the relationship of a new stepparent will depend pretty much upon their actions and reactions.

STEPMOTHER AND MOTHER

Without much hesitation, the biological mother becomes the number one rival to her children's new stepmother. And very few stepmothers express any feelings of compassion for their husband's ex-wife. The natural mother's motive might well be self-centered, rather than for the child's welfare. Whatever her motives, she will—more often than not —cause trouble.

Mothers have a natural tendency to be possessive of their children, especially after a divorce. When her husband initiated the divorce she feels deserted and also fears losing the children as well. It is unusual for any natural mother to respond with joy when her children begin forming relationships with their stepmother. And, she will also resent any gestures of maternal affection the stepmom makes to her children. "Why wouldn't the kids rather live with you?" A frightened mother told her ex-husband. "You're remarried and have a family and home. I can't give that to the kids. I work all day and when I do get home there's very little of me left to give." If a mother didn't struggle to hold on to her children people would begin to question her maternal concern.

Just as they do in many situations, children end up in the middle of the conflict between stepmother and mother. Their loyalties are constantly tested. "Mom needs me now because she's all alone." Or, "I lost Dad once and I don't want it to happen again. If I don't get along with his new wife he might hate me." Many confusing thoughts pass through a child's mind, but they usually will side with their mother, the one with whom they have the deeper and more important relationship.

In some situations there are advantages to the children living with their father and stepmother; better opportunities, a complete family, and material gain. But a mother who loves her children will not be willing to give them up without a fight. And the father is fantasizing if he thinks his former wife and new spouse will have anything better than a cold, formal relationship.

The stepmother has no desire to see her husband and his former wife getting along well, for any reason. She doesn't want *any* other woman competing for her husband's time, interests, money, and involvement, even if it is only fulfilling his legal and financial obligations. The former wife poses even more of a threat if she initiated the divorce. The husband might have lingering affectionate feelings for the mother of his children. Whatever the involvement, the stepmother is correct in wanting it stopped.

Children become spectators like spectators at a tennis match, looking from side to side and recognizing a point won here or one lost there. "Ted and I wanted to buy these underpants for Julie. We could see how much she needed them." Score one for the stepmother, who met a little girl's need and threw it into the mother's face. Or, "Your wife looks better now that she's dyed her hair again." Score tied.

No matter how hard the stepmother tries, she must face the obvious. The odds are against her forming a loving relationship with the stepchildren equal to the one enjoyed by the natural mother. Even when the natural mother has abandoned or totally rejects her children, the stepmother may still find herself the victim of misdirected hostility. Though it may be hard to do, and the reward may be slow in coming, it's better to teach the child to love his or her natural parent no matter what. Someday the stepparent will be "paid back," in one way or another, for such positive actions.

THE STEPMOTHER AND THE CHILDREN'S FATHER

The relationship between a stepmother and the children's father differs from the husband and wife relationship. For example, a young girl might be employed at a company owned by her uncle. The business relationship is employer and employee, but the relationship away from the office changes to niece and uncle. The same two people, but the relationship changes as the location changes.

The stepfamily consists of a natural parent and a stepparent, with either or both spouses sometimes bringing the children of former marriages into the new union. The couple would like to concentrate on their happiness, but that exclusive focus usually is not possible. "If it weren't for the children, everything would be all right." Many have used this as a defense for a struggling marriage, but the issue must be accepted, not avoided. The children will remain in her husband's thoughts even when they are not in his house.

The ghost which continues to haunt most stepmothers is a lack of information about the natural mother. How good was she as a mother? Did she work outside the home and still maintain a successful household, serve hot meals, and attend meetings at school? If the children live in the household with the stepmother she can learn about the absent parent's motherhood, but little information can be obtained from a child who is just a weekend visitor. Preconceived ideas might send a stepmother into panic as she tries to compete with a supermom, when actually the kids' mother was a real failure as a parent.

An alert new wife will understand her husband's fatherly love, accept the situation, and build from there. She can make it easy or difficult for the husband-father. If she complains about the affection he shows his kids and the things he buys for them, he will only hide his actions and, in turn, grow resentful toward her children. But when she allows him the freedom to express his love to his children without showing any jealousy, he will come to appreciate her more for her understanding.

"At first my wife showed animosity every time I did anything for my kids," said Jeff. "Instinctively it made me 'not' want to be around her or her children. Now she accepts me as the father I am and realizes that I'm going to love and do for my kids no matter what she says. It's let me relax when they visit and we are finally beginning to be a family, even if it's only part-time."

As in all relationships, the motive behind any action usually determines the outcome, and selfish intentions are almost always revealed—if not immediately, at some time later. Pure, genuine desire for a caring relationship will not guarantee success, but it improves the chances considerably. Equally important, it allows the person to know he or she is doing the right thing.

STEPMOTHER AND STEPFATHER

The connection between stepmother and stepfather, father's new wife and mother's new husband, is one with little face-to-face contact. In cases where one parent has remarried and moved away, there may be no personal contact at all. The link between stepmother and stepfather is not like the bitter rivalry amidst stepmother and mother, yet it still can play a significant part in its overall effect on a stepfamily.

Relationships are not entirely dependent upon the actions of the parties directly involved. They can be greatly influenced by outside forces. For example, a stepmother might be genuine in her concern for the child's well-being, but the mother's actions can destroy everything she has worked to build. A good relationship between the stepmother and stepfather might also encourage him to influence his wife, the child's mother, to back away, to allow the stepmother to be an effective stepparent.

On the other hand, the stepfather has his new bride and is moving ahead to establish a happy stepfamily dwelling. To succeed he needs a silent partner, the children's father. A wise father, who is more concerned with his children's happiness than his own selfish desires, will allow the stepfather the freedom to be a stepfather without interference.

Stepmothers do not have a direct link to the stepfather, yet they do have influence with the children's father. If a stepmother is wise, she will stay out of the picture and put her energies to use in her own home. But if she is jealous, and uncertain of her husband's love (because of the children's influence), she is like a volcano ready to erupt. If she gives voice to her insecurities, her interference could have a devastating effect on the stepfather's achievements.

When a stepmother uses the knowledge of herself and her children's needs truly and sincerely, she can be a good wife to her husband and a confident stepmother to another woman's children. She also helps herself and her opposite figure, the stepfather, to accomplish the marriage relationships they both desire. Such a stepmother allows everyone to fulfill their respective roles free of interference. All are enriched by this, she most of all.

BASIC TIPS FOR A STEPMOTHER

Investigate Your New Husband-to-be

Find out what kind of father he is before you officially become the stepmother to his children. A surprise visit on the weekend he has the kids will reveal more truths than an expected visit with every detail planned for your arrival. If he lives across town or across country, just show up with the least notice. If you have children be sure to take them along. Whether his children live with him or visit on weekends is not important, what matters is how he handles the two groups together. There are a lot of weekends in a year and you'll need to know what to expect.

Make sure the future husband and his children visit you in your home. You have created your home and lifestyle to please you. Will he be comfortable or restless sharing in your way of life?

Don't Take Anything for Granted

Marriage requires giving from both sides, but will the giving be so unbalanced it will affect the success of the marriage? When the husband

and wife have lived in different localities, will they and any children involved be compatible? A child raised in New York City will have far different social values than one raised in the deep south. Children are cited as the number one cause for failures of second marriages. If they can't adapt to their new situation, chances of the marriage succeeding are slim.

These pre-wedding visits are unlikely to change anyone's mind, but at least they will prepare both parties for what is to come. Neither will be able to say, "I had no idea they would act like this."

Remember Who Is the Adult

Many stepparents act less maturely than the children. One father said, "I finally had to talk to my wife. She complained constantly that my kids wouldn't reach out to her, but that she was willing and waiting. I said, you're 32 and they are 10 and 12. What can you expect?"

After the wedding it's too late to say, "But they're impossible." Start off on the right foot. Be an adult. Let them know you expect their co-operation when it's necessary for family unity. Understand what problems are hindering the adjustment period and accept their hostilities for the time being. As an adult, you understand the difficult adjustments they are having to make.

Be Impartial, but United with the Husband

The children have experienced the break-up of their traditional family. Arguments and disagreements have destroyed their home. What they need now is the comfort of knowing their new home will last. The husband and wife can disagree on major issues, but not in front of the children. Let them see a united front. It will also alleviate problems that could develop later; for example, playing dad against stepmom.

Children or parents cannot take sides in disputes. The father may be the authority figure, but children should be made to know, without question, they cannot undercut their stepmother's stand and get away with it. Make a stand with your husband immediately. Don't let him challenge your authority. "Well, I'm sure she didn't mean you had to do that." Take him aside immediately and reiterate your position. If he does not see a need for a united stand, discuss with him how you see it affecting both the marriage and the children.

Talk Things over that Concern the Children

Listen to his views on education, money, and recreation. Remember that differences of opinion do not have to produce arguments. Stepfamilies require giving, a lot of compromises, but no one person should do it all. Janet, a Los Angeles widow who married a divorcee, says, "John and I had much in common on our views about raising children, but there was one difference. His children had more privileges. I changed that instantly. I set down the rules which I was accustomed to. One of them was no kids out after dark. The kids fell into line with their new limits and John went along with me all the way. He never failed to say, 'Mother is right,' even when he thought differently."

Discuss less important, less emotional matters in the children's presence. Sometimes it's good for youngsters to see there are different ways of thinking and peaceful ways of resolving conflicts. No one is going to be right all the time. Ideas will be challenged and there will be times when each person will have to rethink his or her plans.

Be willing to give in on small matters for the sake of the family. You expect your husband and the kids to make allowances. Give them the same consideration.

Practice the Rule: "Praise is More Effective than Punishment."

Say, "Scott, you're doing very well in learning how to make your bed" rather than, "Your room looks more like a garbage dump than a bedroom." Or try sentences like, "You might have less trouble if you do it this way, but what you're doing looks nice." Give them a model to go by and then reward their efforts. A positive approach gets more response from children than insults or complaints.

Be Honest about the Children from the Outset

A concerned opinion about a child's behavior will be received more openly than a nagging comment. There is nothing wrong in speaking to the kids or about the kids to their father as long as it's done constructively.

One woman became stepmother to two teenagers. The boy immediately rejected any communication with her. One afternoon she took him aside and said, "I don't know why you choose to treat me like you do, but I do know you're hurting your dad and our chances of becoming a family. You might as well accept the fact that I'm here to stay, like it or not."

Let the husband and kids know what you do like. If you don't tell them they will think you don't know what you want.

Find Time Alone with Your Husband

A good husband and wife relationship is essential to a stepmother. The closeness she finds with her husband provides the strength and support she needs for the difficult task of developing ties with his children. He may not be as aware as he should be of this need, but point it out to him. If possible, get a sitter or in-laws to stay with the kids on occasion so the two of you can get away for a weekend. Nothing will compare to having an evening alone and waking up to peace and quiet, knowing there are no little creatures about to intrude on your privacy.

Go out one night a week. Many couples complain they can't afford it, but you'll agree you can't afford not to when you realize the benefits you will reap. The evening does not need to be extravagant; it is the time alone that is important. If it can't be afforded on your husband's income, earn the money needed yourself.

Thomas said, "My wife went to the doctor for her nerves. His first question was, 'When was the last time you and your husband went out alone, without the kids?' My wife couldn't remember and when she asked me later, neither could I. The doctor told her this was the cause of her nervous condition."

Never allow the children to violate the privacy of the bedroom. Let them know quickly and exactly what the rules are. The younger ones will want to know why, but a simple, "Your daddy and I need to be alone," will be good enough. Don't try to elaborate on the subject or make up some foolish answer. It only causes the children to become more interested. When the kids begin to see and appreciate a successful home life, they may begin to realize their dad and stepmother need time alone together to be happy, good parents.

No matter how many children there are in the home a couple usually can find a few minutes alone. "We meet at nine-thirty every evening and have a soft drink and sometimes popcorn and just talk," says Joan. For Karen, "Our bedroom door is always locked. The kids can knock, and they do, but they can't get in unless we let them." Martha says, "Our offices are close enough that Mike can pick me up for lunch. I wouldn't take anything for those few minutes each day."

How or when you find private time with your husband is not important. What is important is that you have it. Set the precedent early in the marriage or you may lose the chance.

If it's Economically Possible ... Move

If you can afford it, move out of the house you shared with your ex-husband or the one your new husband shared with his former wife. Don't burden the relationship with unnecessary stress. "Mom wouldn't want you to move that picture." Or, "This was mom's favorite room." Also, your new husband doesn't need to be reminded of the material things your ex-husband provided you and the kids.

"In my divorce I got the big house," says Barbara, a friendly divorcee from St. Louis. "I just stayed there with the kids, and when I remarried, my husband and his son moved in with us. At the time, his assistant manager's salary was modest and all the glamour of the house made him feel uncomfortable. I should have sold it at the beginning, put the money in a mutual trust, and looked for a house together that we could afford. My failing to do so put a strain on the earlier stages of our marriage."

The move into a new house gets everybody off to a new start. It's no longer mine, but ours. Even if you and your new husband own houses, it's better for the marriage to sell both homes, pool the money, and buy a home that belongs to you both. In the old house, one family is the intruder. "We put our winter clothes up here." Or, "Didn't you know there was a hidden stairway here?"

A move also serves to bring the stepfamily closer together. The excitement of finding a home that's comfortable for all, the plans of the move, and the decisions as to who will share bedrooms with whom. It's much nicer to be able to fix a room together than to hear "Doris, you'll have to move into Tonya's room." Doris feels out of place and Tonya resents the forced sharing. After the move, the furniture from both households can be redistributed and the attitude, "This belongs to my family" eliminated.

Not all problems will be solved by a move, nor is it always impossible to remain in one spouse's original house. However, the advantages are in favor of a change. If the man refuses to move it may make for a poor start; not only because of his refusal to move, but because he is signaling he may not be flexible in other important matters.

Run the Household as You See Fit

Don't hesitate to establish your position in the family. You may not be the mother of the children, but you are the mother of the household. If you do not establish this position early, it may never happen. Be kind, but firm. Be precise with wording, "No, I'm not your real mother, but I'm the mother here." Explain the rules. "What we're trying to do will not be easy. You kids will have to cooperate."

Be understanding of the children's position and their insecurities. You want them to understand you. A child who screams, "You're not my mother," is not a monster, but a sad little creature crying out, "Who am I?" If their father says, "Their mother never made them do that," tell him, "I'm not their mother, but I am the mother here."

While going through the reorganizing process, be thorough. If there is a housekeeper, get rid of her. You're in charge now and chances are she will resent your authority. A woman from Atlanta said, "My husband's wife had been ill for five years before her death. The housekeeper had run the home and the children. When she was there the kids asked her instead of me. I had no job. At first the kids resented me for firing her, but soon it smoothed out."

Don't Criticize the Former Wife

Frances O. says, "I have two girls of my own and a stepson, Paul. His real mother calls from Cleveland once a week, if it's convenient for her. She gives him advice and listens to his complaints, but I'm the one who washes his clothes, prepares his meals, and cleans up after him. I can't stand my husband's ex-wife. She is lazy and thinks only of herself, but I never tell Paul. He idolizes her and he should; she's his real mother. If he thinks about why she didn't want him, he never talks about it. When I get upset, I just bite my tongue and keep quiet."

Whatever the situation, it's better to welcome what the absent parent does; gifts, visits, and telephone calls. In the end it's up to the child to decide how he or she feels about the parent. A child can make room in her heart for both, the real parent and stepparent. Don't force her to make a choice prematurely. Give her the freedom to choose.

The In-laws

Be prepared for some of the most awkward times in your married life when the in-laws visit. "Grandma took over when mom died." Where a father has been widowed or given custody of his children, grandma usually comes in as an intermediate caretaker. At the wedding, she's not too willing to relinquish her authority to an inexperienced bride. And no matter how hard the new stepmother might try, she may never be quite good enough. In the back of the in-laws' mind lingers the question, "Did she break up our son's marriage?" Frequently a move away from them becomes necessary simply to relieve the pressure imposed by their interference.

Not all in-laws will cause trouble. June recalled, "Tim's mom is closer to me than my own mother. I feel free to talk things out with her without fear of condemnation, which I usually get from my mom." When awkward situations arise, and you wonder if it's all worth it, the important thing to remember is how much you love your husband and how important your marriage is to you.

The Problem Child

There are no basic rules for dealing with a problem child, but it's an issue one must consider. A problem child can be discovered during pre-marriage visits, while the father has the children. If he has permanent custody, you will be the full-time stepmom. Will you be able to handle it? The belief that "Our love can endure all things," will not get the job done. A problem child creates overwhelming tension in a traditional family where both natural parents love and care for his welfare. But a stepfamily, with a stepparent and possibly stepsiblings, will not have that same degree of patience, and the child is apt to have a very destructive effect.

A problem child, one who refuses to adjust to the new situation or who has serious psychological problems, leaves the stepfamily with limited options. A therapist may help. Removing the child from the home and placing him in a boarding school removes the problem, but may not help the child. You could smother the child with love and risk jealousy and hurt feelings from the other children, or you could discipline him severely.

There are no guarantees but as long as the husband and wife work together, there is less chance of a major battle over, "that impossible kid." But if the husband refuses to admit a child has a problem, he's insinuating that you have serious shortcomings as a mother.

Patty B. recognized the problem of her husband's twelve-year-old daughter ahead of time. "He wanted Janie to live with us. Her mother made no arguments, but I said no. The kid wanted to make the move and reach out for my love, but I knew what I could do and what I wasn't able to do. This was too much. I was honest with my future husband right from the start and told him I'd never want Janie to live with us. She's too disturbed and I just can't handle her. Alan got mad at first, but I'd have never married him if she came along. Even now I panic on her scheduled visits." Honesty up front may cause anguish at the time, but it will make for better relations later.

The troubled child may not always be the husband's. Betty married a widower when her children were thirteen and nineteen. His, both girls, were sixteen and twenty. "My younger child said he hated me for getting married. I told him, 'I'm marrying because I love Ted and he loves me. It's time I think of myself a little more.' My son is nothing but trouble for my new husband. He dropped out of school, won't work, and lies around the house all day. For five years my husband has endured this for me. I finally had to tell my son to get out. I wasn't going to give up a man who loved me as much as Ted did, for a son who didn't."

In a stable home and with a united family, some problem children can change. But even in the best of situations, many do not.

Parents and stepparents in the combination family must learn to deal with guilt. Evelyn said, "Maybe Jonathan would not have turned out this way if we hadn't divorced." Maybe he wouldn't, but Evelyn will never know. Because of its impact on individual lives divorce can be tragic, but life must go on. The stepmother cannot relive yesterday.

Stepmothers must face the fact that they will have problems, like all other parents. Adolescents have problems with all authority figures, their natural parents as well as a stepparent, but "they'll grow up some day." Even an adolescent stepson who hates his stepmother, can change with time, learn to respect her, and eventually leave the nest. It may not be in that order. Years after he has left home he may come around to say "Thanks."

Accept it, and hug your husband.

CHAPTER 10

I'm Just A Stepfather

A man who has the courage to become a stepfather is more important to the children than he is led to believe. To uncover the significance of his status he must first sift through biases similar to those a stepmother would encounter, plus the devastating "You're only our stepdad."

The stepfather often becomes the forgotten man. Because he is not their real father, the children tend to overlook any authority he tries to assert. "Mom's the head of our home. Now that dad's gone she gives all the orders." In-laws are anxious to exclude him because he represents the failure of their daughter's first marriage, and they're not sure he wasn't partially responsible. To top it all, his lovely new wife wants his love, financial security, and concern for her children . . . "But don't tell my kids what to do."

Stepfathers face many of the conflicts in relationships stepmothers do, but they are different in nature. The expectations imposed on a stepfather are extraordinary: Be a good male role model for the children, but don't over-step the boundaries; Develop good relations with the wife and strive to meet her needs; When the kids' father arrives to pick them up, be nice to him; And when the grandparents, your new in-laws, come to visit, don't overdo the father routine—after all, you're just the kids' stepdad.

Sound inviting? Not really, but in spite of these inhibiting "ground rules," the country's stepfather population continues to increase dramatically.

The intent of the chapter is not to show any bias, but experts agree stepmothers face more serious relationship problems in new blended families than stepfathers do. The argument is that the stepmother is more conscientious in her role. In other words, it's more important to the stepmother that the children like her. A stepfather is more likely to give up more quickly if he sees the stepfather/stepchild relationship not working. Stepmothers are more concerned about the opinions of others. Most men would say, "I did my best, but that wasn't good enough for her kid."

Although custody laws and attitudes continue to change, more children will live with their divorced mother than with their father. While stepmothers prepare for the weekend invasion, the stepfather lives with the children during the week and eagerly awaits the natural father's weekend arrival. Although it may seem insignificant, the step-father's role is vital. He is the one who is living in the home daily.

Men who marry women with children bring the same illusions to the relationship women do. "Our love for one another is so strong it can overcome anything." A man will naively compare his new bride's children to his own, then later find they are not at all alike; no man-ners, disrespectful to their elders, and spoiled. The divorce (or death) and loss of a parent has been difficult for them. Their mother, in turn, has smothered them with her attention, trying to compensate for their loss.

Many stepfathers are disappointed when they become aware of the actual role they will play in the stepfamily. The man comes expecting to be head of his home, but existing circumstances prevent his taking that position. His wife has a responsibility separate from him, that she shares with another man, the children's father. The stepfather lives the live of a family man, but he also lives in the shadow of the family be-fore. There's no way he will try to be a father to the children whose natural father shows up on weekends to take them away, sends them money which supplies their needs and buys them clothes, and is the father image they want to maintain. If his wife interferes with the ac-tions he tries to take, his leadership role is further jeopardized.

What the stepfather can be, if he doesn't push too hard or too fast, is much different from what he had first anticipated. He can be the genuine strength his new family really needs. Patience is waiting for his wife to give up trying to raise the children by herself. Even though she's married and has a new mate, she feels they are her responsibility and that her husband should not be burdened with them.

There also are some mothers who simply resent any other person, especially a stepdad, telling their children what they can and cannot do. These same mothers probably had similar problems with the chil-dren's real father, possibly contributing to the break-up of the first marriage.

Husbands and wives constantly play games with one another. She might say it's not necessary for him to bother with her children, and at the same time need his help. When she becomes aware of this, be un-derstanding, knowing it is difficult for her to ask. The last thing she needs to hear is, "I told you so."

The child's dependence upon a stepfather grows with time. In most cases the stepfather lives in the same dwelling as the children, and as time passes they become more acquainted with him and his way of do-ing things. The convenience of him being around in the absence of the natural father automatically develops a closeness. The stepfather is needed, but the family must become aware of the need without his pushing it.

The stepfather has the same relationship challenges to conquer as a stepmother. The only difference is that he is a man and he will greet and will handle the conflicts differently.

STEPFATHER AND FATHER

Stepfathers usually do not show the animosity toward the children's natural father that often is manifested between the stepmother and the children's natural mother. Usually there is very little contact between the men, and that eliminates most of the chances for friction. Men, it seems, are not as jealous and possessive as women, with respect to the children developing affectionate relationships with others. It does not indicate men do not care what happens to their children, just that they are more accepting of the situation. "I'd like to see things different from what they are, but I can't do anything about it."

Human nature accounts for the difference. The mothering instinct is different from a father's paternal nature. Bill says, "I have two girls living with their mother and new stepfather. I'd like to do more for them, but they live seven hundred miles away. My only hope is their stepfather will care for them like I do my stepkids."

More women are entering the work force than ever before, but society does not provide most of them with opportunities for meaningful fulfillment in areas other than child bearing. That condition is likely to produce women who jealously covet their children. A mother who finishes a day's work in a factory will leave work with less satisfaction than a man. She is just supplementing the family income. As important as it is, it still leaves her with less satisfaction. And she is burdened with guilt because she has left her child.

In such a society men receive more ego gratification outside the home. Their careers and outside interests make them less dependent on home and children for a meaningful life.

The relationship a stepfather has with the child's natural father is also affected by the degree of understanding between the two men. The stepfather enters his new family with a lot of awareness of what the real father is going through. Since he too is divorced, he also has become a part-time father and can identify with the loss the real father is experiencing. Weekend visitation is a poor substitute for coming home at the end of a day and finding the kids waiting enthusiastically in the yard. If he is going to enjoy quality time with his children, he must do it within the forty-eight hour period and in the presence of a stepmother with very differing views.

If the stepfather wants to have a good relationship with the father, as well as with the children, he should never criticize the natural father in front of the kids. When the stepfather is asked questions about the natural father, he should be non-judgmental in his answers. If he is critical, he either puts the children on the defensive or places them in the middle of a controversy. The best thing is to stay away from any potential conflicts.

STEPFATHER AND STEPCHILDREN

The stepfather and his stepchildren begin on a footing that differs from that which exists between the stepmother and her stepchildren. His children will live with their mother and visit occasionally. The stepfather, in turn, will live in the same household as his stepchildren and he will be there when they wake in the morning and to hear their grumbling every night.

The journey to a successful relationship is difficult and time-consuming, often requiring more than a man is willing to give. "I just don't care about those kids anymore," remarked Chad. "I've tried to reach out to them, but their mother stops everything I try to do." The kids' mother means well, but she is her husband's biggest obstacle. The wisest thing would be to let her husband be the head of his home, but he can't be the one to tell her. He will never gain the children's respect if their mother constantly undercuts his leadership.

"I love my wife, and before we married all I heard was how she wanted me to be a father to her two boys. Now she won't let me." A divided home cannot stand. Someone must lead and there can be only one leader. The fact that the father assumes this position in most families *does not* downgrade any other family member, or make a wife and mother less important, but it is a system that has worked for centuries. Every organization needs a chain of command to function efficiently, but husbands, fathers, and stepfathers must not interpret their role as giving them dictatorial powers. Proper leadership is displayed by acting with authority thoughtfully and with love.

The age of the child also has a bearing on the relationship. In later chapters each age group is discussed in detail, but here the focus remains on the stepfather. "It's been fifteen years since I heard a small child cry out in the night," said Cliff, who is 45 and a divorce with two children, the youngest 17. His new wife is 27 and her two children are four and two.

When a man remarries, it generally is to a younger woman—sometimes a much younger woman. The romance and courtship were exciting and without the involvement of children (thanks to a reliable sitter), and by the end of the evening the children were conveniently asleep. But if a man is in love, that love naturally overflows to include the children. During the courtship they seemed to be no bother. Even if they did get on his nerves from time to time, it was such a small price to pay for their mother's love.

After the honeymoon, however, things change. Now if there's an evening out, they take the kids with them. Sometimes he even hears remarks like "What a lovely grandchild."

The stepfather has to decide if he wants a close relationship with young children or merely a convenient one. The ball is in his court and if he does not make the choice early in the marriage, the relationship almost inevitably will end up as one of convenience.

A stepchild of grade school age is a more frustrating challenge for the stepfather who wants a close relationship. "You're not my dad." Eight-year-old Johnny doesn't understand why his father had to leave. His mom's boyfriend, now his new stepfather, wants to play ball and take him to special places, but all Johnny wants is his father. A stepfather's only option is patience. Don't push the real father out of the picture or try to take his place. Living in the same house will be an advantage, but the son has too many fond memories of his real dad, no matter how he might have failed as a husband.

Teenagers respond in much the same way when it comes to accepting the stepfather. Their dad had been around too long for anyone else to fill his shoes. Alex said, "Janet's two teenage girls were very close to their father. From the beginning I respected that closeness and never once criticized any of his actions or ridiculed him in front of the girls. Since I live in the same house with them, time has drawn us closer together. Now I am the available one and they call on me when they need something around the house or help with their car. He is the one they turn to when they need advice. They visit him regularly and talk freely about him in my presence. I suspect it's the same way when they are with him. I don't know that I would want our relationship to be different in any way."

No matter what age children are, they want a happy life even if it includes two "father relationships," one with the natural father and one with the stepfather. If all the parties involved are willing to work at it, a satisfactory conclusion can be reached.

STEPFATHER AND MOTHER

The relationship a stepfather finds himself in with the children's mother is far different than the husband and wife relationship he obtained through marriage. It's the same man and woman, but these relationships represent two different areas of the stepfamily. The husband is now the stepfather; he represents new leadership, different values, and another adult with whom to share the kids. The adoring wife also has the role of mother-protector; she resents anyone other than herself instructing her children, and wants to keep them all under her wing. "But we've been through so much together." Stepfathers agree they would have an easier time establishing themselves in their new home if the mother were not so fiercely protective of what she sees as her rights in this area.

When problems do arise, a smart stepfather calls for a husband

and wife talk. Tell her how the conflict is affecting you and what long-term effect it may have on the marriage. The mother may not be aware she's jeopardizing her husband's position in the family. Her sole intent may be to lift responsibility for the children from her new husband's shoulders. The talk may not solve the problem, but at least it provides the opportunity to clear the air and gives the husband a chance to express his feelings on the matter.

Stepfathers are not as apt to fear the absent parent's shadow as the stepmother does and there is not the continuing feeling of competition. "I don't think Sharon would have married me if she didn't think I was going to be a better husband and father," said Chet. "There is no need for me to compete with her first husband.

A wise stepfather will not put off establishing his rightful position in the home. The mother may not mean harm by interfering with his actions, but it can disrupt family unity. "I love you and believe we can have a good home, but only if each of us assumes only our individual responsibilities—not the other person's as well.

BASIC TIPS FOR A STEPFATHER

Don't Back into the Marriage
Find out what kind of mother she is before you become the stepfather to her children. During the courtship the man usually spends more time in the woman's residence than she will in his. Observe her actions around the children. Is she on edge when you move into the role of father? Her reactions are no guarantee they will not change after the wedding, but in many cases the about-to-be stepfather can prepare for what is ahead.

She will always be the children's mother. Her natural instinct will be to protect them, but how she responds to your influence on them can tell a great deal. If the children respect you and begin to trust your leadership and she is happy with the situation, this probably is a good sign that she'll encourage a close relationship after the marriage. But if the bride-to-be reacts jealously when her kids become close to you, there might be fireworks ahead. Discuss the situation immediately. If it is not worked out before the wedding, chances of it improving later are slim.

Ex-wives usually will discuss their former marital problems with their new fiance. Listen intently and hear all of the real facts. If there is a close relationship with her friends, you might ask them about her first marriage. Many men have been led down the aisle under false pretenses. If there were arguments over the children in the first marriage, get her side of the story. If, based on what you hear, you think her first husband—the children's father—was right, don't expect her to change just because she is remarrying. And you will only be the stepfather, without the negotiating position of the natural father.

A visit into the home will not only show you the kind of mother your prospective wife is, it will also introduce you to the children in their home environment. "Those kids didn't act that way before we married." Chances are they did, but a man who has fallen in love is not a reliable observer. Psychologically you didn't want to see anything that would interfere with pre-arranged plans.

A person can learn a lot about the kids when he spends the whole evening in the home, *if* he is looking. When they have to be reminded about how to behave, it indicates that good manners are not part of their nature. If they are corrected, how long does it take for them to obey? Do they have to be coaxed or is there an argument? When the mother is in control of her children there will be no back talk when an order is given. Are these children more than you can cope with later?

Resentment is a common characteristic in the stepfamily, and difficult to handle. Some children speak their feelings freely. "I don't know why my dad is gone, but I sure don't want you trying to take his place!" At least the stepfather knows where he stands and mostly what he can expect. A relationship can be built on this foundation. Other children allow resentment to build up inside, with no outward signs until their feelings erupt. "Why didn't you tell me? I had no idea you felt that way."

Not all the questions and answers are going to be uncovered during visits and before the marriage. But no marriage benefits from unexpected surprises, especially bad ones. The more that can be discovered ahead of time the better prepared the stepfather will be. A sad little boy, having to move and giving up his favorite room after already losing his father, can become a friend when he is shown his new room in the new house.

You Are the Grown-up

Too many adults behave worse than the children. Stepfamily relations are not to improve if the stepfather says, "Well, I'm just waiting for her kids to come around." The kids probably are waiting on the adult to set an example and be the leader he is supposed to be. Any family unit would be weakened if the leadership were turned over to the children. Yet stepparents are doing it by waiting.

Start out right and behave like an adult from the beginning. Many stepparents feel they can win the kids over by trying to act like a child, but the child would rather have an adult friend. They already have friends their own age.

Adult behavior has two components: It will insist on cooperation when it is important to the family unit; and it will understand the adjustments the kids will be making, even accepting their hostility because you are aware of its source.

Remain Impartial, yet United with Your Wife

A united stand by the parent and stepparent is essential. This is as true for the stepfather as it is for the stepmother. There is nothing wrong with disagreeing on major issues, but don't do it in front of the children. When children learn they can instigate an argument between parent and stepparent, they will begin to play one against the other.

Come to a decision with your wife and stick with it. Many family disagreements are founded on misunderstanding. Your wife, the children's mother, has been around the kids all their lives. Learn from her expertise. She should be more than willing to work with you concerning her children, provided you don't come with an, "I know it all" attitude. Her four-year-old could very well have a physical problem which causes his bed wetting. A sarcastic outburst from an ignorant stepfather at such a critical time will do nothing to help him in his position in the new family.

The united family has no room for undercutting, playing favorites, or taking sides. "If your mother said do it, that's it. Do it." Stepfathers tend to be lenient wanting the kids to like them. But if he's weakened once, it'll be harder to be forceful the next time.

One person should not do all the giving, nor should anyone try to bull his or her way through. "Janet brought her two children with her into the marriage, and mine visit on weekends," said Frank. "My kids were used to more privileges, like playing outside later and not having a set bedtime. Janet quickly stepped in. 'It's not fair to have two sets of rules in one house and I don't want my kids complaining that yours don't have to mind.' I knew she was right, and though my boys resented it at first, it made for better weekends. After we put the kids to bed, I also enjoyed the relaxed time with my wife. The tension in our home had hindered our companionship."

Do Things Together

The kids belong to her and they expect her to mother them and chauffeur them around. But when the stepfather comes up with a terrific idea for the weekend or evening out, it means so much more to them. "My new stepdad's not so bad after all. Do you know what he wants the whole family to do next weekend?" When a stepfather suggests the idea it makes the kids feel that he wants them around. Many households are unhappy places because its members feel out of place or unwanted.

Don't let them down, for any reason. Even if second thoughts show they're not so terrific after all, when plans have been made go through with them anyway. The last thing a stepfather wants to do is to allow his stepchildren to lose confidence in him.

Be Prepared for an Awkward Time with the In-laws

In some situations the stepfather will not always be as welcomed as the son-in-law as he would like to be. For example, if the new couple is employed by the same company, he probably learned of her bad marriage and pending divorce before her parents did. Their friendship blossoms and after the divorce the courtship begins. His new in-laws, the stepchildren's grandparents, believe he moved in too quickly, not giving their daughter time to think or to reconcile her marriage. It takes two people for a courtship, but in the eyes of her parents he is the bad guy. Many parents refuse to accept the fact that their daughter had marriage problems she could not resolve.

Grandparents also do not appreciate a stranger telling their grand-children what to do. "When I first married Marsha, her parents commented on how well the kids behaved and they thought I was doing a good job as stepfather, said Ken. "Six months later they told Marsha I should back off since I wasn't their real father. What her parents resented was the fact the kids obeyed me better than them. They spoil them by trying to buy their love and never learned to discipline them. I asked Marsha how do they think kids learn to behave if someone doesn't tell them. Now her parents refuse to visit when I'm home and they look for things to discredit me."

In uncomfortable situations the wife and family have to come first. Don't let such outside annoyances as in-laws upset the marriage. The wife cannot make her parents change, and she probably doesn't like the circumstances any better than you do.

ADVICE FOR THE STEPFATHER'S WIFE

Accept the fact that a stepfather will never love your kids as well as he loves his own. Don't resent the feelings he has for his kids; after all, you love your kids more than you'll ever be able to love his. When a husband learns that his wife understands this basic need, he can relax, not feeling guilty for loving his kids. The relaxation permits him more freedom to take on the responsibility of being a stepfather.

Don't Try to Be Boss

When the natural father does not live with the children, it is important that the household not be dominated by the mother. A boy needs a male figure to emulate. If the mother dominates, the son likely will be dominated by his wife when he grows up and marries. The son also needs to know there is a strong male in the home to protect him, not some weakling who won't even stand up for himself. The stepfather also should be the one to encourage a son's aggressiveness, just as he will encourage a daughter's femininity. It's not so important if he's liked or disliked. What would matter would be his passive role in the home, his always responding to the kids by saying, "Ask your mother."

Pat B. says, "The right kind of stepfather can give guidance when it's needed. Chet's own father never gave him any real direction. Whatever Chet wanted, Chet got. After my divorce, I married a man who was really firm with him." Shortly after Pat's marriage to Cleave the first real stand-off came. They were in the middle of preparing for a dinner party, and Pat was beginning her shower, when Chet announced he needed typing paper for a report at school. Out of habit Pat quickly dressed and started to leave for the store with her demanding son. Cleave stepped in immediately. "You're not going anywhere right now and neither will I. We have a party to get ready for and he had most of the day to inform us that he needed the paper. One of us will take him tomorrow, but not now."

Chet did not know how to react. His father had never talked that way to him before. Two weeks went by without Chet saying a word to Cleave, but when he finally did speak, it was clear a new and better relationship had started.

The wife must help establish her stepfather-husband in his role in their home. He either will be a leader, helped by her encouragement, or he will be shunted aside by her dominant behavior.

Donna had a fight with her ten-year-old son, who retaliated by kicking her in the shins. At that point the stepfather took the boy to his bedroom and scolded him for his actions saying, "You can't treat your mother like that." Then he spanked the boy. Donna thanked her husband in front of her son, and said, "I'm glad you are a father to my child."

If she had reprimanded her husband for handling the situation as he did, the outcome would have been entirely different. But her approval established the stepfather's authority in the home.

When the Husband Has No Children of His Own, He Must Be Taught to Be a Father

The marriage requires the wife to let go of the double roles of mother and father to her children, roles she assumed after the divorce. Until this happens her husband will not be aware of the demands of his new paternal role.

Margaret L. married Phil, a childless widower. He had no money and worked at a blue collar job. "I was arrogant toward Phil, because of his financial status, and my children followed my example. I never gave him a chance with the kids. They were fed and bathed by the time he got home so that I could be alone with him. I never discussed the children or their problems and they became playthings to him rather than stepchildren. I wouldn't let them become his responsibility. What I should have done was include him in our family and respect him for what he was, their stepfather. Also, there were books I could have suggested which would have helped and encouraged him to take over certain responsibilities."

Some stepfathers do not want the responsibility of being a father figure. Julie met it head on. Her husband stayed annoyed at her teenage daughter because she talked on the phone too much. "He picked at her so that I finally had to choose between him and her. I chose my daughter, but if I had prepared him in the beginning it might not have come to this."

Don't Blame Him for Your Financial Losses

A new bride should have considered all the financial realities well in advance of the marriage. If she cannot stand a drop in family income, she should not remarry. It's possible that her children may too be forced to do without some of their luxuries while his children continue to enjoy theirs; dance lessons, piano instruction, gymnastics, or private schools. His obligations to his first family will continue, but her alimony payments may stop because she has remarried.

In retrospect, a wife may want to continue enjoying the more-than-adequate child support payments. Consider the new husband's feelings about your needs being satisfied by another man's money. "She puts all of the child support check into a separate account. There's no offer to help with the regular household bills, and when I ask her questions, she says it's for the kids. Then when she wants new clothes for herself, which I can't afford, she draws out of the special account and goes shopping. When I see her with a new outfit, I feel she's wearing something 'he' bought her."

Don't Make it Hard on Him When His Kids Come to Visit

Divorced fathers get to spend very little time with their kids through out the year; just a few days or weeks to show his love and teach them his values and ideas. Don't resent those few precious days. Your children may see his kids getting away with things they cannot. Explain to them he's only doing it because he knows they soon will go back to their mother and he will not see them for quite some time—just as their father sees and pays special attention to them. Don't add to his problem by criticizing or being demanding. Discipline the kids fairly, but don't nag them.

When a stepfather finds his place in the new home and begins to feel comfortable with his responsibilities, the home takes on a new meaning. No longer will he think, "If I can only hang on till these kids leave." Once stepfathers relax, the children bring more pleasure to him and to themselves because they too feel comfortable and not pressured. The reconstructed family should be regarded with the same concern as the traditional family, and stepparents should do everything possible to make their "step" role as natural as the "real" thing.

CHAPTER 11

Discipline in the Stepfamily

When it comes to discipline, caretakers of children do not have a choice. Whether it be a traditional, single parent, or stepfamily home, when parents or stepparents do not discipline children, they have failed them.

Most parents and stepparents flounder in this area because they do not have a proper understanding of discipline. "I love my kids too much to discipline them." Dictionaries define discipline as, "Training that develops self-control, efficiency, etc." What parent could say he loves his child too much to teach and train him for life ahead?

Discipline takes time, effort, patience and concern—and a lot of energy. The stepparent often is not willing to make such an effort for someone who is not a blood relative. "Why should I; he's not my kid." But no excuse is good enough to justify bypassing such an important responsibility. One stepfather recalled, "When you get married and have children the parents learn gradually as the children grow through their various stages. But when a person marries someone with kids, their rules have already been made and put into practice. If anything positive is to come from the relationship you have to renegotiate everything."

Whatever the cost, discipline is necessary for the stability and satisfaction of the children and for peace in the home. The future of the marriage can depend on it.

Discipline is used for two reasons: to promote desirable behavior and to avoid undesirable behavior. No one approach will work at all times with every child. Many parents and stepparents become confused rather than enlightened after reading books and articles on raising children. The new stepparent who comes into the stepfamily childless and without experience is even more frustrated, trying to fit his new stepchild into a particular mold described in one of the books. Writers on the subject of discipline should warn their readers that "all children are different" and that what works for one child might fail completely with another.

Many factors must be taken into consideration before positive results can be seen. To apply discipline properly, the caretaker should regard the age and background of the child. It would seem obvious that one would not use the same technique on a three-year-old as with a ten-year-old. But then there are no guarantees that something which worked with one three-year-old will work with another.

The stepparent is handicapped from the very beginning by his or her lack of background knowledge and patience. "Why do your kids act like that, mine never did?" While that might be true, it is not always the kids' fault. Or a stepfather who never has been married has "observer" knowledge only. "My cousin's children go to bed on schedule. Why is it that you let your kids stay up as late as they want?"

A child's behavior depends on the training he has been given by his caretaker. Most behavior problems can be traced back to improper training. Whatever you do, don't look back on past practices and criticize, look to the possibilities ahead.

DISCIPLINE: MORE THAN A RIGHT OR WRONG

A husband and wife will enter their new family with a sense of right or wrong that is derived from the training they got as children. Developing rules and roles for a new family is complicated and takes a considerable amount of time and energy. It's especially true for the remarried partners, each of whom brings to the stepfamily values formed in their previous households, along with a pattern for handling deviations from accepted behavior. In one home a child might come in past curfew and be physically punished. In another home the child might be deprived a few privileges. And in a third, the youngster would know he is in for a stern lecture.

MORE THAN A SET OF RULES

While commenting on their differences, William said "Alice and her children had a relaxed, free-and-easy relationship. On the other hand, I tend to be more formal." said William, while commenting on their differences. "Alice believes that her children should only be required to clean and straighten their rooms on weekends, while I always believed that an orderly mind functions better in an orderly setting. My boys, who live with their mother, attend an academy where ties and jackets are required. Alice's kids wear jeans. The argument in our home is that she is too slack with the rules and she complains that I am too stern. In calmer moments, we realized that no one of our differences was a matter of life and death, only that they were building up dangerously."

William continued, "One day, Alice and I looked at one another and decided that none of our quarrels made any sense. We needed to set some standard rules which we and the children could live with, and we did. My stepchildren still aren't required to straighten their room every morning, but it must be attended to first thing when they return home. And I think my boys, when they visit, enjoy the relaxed environment."

Conflict over rules, discipline, and authority seems to be one of the predictable consequences of remarriage when children are involved. These are not irreconcilable, but they do demand a lot of time and understanding from everyone.

WHO HOLDS THE AUTHORITY?

The new stepfamily begins somewhere during the course of the child's developmental process. Unlike the traditional family where children are born into the home, allowing time and the kind of experience that enables parents to become capable of raising children, the stepfamily begins anew. Discipline, how it will be administered and by whom, is a major conflict in the blended family. Should the authority flow directly from stepparent to stepchild, "Alan, you will need to clean your room today," or should it flow indirectly, taking a detour through the parent. "Ted, I want you to make Alan clean his room."

Each person has his or her own opinion. Even professionals disagree among themselves as to which is the best answer. The stepparent looks at the situation and ordinarily chooses to take the easiest path, sometimes not considering the child's best interest. If the couple has not decided before the wedding which procedures they will follow, they should not delay the decision any longer than necessary. The children's developmental process has been disrupted already, and it's best to get them back on the right track as quickly as possible.

One view is that the stepparent should establish his or her new place in the family right away, showing the child that both partners, natural parent and stepparent, have equal authority. Another concept, one which seems to create less friction, suggests the stepparent would approach a position of equal authority gradually, giving the natural parent time to relinquish the sole right to control the child. Either way, the stepparent must face the problem of sharing authority. And it is something that must be done in the fragile, early days of the marriage, when the child has an irresistible opportunity to play one caretaker against the other.

Anytime there is a dispute involving the children in a reconstructed family, the parent—right or wrong—can always pull rank over the stepparent. A father interrupts his wife while she is talking about his children saying, "You don't have any idea about the children's first five years of life. What makes you such an authority?" The stepmother replies, "Well, no but..." "You don't," he insists, and he wins the argument hands down because he was there when the kids were small and she was not.

One stepmother recalled, "I wait each day until my husband comes home to have him speak to his children about their misbehavior throughout the day. They'll listen to their father, but they won't pay any attention to me." Perhaps they won't listen, but they also will lose respect for a stepmother who carries tales rather than trying to be an effective parent. If the children don't listen to her, it's because proper authority has yet to be established within the home.

In some blended families the husband disciplines his children and the wife disciplines hers. In doing so, the couple perpetuates the division between their families saying, "What's mine is mine and what's yours is yours." This makes it even more difficult for the children to become "ours." Experts agree that stepparents abdicate their position as authorities when they leave all discipline to the spouse.

However, stepparents should be aware that their early efforts in assuming authority are likely to be met with criticism from an opinionated audience of one—the "real" parent, who is apt to be "sitting in the stands" watching every move. "Even if you impose discipline in what you think is a fair manner," said a hurting stepmother, "the real parent is listening to your every word and judging your actions, often saying, 'Don't you think you are overreacting to my children?'" In blended families, he also is apt to add "and you're too protective of yours."

After a reasonable adjustment period, and for the good of the new family, the stepparent should not delay taking an active role. The biological parent is advised against hovering over the proceedings. Unless a youngster may be in physical danger, stepparent and stepchild should be given room in which to work out their relationship.

The adults should discuss their differences, but not in front of the children. Unity in the couple is important in every aspect of the newly-blended family. And the stepparent who feels the freedom to yell at a child should also be free to hug that child. The ability to react spontaneously is important, despite the fact the natural parent is observing what is happening.

Understand this basic "rule" from the onset: Whether the authority is direct, indirect, or shared, there is no task in parenthood, traditional or step, more challenging than discipline.

WHAT IS IT?

Many caretakers confuse the word discipline with the word punishment. "I'm the disciplinarian in our home. I do all the spanking." Most believe that a needed spanking at the right time will do wonders for a child's developmental process. But, proper discipline is not something we do *to* children. Rather, it is a system we employ to help them live responsible, productive lives. It includes both corrective and preventive measures for helping young people take charge of their own lives; to make decisions, and to learn from the consequences of those decisions.

Begin by realizing that discipline is not a way to be in charge, but a learning process for the child. Punishment is negative, but discipline is not. If the discipline provided by a caretaker is meted out properly, it can teach the child self-discipline and guide him toward responsible independence.

Not only are caretakers responsible for providing proper discipline, they must also serve as role models—exemplifying the mature, responsible behavior they wish for their kids. For example, if parents who smoke cigarettes are serious about their kids not doing likewise, they should do something about their habit. Parents who drink alcoholic beverages or rely heavily on prescription drugs should be aware of the examples they are setting. A demonstration of restraint and sound judgment will encourage a struggling child to act similarly. Actions do speak louder than words.

SETTING THE LIMITS

Discipline and punishment are two distinctly different topics. "Losing Privileges" would fall within the category of punishment, while "Setting Limits" is a wise example of discipline. Discipline involves a discernible pattern, a structure within which the child can operate with a feeling of predictability. They need to be able to predict what they are about to experience, to some degree, in order to prepare themselves to adjust to it. When they are uncertain, feelings of frustration and anxiety develop. There is less apprehension and a greater measure of security when a young person knows pretty much about what rules will be applied *consistently* in his or her life.

Children who are exposed to an inconsistent environment, where limits are vaguely stated or where they have no way of knowing what will happen next as a reaction to their actions, are frustrated and often very destructive. Usually their destructive behavior is not the acting out aggressive instincts; actually they are begging for a caretaker to stop them, to tell them the rules. Janet D. from Ohio said, "I overheard Bill's daughter telling a friend, 'My stepmom won't allow me to do that!' That evening she told us that Ellen's parents couldn't love her very much. They let her take too many chances."

Certain species of animals are known to reach the outer limits of their territory and challenge the animals in the adjacent area only to establish who belongs where. Similarly, a child who misbehaves sometimes is asking his caretaker to tell him, "No, you can't do that!" Children feel safer and are known to be more productive when they are part of a secure, structured environment—when they know the limits.

An atmosphere of complete freedom only leads children to feelings of insecurity and various kinds of provocative "testing" behavior. Problem children become more productive in surroundings which are structured, but which allow some gradually increasing freedom within that structure. Occasionally when a person sees a destructive behavior in their child, he or she may be reacting to limits that are beginning to feel too restrictive. Limits are essential, but should be reviewed frequently and moved outward to allow for natural growth. But the expansion should be monitored closely.

ARE EXPLANATIONS NECESSARY?

Explanations are needed at times when giving instructions and defining limits, but there are occasions when the caretaker must exercise ordinary common sense. Some adults believe a detailed explanation is necessary for every instruction, but there are certain factors which should be taken into consideration—starting with the age of the child.

The stepparent should not try to reason with a toddler who will not understand any but the simplest instruction. The more complex the explanation, the more confused the very young child will be. A complicated explanation only leads the child to engage in provocative behavior, just to test the limits that seem so confusing. There will be time for reasoning with him later, when he's older. For now, an assured "no" will be sufficient for most situations. "But I'm afraid he won't like me." says one stepmother. When a child likes a caretaker for what he can get from her, it's not the person he likes, it's her leniency.

Sometimes explanations are needed to prepare a child for something new or unexpected; for example, going to the hospital, starting nursery school, or taking a plane trip. Overly detailed explanations can exhaust the child. "Okay (he thinks), I'll put my boots on. Just please don't keep telling me why I have to!"

DECISIONS, DECISIONS

Making the right decision about discipline is important to the struggling stepparent. It's hard for caretakers to know just when to get down to business or when to overlook a child's misdeed. Most stepparents are afraid to step out and take control. Others have to realize they cannot keep after the kids all of the time. "I know John's two girls must think I'm terrible the way I stay on them."

When to discipline and when to excuse a child's behavior can be a difficult decision for a new stepparent. Here are a few objectives to consider:

Immediate action should be taken when:

1. The child exceeds his safe limits and heads for serious harm.

2. The child is hurting others.

3. The child disobeys deliberately.

4. The child steals willfully, knowing what he is taking is not his.

5. The child is caught lying beyond his imagination.

Each of these areas of misconduct present a child's way of testing the control of his or her caretaker. All of them can hurt the child, or others around him, either now or at a later time. The intent of the caretaker's interference should be protecting the child from danger, but not to the extent of eliminating all of life's bruises.

Just because a stepparent is inexperienced and/or new to the family does not give him or her an excuse to stand idly and overlook bad behavior. Discipline is needed to guide the child toward a safe and healthful way of life.

CHILDREN NEED DISCIPLINE

Like adults, children have wants which are different from their needs. Without discipline, children would eat and care for themselves like animals. Out of control they could not live in a controlled social environment because they would not have the attributes needed—appropriate language, manners, decency, and kindness — to interact with other people.

Discipline is helping a child know what is expected of him without confusion and getting that child to want to do what's right. It is fairly easy to communicate to the child what is expected of him, as long as his level of development is considered. Convincing him to want to do what is right can also be less difficult than expected when persuasion is done with love. A child loves his parent so much that he wants to please that person. That's not the case with a stepparent. Stepparents who think their stepchildren should love them as much often bump into considerable resistance. Frequently, stepchildren will resent their stepparent. Instead of responding with love, and they spitefully will do the opposite of what's asked them. Time is the only possible answer, and that does not always yield a positive answer. Some stepparents have admitted they have never received a stepchild's love.

Whenever a stepchild will not respond positively out of love, the stepparent must recognize the fine line between love and respect. If a stepparent can gain a child's respect, love often comes later. "You don't have to love me, but as long as you live in this house, you will respect me."

Discipline must be clear and firm with few exceptions. When a child is told to wash his hands before he eats, he should know this means every time and not just when the parent is tired or upset with him. If exceptions to the rules are made often, the child does not know whether it is meant for this time or not. Make every rule clear, firm, and simple enough to be followed at any given time.

STOP THE BAD BEHAVIOR AND LOVE THE CHILD

Correct terminology is vital in discipline. No matter what the age of the child, let him or her know it's the bad behavior that is the problem, not the child. Instead of saying, "Tom, you're a bad boy." Change it to, "Tom, what you did was wrong. I know you'll learn to do better." Telling a child he is bad can make him believe you, and his image of himself will be that he is a bad person. If you let him know you think he's a good boy, even though he did something bad, it gives him a chance to redeem himself, and an opportunity to live up to the "good boy" image.

WHY NOT LET THE NATURAL PARENT DO IT ALL?

When discipline is required, the stepparent should not stand idly on the sidelines, unless the natural parent refuses to allow any participation. When this occurs a good husband and wife talk is needed. If stepparents want to have their own basic rights and values protected they must share in disciplining the children. There should be adequate control over the children to assure order in the blended home, and there must be discipline for each child; not only so he can be a credit to the family, but so he can find happiness and satisfaction wherever he goes.

Discipline will never be easy, but caretakers need to develop a method of discipline which will work for their situation. Even in the same family, some children require a firm hand while others respond to a lighter touch.

TIPS ON LENIENCY

A stepparent who has never experienced parenthood is handicapped when it comes to administering discipline because he does not know what is normal behavior for a child. Also he cannot relax and begin to accept the child's normal behavior until he is sure of his own position in the new home.

A stepparent should not overreact when:

1. The child does not know any better. If the action is uncalled for, teach him or her instantly what is allowed and what is not.

2. The child has an accident or makes a mistake. No one is perfect.

3. The child is sorry for the misbehavior. Don't stay on his back. Accept the apology and love him.

4. The child is acting his or her age. But beware of stretching the limits. "Since I got away with it once, I'll try it again."

5. The child is improving his skills and testing what he thinks he can do. Be sure he is safe, but do not be over-protective.

WHAT ABOUT SPANKING?

Experts disagree on the issue of spanking. Some say it does no good, while others say it can be helpful if handled properly. There probably is nothing wrong with a moderate spanking if the child is given adequate warning and if it really doesn't hurt him. Sometimes it becomes necessary to say, "If you do that one more time I'm going to spank you," and when he or she does it again, to follow through as promised.

You do not have to hurt a child to get the point across. Eventually he will get the message: "She means what she says." It should also be pointed out when you spanked the child you had no other alternative; he or she had disobeyed a direct and clear order. In fact, you have given the child freedom of choice, rather than making him feel powerless and uncertain. "Be naughty if you insist, but this will be the consequence." He has the choice and he can determine whether or not he'll get the spanking. However, if a caretaker hits the child without warning, you have a totally different situation. It's not discipline, it's punishment. Punishment only teaches a child to be wary of getting caught.

Parents and stepparents often can avoid direct confrontations when they see what the child is about to do and prevent it from happening. He or she can be distracted, a much more constructive way to handle a potentially bad situation.

A preschooler who does not want to get dressed so he can be taken out will sometimes be distracted by a picture book while a snow suit is put on. If all else fails and there comes a time for more direct action, use a method of related consequence. For example, if a caretaker decides to withhold television for the following day, it makes television the important object and the consequence is so far ahead it has no meaning at the present. The child figures, "I'll deal with that later," and the caretaker will have forgotten about it by then. Take a firm stand, "We're going out now. If I have to hold you and dress you like a baby, I'm going to do it."

Stepparents generally feel insecure in the relationship with their stepchildren. They will back off when the child is disrespectful, then later blame the child, when respect was never demanded. There are times when discipline requires strength. If the child is to understand reality and feel secure in the world, the caretaker must be the one to help him acknowledge there is a difference between children and adults. When a stepparent puts herself on the child's level, communication begins to break down. But when she says, "Look, I'm the mother of this household," even if she is the stepmother, "and you must obey me," the relationship has been defined.

It does not need to be hostile, even though the child's response at the time may not be positive. What is happening *is* positive; the child is learning he lives in a consistent, stable universe and he can learn to function in it because there are some definite rules.

BARGAINING IS NOT A GOOD IDEA

Trying to reach a decision with a child by bargaining is not a good idea. "You know you're not hungry enough to eat dessert." What the child knows is that he wants some of the cake he sees whether he's hungry or not. It's better for the stepparent to use her own feelings as the negotiating currency. The child learns that his caretaker is happy with him if he behaves one way, unhappy with him when he behaves another way, and that she gets so irritated sometimes she won't play with him. If the child desires parental attention he'll soon learn that obedience earns it, but misbehavior does not.

Some stepparents are troubled with this approach because they want to win a child's approval immediately. Many will leap into the relationship doing anything to please, instead of taking it one step at a time. In most circumstances the child is just as anxious to please the stepparent, and he is looking more for stability than favors.

Uncover all the facts. Be straightforward and honest with the child, and don't try to bargain for his or her affection. Take charge.

BE CONSISTENT

Teaching social behavior is one way to help a child learn to adapt to the real world. Testing limits does not stop at any certain age. Adults continue to test the limits throughout life just to see how far they can go, how much can be accomplished. If humans did not have that instinct, we still would be in the horse and buggy age, not the space age.

Children continue their testing as part of the process of learning about their environment. It's their way of finding out what the world will and will not allow. If the limits become inconsistent, if the person in charge allows something to be tolerated one day and not the next, the child is uncomfortable. He is uncertain about the future consequence of his behavior. He then has a much greater tendency to challenge the caretaker, to find out for sure what the limits are.

When a caretaker over-disciplines, the child is not likely to accept the rules unless the adult is there to enforce them. A dog that jumps off the couch every time its owner enters the room has not learned what not to do, only that he shouldn't do them when the enforcer is around. The dog does not know it's wrong to sit on the couch. He merely associates his owner with the punishment he receives when he is discovered on it.

When a caretaker is too harsh, the child learns to be cautious. He won't do the things he knows are objectionable as long as the caretaker is present. But when he is alone, he will do as he pleases. If on the other hand the caretaker is generally firm, consistent, and fair, he or she will gain the child's trust and dependency and will no longer need to be present for the child to behave. "I know my parents are out of town this weekend, but I'm still not going to do that." The parents' rules have become a part of the child's value system, and his conscience begins to take over.

A new stepparent coming into the home may see the existing rules are vague, or have deteriorated since the divorce, and need to be explained. It matters less exactly what the limits are than that they are consistently enforced. The area in which the caretaker is most ambiguous is the area in which the child will try to manipulate them into taking a firm stand. A child wants to know if there is anybody around strong enough to provide consistent discipline, so he or she can relax. "Okay, I know what the rules are."

Some adults have the misconception that children should have no frustrations, believing that each child should have complete freedom to express himself, and feeling that inhibiting this freedom would in some way hold back the child. The best time to teach a child how society expects him to behave is when he is ready to learn it. There comes a time when the child is receptive and derives a sense of satisfaction from mastering certain accomplishments. If a caretaker passes by this opportunity, and doesn't help the child learn to master socially unacceptable desires and impulses, the child will not be prepared for the next stage in the developmental process, when he will need to use this control.

A proper disciplinarian is not one who pushes nor one who overprotects by always doing for the child. "I never let my kids do for themselves. I always stayed one jump ahead of them. Later, it hurt seeing them struggle so hard with things they should have learned in our home." The intelligent application of discipline requires a sensitive touch. If too much is done for the child you risk hindering his growth. If demands are made he's not ready for, you can put him under undue pressure he may not be able to withstand. Walk slowly, keep your eyes open, and be aware of every action and reaction

WHAT ABOUT REWARDS?

Rewards and punishment seem to be leftovers from a past society. Some may say this hasn't worked and others would be quick to say it has. Probably the more common belief is that young people who seem to be motivated by rewards and punishment can eventually become dependent, unsure of themselves, and fearful. By the time they reach their teenage years, they may feel they have no control over their own lives.

A reward is something given by someone in a superior role to someone in an inferior role. In family relationships rewards often get turned into bribes, sometimes with strings attached. "If you do this for me, then I'll do something for you." The strings might even become tied at both ends. The child may respond, "I'll do that, if you'll give me this." The whole system can reach a level very close to blackmail.

When Chet was 12 his parents paid him a small amount of money to mow the lawn. Now that he's fifteen, Chet told his parents, "I'll be glad to mow the lawn for the same amount a professional lawn service charges." Chet has not learned how to cooperate, only how to drive a hard bargain. It would be nice for each of us to get everything we wanted, but there are times when life requires cooperation. A stepfamily needs everyone pulling together, not certain individuals pulling in their own direction. Life will not always offer us something for everything we do.

Parents' approaches to discipline range from one end of the spectrum to the other. Some employ a "rewards and punishment" system, while others are generally permissive. A better alternative is to establish a relationship between stepparent and stepchild; a relationship based on equality and mutual respect. The challenge is to find ways to cooperate and encourage each other.

Stepparents should begin by challenging themselves. If they want cooperation, they should be cooperative. If respect is the objective, be respectful. The child should be treated in the same manner as the caretaker wants to be treated. For a teenager, for example, it would be a good idea to arrange time for him or her to use the family auto. By demonstrating respect and a desire to cooperate, it lets him know he is looked on as a worthy person, on equal terms with the stepparent.

DISCOVERING NATURAL CONSEQUENCES

"My stepson thinks the world owes him a living." The child never learned the natural consequence of not working. If a person fails to pay his electric bill, the service will be disconnected. When he's late for work, his pay likely will be docked and he will be reprimanded by the boss. These are not forms of punishment, just predictable reactions to simple violations of natural order. Punishment can be angrily resisted by a child, but natural consequences deliver a straight message that's hard to overlook.

Caretakers also can put natural consequences into practice if they are willing to be creative and work at it. If a teenage son misses dinner, the natural consequence will be he will go hungry. A caretaker may offer the boy an opportunity to fix himself something to eat, if he agrees to clean up afterwards. If he fails to do so, the next time he goes without eating.

How many times has a stepparent impatiently waited for their stepchild to the point of making themselves late for an appointment? "I'm leaving in ten minutes. If you are riding with me, be in the car!" Be consistent. If you say you're leaving in ten minutes, don't wait a minute later. The child may show hostility because she was left behind, but you will not miss your appointment. And the next time the child will be ready when you are.

"I nagged my husband constantly to make his teenage son save some of the money he earned." recalled Evelyn. "He had a good paying part-time job while in school and an excellent opportunity to put some money away for the future. Alex told me to let him learn the hard way. I disagreed, but since it was his son I decided to keep my mouth shut. A year later, when it came time to purchase his first auto, my stepson did not even have enough money saved to make a good down payment. Now he works hard and knows if he misses one payment that his father will sell the car. I wanted to tell my husband, I told you so, but instead his son learned a real lesson in life.

Natural consequences are always going to be there. The sooner a child learns of their existence, the better off he will be.

STANDING FIRM

Standing firm in matters of discipline allows the caretaker to avoid a great deal of conflict. "Bill, I'm not going to nag you about your room. If it's not kept clean, you do not go out." The decision to go out is not in the hands of the caretaker; it's in the hands of the child. If he does as he is told, he receives permission to go. If not, he stays home — with no one to blame but himself.

Youngsters test adults until they know the rule stands firm. Guidance should be given according to the developmental readiness of the child. Most stepparents are unaware of where in that developmental process the new stepchild is. Also, when a person does not understand the normal process of development, he or she cannot know what to expect of the child during each stage. You can be frustrated by not knowing if the child's actions are normal or not. The uneasiness keeps the stepparent from relaxing. Don't try to do everything at once. Try to meet the child's most critical needs at the time.

THE DEVELOPMENTAL PROCESS

Libraries and book stores are well-stocked with material on child care, from birth through adolescence. This book cannot give a detailed description of each stage of a child's development, but here are a few key points which should be helpful to an unaware stepparent:

Infant

An infant's greatest need is tender loving care, cuddling, and confidence. As a stepparent, relax and enjoy the baby. There is no need to rush into toilet training, teaching table manners, or how to share toys. All of those will come when the child is ready for them. Focus your attention on making the youngster a happy, healthy child.

Toddler

Toddlers need to handle and touch the things with which they share their world. They love to explore. You will want to help them indulge this natural instinct, but you should provide them — with as little restriction as possible — with safe limits. The limits on his activities should be established well ahead of time, so he can have freedom to explore and the caretaker can be free to get on with her work. The caretaker also can save the toddler a lot of frustration if she will give him time to learn what is expected by example and encouragement. He should not need eating training until he is ready to use the appropriate utensils.

Young Preschooler

The young preschooler, age eighteen months through two years, is a babbler trying to communicate with others. The discipline should be positive in talking with him, answering his many (sometimes annoying) questions, and encouraging his communications. When he enters the negative stage which comes between two and three, caretakers should be prepared for sudden outbursts of anger. Give him outlets for his frustration at this stage; for example, clay and other materials he can manhandle. Do not make a big issue of the occasional outbursts of temper that come with his push for independence. Calmly separate him from the others, and move him to a quiet corner until he is ready to rejoin the group. Avoid conflict as much as possible. The child soon learns that tantrums will not give him his way.

Older Preschooler

The younger toddler explores his new world in the home, while the three and four-year-old turns his interest to the outside. He is learning more about other children in the neighborhood and in his day care nursery. He develops great interest in finding out what other youngsters are supposed to be doing. This age is quick to learn that other families differ from his in some ways.

New words and actions that get learned on the outside will also be tried and tested in the home. When he or she hears an objectionable word, a caretaker should calmly inform the child when that word is not suitable. Don't panic or over-react to objectionable language or behavior. Any overreaction only tempts the child to try it again.

School Age Children

School age children are eager to become responsible. They want to be helpful to the teacher at school and also to the caretaker at home. This age has much to learn about what school expects of them, as well as how to conduct themselves. The discipline should be to assist and encourage as they attempt to measure up to their new roles and responsibilities. Don't be too quick to criticize. The child already feels insecure.

Ten-year-old Patty came in from school and went directly to her room. Her stepmother found her lying on her bed, looking as if she had lost her best friend. The stepmother lovingly asked, "What's wrong honey? Don't you feel well?" Patty answered, "I've been miserable all day and I thought I'd take a nap." The wise stepmother did not nag or coax a reason from her, she merely replied, "I have days like that too. Sometimes we bring them on ourselves. A nap might help." The stepmother's response told Patty that life is not always going to be pleasant, but that she would do her best to stand by her.

Adolescent

The typical teenager wants to be more grown-up than he is, and they want parents and stepparents to give him guidance suitable for a grown-up. Teens resents it when adults try to treat them like children. If they have had the benefit of proper discipline through the earlier stages, teenagers should be prepared to manage their own affairs. Though they want to be grown up, there still are some things they need to learn one step at a time. If a good relationship exists with the caretaker, he or she will be called on when the youngster gets into a jam. A wise teenager is aware of his need for a parent.

Tom turned eighteen in September and enrolled in college the same month. "During all his preparation, never once did he consult me or his stepmother for advice," recalled Dan. "When registration started, all of his plans fell through. Classes were closed, expenses were more than he anticipated. He was one frustrated teenager. Since his stepmother was younger than I, and a more recent college graduate, he turned to her with all of his questions. We both could have helped along the way if he would have let us, but his teenage girl friend knew all the answers, so he thought, and when we tried to help, he said we were butting in. All we could do was stand by and wait." Although there will be times you will want to step in and help without being asked, that is not the kind of discipline teens need or want. You want to be open and helpful, but sometimes you have to wait.

THE VISITING CHILD

It is more difficult to apply discipline to children who visit the home for short periods of time than it is to establish ground rules for youngsters who live in the home. Often the non-custodial parent, whether or not he or she has remarried, feels frustrated by the inability to have a continuing influence on the behavior of a child she does not see daily. "I know my daughter watches too much television," said one father, "but it doesn't do much good for me to be strict about it on weekend visits when I know she'll be allowed to watch whatever she wants the remainder of the week. That's when control is more important."

While the parent does not live with the child he must become reconciled to losing power, the stepparent has to face the fact that his or her role will be even less important. The stepparent often is in a situation of responsibility, but without any authority. "I feel like a maid," complains one stepmother after another.

Though it might accidentally happen on occasion, it should not be the prevailing situation. The stepparent has a right to be consulted and included in the decision making on matters involving a spouse's children. She has a right to feel comfortable in her own home. The non-resident child also should be given a say in the process that establishes the rules by which all the children are expected to live.

USE COMMON SENSE

There is no one particular rule which will work every time. It almost always comes down to using common sense. A little permissiveness is not wrong, but too much can ruin the child. Consistency is essential, but it won't hurt to give in a little on certain occasions. Experts tell us not to use punitive measures, but sometimes nothing else seems to work.

Donald, father of three children and stepfather of two said, "When my kids were young a friend publicly criticized me for spanking my five-year-old daughter for her misbehavior. She told me I was too hard on my kids and they would grow to resent me. Her children were caught in the same misdeed as mine, but she did nothing about it. Fifteen years later, my daughter is a successful business woman who calls me regularly just to say, 'I love you dad.' My son is in college and keeps close contact with me. My youngest, who was not born at the time of the incident, is in high school doing well. As for my friend, her oldest child died from an overdose of drugs, and the other was killed as the drunken driver in an auto accident."

Discipline should be maintained in keeping with the child's capabilities, age, development, and temperament. No two children will respond the same way; and, more than likely, no adult will administer discipline the same way twice. A caretaker must think and "adjust" the required guidance to meet the need at the time. A natural parent learns and grows along with the child but the stepparent will not have had this experience. The parent has to be on her toes, but the stepparent must walk on egg shells. Sometimes a stepparent does the right thing and everyone feels good about it. Other times he or she will make a mistake and it seems as though the whole world comes down on them. They go through torment trying to make things right. Keep trying. The world goes on.

ADULT FEELINGS AFFECT THE DISCIPLINE

Much goes into the establishment of positive discipline. Much has been said about the child, but what about the adult's feelings? A caretaker's feelings about the child, himself, and about discipline overall will affect the situation more than any advice from a spouse. When relationships with other people are going well, the feelings will be positive. The discipline will reflect an inner peace. If he has good feelings about the child, a caretaker will handle him more lovingly and with care.

But it is difficult for a stepparent to attain peace and harmony with a stepchild. A feeling of uneasiness about the child keeps the stepparent on edge, adding tension to the administration of discipline.

Even a reasonable and mature adult will be unable to cope properly at time. There will be occasions when a person becomes so exhausted with the child that he or she will lash out in uncontrolled anger. It would not be normal if extreme frustration did not cause this to happen. Even though a stepparent knows the population of stepparents is increasing daily, all feel alone and defeated when these outbursts occur. If there is any relief to be found, it would be in knowing others are going through the same frustrations.

A sudden, frustrated outburst is not going to destroy a relationship. The child can handle an occasional lapse of control if he feels a basic sense of security in the blended family relationships. A "blow-up" may even reassure a stepson or stepdaughter. "My stepmother is human, too."

Stepchildren need to learn as much as possible about the stepparent. Adults are inclined to hide their weaknesses—their occasional emotional moments—when they should let them show. "Wow, I didn't know your mom did things like that!" A stepchild learning he is not the only one in the home to explode now and then is not necessarily a bad thing.

APOLOGIES

Is it good to admit to being unreasonable? When it happens the stepparent has made a great stride into stepparenthood. Acknowledging to a child that you "blew it" gives him an acceptable way to handle his own mistakes. Apologizing openly after you have been unfair provides the child with an opportunity for forgiveness, a capability youngsters need to develop in their contacts with other people.

When Joan realized she had been unfair in settling a dispute without taking time to gather all the facts, she apologized to her stepdaughter. "That's okay, I've done that before too. Don't worry about it," was Kay's response. Kay had fumed at her stepmother's partiality. Hearing the apology, she developed a better understanding of how much pressure was on her stepmother in the new home. This understanding made them closer.

No matter how stepparents look at themselves, it is unlikely there has ever been one who is completely satisfied with his or her own behavior. Stepparents must learn to live within their own strengths and weaknesses in their disciplining of the child. Sometimes things will go right. Other times, sometimes inexplicably, they will go wrong. When a stepparent acknowledges that "fact of life," accepts his or her mistakes and learns from them, all the family problems will be resolved much more easily than if the stepparent pretended to be perfect.

Always remember, the success of the blended family is at stake.

Children in second marriages are at a high risk for divorce when they grow up. Proper discipline in a home will not eliminate all the problems, but it will help the youngsters involved take a step in the right direction.

CHAPTER 12

Stepsibling Rivalries

The stepfamily has been identified as a family unit put together with fragments of other family units—a husband and wife, with children from at least one of the former marriages. In many cases the husband and wife both bring children into the recreated family. In some second marriages, both husband and wife will have custody of their children. In other situations, one spouse will have custody and the other only visiting privileges. Whatever the situation, the new closeness will inevitably lead to rivalries among the stepsiblings.

The quarreling which develops between the two sets of children will be one of the most exasperating problems couples will face. The squabbles often are over such trivial things it's hard to understand how they can become so violent. Stepparents often are at a loss as how to handle these disputes, and when a particularly difficult situation has been solved they wonder what they can do to prevent a reoccurrence.

Just as the myth of instant love imposes unreal expectations on different family members, so does the fantasy that stepsiblings will enjoy instant friendship. Why should they? The children did not meet and court, nor did they vow to love and cherish each other. Strained relationships between stepsiblings, particularly those forced to live in the closeness demanded by a shared household, can range from hostility to secret romance. For the sake of the new home, family leaders must learn to deal with any crisis that develops.

IS QUARRELING INEVITABLE?

Virtually all children fight at some time in their growing years. Some are more aggressive than others and seem determined to start arguments. Others have more mild temperaments most of the time, but even they become embroiled in struggles with brothers and sisters on occasion. The difference between stepsibling rivalry and biological sibling rivalry is the not-surprising fact there are more things to fight about in the step-family household.

These rivalries are nothing more than a test of supremacy between two opponents. A simple phrase like "Mine's better than yours," sets the stage for a scrimmage. I stated earlier that a new stepfamily would encounter fewer frustrations if they could start out in a new home—a neutral ground for all parties. The child who moves into an existing home feels he's the outsider and has to prove his worthiness. Trivial disputes may result from nothing more than a child's way of conquering what he sees as enemy territory. "That's nothing, watch what I can do!" Or, "Is that all you know?" The child who lives in the home is also forced to share with someone he may feel does not deserve to be there. That feeling can kindle a flame of resentment. "Before you moved in I had my own room." The feeling of giving up something festers.

A good understanding of the child and his or her situation should uncover many of the reasons why the stepsiblings argue. Only then can a caretaker begin to help put harmony into their home.

JEALOUSY

The number one cause for rivalries is jealousy. Jealousy runs rampant in the typical stepfamily because of the many areas in which it can erupt. Stepbrothers and stepsisters share the same house, its furnishings, and facilities. Cramped quarters, shared bedrooms, and longer lines to the bathroom can strain the patience of youngsters and turn the dwelling into a battlefield. "What right do you have to be in my room?" Or, "I don't like your crummy room anyway."

Age, sex, and temperament affect the relationships. Children of the same sex who are close in age may see themselves as rivals for the same offerings. Caretakers should try to avoid making any comparisons. "Why does your stepsister get her work done on time and you're always late?"

Whether all of the children live in the same house all the time or some of the time, there is a certain amount of sharing which must be done. And sharing causes jealousy. When one child feels he is getting less than the other, trouble begins. "Why does she have a phone in her room and I don't?" "If I stayed in the bathroom as long as he does, you'd get onto me!" After a trivial difference simmers for a while, it can erupt into an all out war.

Struggles for the caretaker's attention also lead to jealousy. This can become a significant issue in the new stepfamily as each member strives for recognition and acceptance. A stepparent who is trying hard to gain the approval of his or her new stepchild might be told "You love him more than you do me, your own child."

The closer the relationship parent and stepchild build, the more the biological child may resent it. Eight-year-old Lora was her father's favorite. Whenever she would see him paying attention to Joan, the nine-year-old daughter of his new wife, Lora would run in and sit on his lap. He would turn his attention to Lora immediately, and Joan would run into her room and close the door.

Attention focused on the biological child may cause a stepchild to say "There's no way we'll be a family. You don't care about me." The stepparent feels he has come into a no-win situation, but neither of these situations reveals a bad approach. Showing love and concern for one's stepchild is positive for the stepfamily. And because she has been through so much already a parent's dedicated attention to his own child's need is justified. It can be worked out.

In Lora's case, the father needed to see he wasn't helping by always giving in to her demands. If Lora came in while Dad was spending time with Joan she should be told she could join them or wait until he was free. A stepchild who feels left out will soon come around when she sees the stepparent's fairness in all relationships.

Jealousy is not a pleasant state for the child, parent, or stepparent. But it is very real, urgent emotion, and it cannot be overlooked. When a child has jealous feelings, he sees no way to express himself but to lash out in anger.

FRUSTRATION AND ANGER

Children easily become frustrated when things don't go their way. The younger child is upset with his size, skills, strength, and power. The older child wants to act and be treated like an adult, but still enjoys a parent's favor and attention. When what they want cannot be, they become frustrated at themselves and the people around them. Being a stepchild only multiplies the problem. Their first home has been disrupted, one parent is gone, and now they are forced to live with people to whom they are not accustomed. Stepchildren are angry with the absent parent who deserted them (their belief) and caused the unhappy predicament in which they find themselves.

They are angry with themselves, thinking they may have been responsible for the separation in some way or that they could have prevented it. The easiest way to release their pent-up feelings is to get mad and lash out at those closest to them, the stepsiblings. The stepparent's first step toward solving these problems is to understand them and to show concern.

OH TO BE FIRST

Children of all ages compete to be first in line, first in favor, first in any activity where score is important. Like adults, no one wants to lose, or even come in second — especially all the time. If stepbrothers and stepsisters are older, the younger child feels he cannot compete and win. When there are few chances to win, a child will cheat, quarrel, and sometimes lie to gain favor with a caretaker, even if it only lasts until he's found out.

When the blended family first gathers in the new home, part of the stepparent's introduction to the home should be to inform all children there is no need to compete for attention or love.

RELEASE OF TENSION

Pressures continue to mount on children as they proceed through their busy day. A school child builds up tension in the classroom and on the playground as he competes in one situation after another. He may be bullied or harassed by a classmate, only adding to the stress. He and the teacher he so wants to please will not always agree on behavior, and his own actions probably will get him into trouble occasionally. By the end of the day he is a boiling teakettle that must let off steam. He releases that steam in the safest place he knows, his home. The target of his attack usually is a stepsibling, an easy "enemy" to defeat.

Before he or she can ease the pressure, a stepparent must try to understand the reason for the child's tension. The absent parent might have been the shoulder the child leaned on, and now that shoulder is gone. Reach out to the hurting child.

Between the divorce and remarriage the child's environment went through many changes. But whatever the situation there was still no need to compete for attention. After the wedding, however, the child became part of a whole new family. The parent and stepparent should work to make the transition into that new family as smooth as possible. Get acquainted ahead of time (before the wedding), and do family things together as soon as possible. Do not expect it to eliminate the rivalries completely, but every move to build a family feeling is a step in the right direction.

TREAT THE CHILDREN AS EQUALS

Jealousy is the anger which comes from believing someone else is treated better and loved more. Every child needs to feel equality and love within his home. He needs that assurance every day. The blended family has taken every bit of confidence away from him and jealousy is his struggle to recover it.

Children should be treated as equals with respect to limits imposed and favors given, but a stepparent should not be expected to love equally. No matter how hard a person tries, the feelings of love between a stepparent and stepchild will never be as strong as those which exist between a parent and child. Honesty in the relationship is helpful when explaining, "Jeff, I'll probably never love you like I do Sharon, but you can depend on me being fair with you. I'll never demand or expect more from either one of you."

Spoken in the beginning, this kind of statement will bring back the assurance each child needs to sustain a relationship with his or her stepsiblings.

EACH CHILD IS SPECIAL

Each child must be cared for in his own special way. One may be a cuddler, another express less need for physical affection. One child may burst into the house after a day at school eager to tell all, while another keeps everything inside and only opens up to a few close friends. Children differ in their actions and in the way they want to be treated. The sibling with an outgoing personality may be hurt if the stepparent doesn't ask about the day's activities. The other child might be offended, and think him or her too nosey if they did ask.

The stepparent's nature has a lot to do with her ability to give and receive affection. Elizabeth said, "My teenage stepson thinks I hate him because I don't treat him the way his mother did. When they're together it makes me sick to see the way they hang on each other. But I don't treat my boys any different than I do him. He just expects it and I can't deliver."

Fortunately, most children have two adult caretakers as well as other relatives, some of whom will match up to their needs. "Karen loves to visit my sister," said Martha, who is Karen's stepmother. "Karen enjoys talking about everything, boys, school, and her friends. I don't show the interest I should, but my sister just lets her talk on. At first I was jealous of their closeness, but I realized our natures were different and now I'm glad Karen has a stepaunt who will listen to her."

Every child comes with certain characteristics that are deserving of praise. It should not make him egotistical as long as the praise comes spontaneously and from the heart. It's one reason a caretaker needs to spend quality time with each child, so he can discover the finer qualities of the youngster. Take them shopping or on general errands, especially when the children are young. Remember that the stepchild is now part of the family. Older children may not want to join you in the grocery shopping, but if they do, take them.

Time alone with the child is necessary because it gives him an opportunity to share his plans and talk over problems. It also gives a stepparent the opportunity to point out possibilities and potentials to him. Doing so assures the child that he is an important human being, and that there is no need to feel inferior in the new home.

CALM DOWN THE COMPETITIVE SPIRIT

Stepsibling competition cannot be eliminated completely. In fact, no matter how much a stepparent thinks she would like to see that happen, it would not be beneficial. People of all ages become apathetic without competition. But competitive rivalries can be minimized by caretakers who care enough to rear their children without putting too much pressure on them to excel. "John, that's just not good enough. I know you can do better." When that pressure is taken away, the child loosens up and the home atmosphere becomes more relaxed.

Grades and sports are the big comparative tests for parents and step-parents. No two kids are the same, and it is not fair to expect them to perform as well as a brother or sister—or a stepbrother or stepsister. Simply because a parent or stepparent likes football doesn't mean the son or stepson will share that enthusiasm. A stepfather who is a football fanatic can drive away a stepson who doesn't care about the sport but who is reaching for his stepdad's time and affection.

Having an interest in a child's progress at school is good, but putting too much pressure on her to be the best in the class can be damaging to the youngster and her relationship with peers and the other caretaker. Stepparents have a tendency to criticize their stepchild. No matter what progress is made, it's not good enough. Lynn, mother of two young boys, ages six and two, married Norman who has his teenage son living with him.

Not accustomed to having a teenager around the house, Lynn did not know how to respond to his behavior. She had grown close to her boys, but there is a big gap between a six-year-old and a fifteen-year-old. Lynn complained about his room, his appearance, about his grades at school. Finally her husband stepped in and said, "What makes you think your boys will act differently when they reach his age?" Lynn had not looked that far into the future. She only "thought" her boys would be different.

Never compare children. Rarely, if ever, will comparing one child with another motivate her to improve. Generally it makes the child feel she is not cared for, understood, or as acceptable as the child with whom she is compared.

Rivalries usually stem from a child's desire to be better than someone else. Normally they are not terribly important. They should not be encouraged, nor should parents be too disturbed by them. Sibling rivalry is to be expected, especially in the stepfamily where stepbrothers and stepsisters compete constantly. But the atmosphere in the home influences the intensity of the rivalries. When relationships are positive, the arguments tend to be trivial and unimportant. When unnecessary pressures exist, even a minor disagreement can explode.

THE PEACEFUL CHILD

Every child needs three things to assist him in life; love, food, and room to grow. When he feels secure, he finds peace within himself. If he is deprived of one or more of these basics, the child struggles — with himself and with others around him. A hungry, tired, or unloved child becomes argumentative, constantly looking for a fight.

If parents provide a sensible routine of eating, sleeping, exercising, and growing, within a loving atmosphere, they show the children by example how to get along with others. Here are a few guidelines for keeping stepsibling squabbles within reasonable bounds:

1. Establish a regular, healthful routine for rest and exercise.

2. Set clear limits which children of every age can easily understand.

3. Feed the children before they get too hungry.

4. Express affection for one another openly, often, and fully.

5. Provide opportunities for each child to achieve at his own pace.

6. Disapprove violence in any form, in ways the children understand.

7. Keep yourself from getting too uptight or out of sorts.

8. Help the children *when* they need it, not before then.

9. Discourage violence in movies, television, and other media.

10. Do not punish the children physically as a regular practice.

11. Let each child know that you love him for the special person he is.

Stepsibling problems become so complex they seem to defy resolution. It's unlikely the remarried partners imagined before the marriage the drain the children's problems would be on their relationship. Some second marriages end in divorce, not because the husband and wife are not compatible, but because they want to remove themselves from the problems created by the children. A couple considering remarriage should devote serious thought to the kind of life they will be leading; not just their own relationship, but the influence of their children as well.

Remarried five years ago, Paul recalls, "When I married Shelly I thought nothing could stand in the way of our happiness. She had her two preschool girls living with her and my teenage son lived with me. Six months into the marriage and I wouldn't have bet two cents we would make it to the end of the first year. Many nights one of us would walk out, threatening to give it up. After cooling off we'd return, realizing the love we had for each other. Our biggest problems were with the kids, coping with their differences, and keeping harmony among them." Paul concluded by saying, "No parent can be happy when he sees his child is miserable. We worked through the hard times and now we're glad we did."

CHAPTER 13

What About the Marriage?

What comes first, the kids or the marriage? Rearing children with care and consideration draws heavily on a parent's time and energy. Studies show that children tend not to enhance the closeness so badly needed between a husband and wife but rather to detract from it. This is true in the traditional family, where the mother and father are present, and a much more painful truth in the stepfamily.

The demands put on stepparents can be staggering. Many spend sleepless nights wondering what to do next. "I love my husband so much, but I don't know how much longer I can put up with his children." Sometimes it comes out as a threat, "I just can't handle your child any longer. It has to be him or me."

A spouse/parent feels helpless when faced with the prospect of giving up one of the two things most sacred to him or her—the children or the marriage. Even when it's not spoken, the implied choice is often there. "If the kids lived with their mother, or father, or grandparents, we'd be happy." A person not in a stepfamily would have difficulty identifying with this, but, more often than not, the stepparent would be happier if the children were living with someone else.

Most people are ashamed and not eager to share their hurt and their problems with others. That is why statements like these are made only in the privacy of the home. This is a "real life" problem. Children can put a strain on any marriage, particularly a stepfamily marriage. A strong husband and wife relationship can weather most of these difficulties, but sometimes not without pain.

THE KIDS ARE HERE. WHAT DO WE DO?

It doesn't really matter whether the kids came with the marriage, were born into the stepfamily, or both, the marriage relationship should be the axis around which all other family relationships revolve. When husband and wife make their marriage the number one priority, it puts all the other relationships in their right perspective. This is especially true in a blended family. The strong relationship between husband and wife, whether it's mom and stepdad or dad and stepmother, is the foundation the children need on which to rebuild their sense of security.

BUILDING A STEPFAMILY MARRIAGE

In a stepfamily, at least one spouse already has been part of another marriage. Chances are it ended in divorce. When it's happened once, it's easy to have the feeling (consciously or otherwise), "If this one doesn't work out I'll just get another divorce." Whether it is the first or second, the marriage must be built on a solid foundation. "If this doesn't work, I'll just try again" is not a strong foundation.

"I've known Karen for twenty-three years," said Donna, "and every time one of our friends divorced she would criticize her for not working harder to make the marriage work. Two years ago Ted divorced Karen. Now, just six months into her second marriage, she's complaining about her new husband and saying that if things don't improve she's going for another divorce."

The most important decision a couple can make is a commitment to make the marriage a success. "This marriage is going to survive no matter what." Not all marriages will make it no matter how much the couples work to make them successful. But when a person accepts the feeling that the marriage is only temporary, she feels no commitment, no desire to build. Erase negative thoughts. The nation's easy divorce laws have crippled America's way of thinking, making it easier to bail out than to make it work.

IT'S FOR REAL

The marriage ceremony marks a step in the process of two people making a mutual commitment to each other. The commitment process does not climax over night and then weaken. It extends over an indefinite period of time, during which the couple must learn by experience as they take on specific responsibilities and assume definite functions. Some divorced couples have admitted that their wedding ceremony was the high point in their relationship. From that point it drifted downward.

By its very nature, marriage is not a simple task for two people. It should be looked upon as a continuing growth process. Through sincere effort, individuals can shape their lives so both partners benefit and create an atmosphere where love can grow stronger as each day passes.

The married couple faces the need to make adjustments as they begin their life together. Each will bring to the marriage predetermined needs and expectations which may differ in degree or kind. Some of the more significant among these are: individual attitudes, personal preferences, habit patterns, aversions, basic temperament, and emotional response patterns. Each of these is part of an individual's identity and the marriage ceremony does not change them.

The early stage of the marriage is important because it is the time the couple works to adjust to one another's differences. The courtship is romantic and should be a time to see if the couple is compatible, but the "real identity" of the partners will not be revealed until after the wedding. Couples in stepfamilies are handicapped during their adjustment period by the interfering presence of the stepchild, and are deprived of the time alone. The romantic meals and quiet evenings needed to discover each other's private lives become only dreams.

Stepfamily couples have to be more creative in providing time alone. And more patient when such times must be postponed. "Wait till I put Tommy to bed and we'll have some time together."

Both partners must be willing to accept the attitude, "This marriage will be different because I'll change to make it different." The willingness helps to overcome some of the basic feelings which lead to internal power struggles. If one partner is forced to make all of the changes, he (or she) will feel he is giving more to the marriage than his partner. "I'm making all the sacrifices and you're doing nothing." It hurts to know one is doing all the giving, and receiving nothing in return.

A person who is willing to change for the success of the marriage does not feel the change is a threat to security. Consequently, he or she becomes a more adaptable person. Whatever the stage of a marriage relationship, it is never too late to make constructive changes.

GROWING A MARRIAGE RELATIONSHIP

The romantic illusion always has been "Man and woman fall in love, marry, and live happily ever after." Years into the marriage, and sometimes on the brink of divorce, one cries out, "Why can't it be the way it was before?" Marriage relationships often are left to drift aimlessly, with little effort put into the "care and feeding" necessary to make it last.

When a plant is removed from light and moisture, it soon begins to wither and die. And so, similarly, does a marriage. When its life sustaining ingredients are gone, the marriage will deteriorate and die. The high divorce rate tells us the idea of nurturing and growing a marriage relationship is new to most people. Either its importance has not been understood or couples are not making an adequate commitment to growth.

Couples choose to marry. In very real terms, they also "choose" to make their marriage grow or fail. Occasionally a marriage will drift in a positive direction and will succeed, with no particular effort made by the partners. The odds are against this happening. A happily married couple usually will confess that each partner has worked hard to make the marriage a success. Helen said, "Why risk failure when some problems can be prevented?"

CAUSES OF CONFLICT

A marriage of stepparents starts with a high degree of difficulty built in. Because of the children there is interference, a lot of confusion, and little or no time to make adjustments.

Conflicting demands place a strain on the marriage. Wife and husband are stressed by new, equally taxing responsibilities. When her husband works extra work hours, for example, she will have added tasks at home. The added income is appreciated, but each person's extra work load can cause the relationship to suffer.

Boredom is not good for a marriage. When marriage partners do not have enough to do that is interesting or stimulating, they become bored with the marriage. Just because a person is busy does not mean she is stimulated by or interested in what she is doing. Washing clothes all evening, bathing the kids, or even being a taxi service are all activities. They also all are boring.

An overloaded work schedule also can be threatening. In most marriages the wife works outside her home. In addition to her outside work, she is expected to fulfill all of her regular household duties. It's hard to get excited about standing over a hot stove while the husband is watching television.

Marriage is a relationship, and as such it will continue to change. Change may be inevitable, but growth is intentional. Couples need to consider whether the changes that are taking place represent growth in their relationship, or something less positive. They should determine what direction they want their marriage to take, then commit themselves to learning and practicing the skills that will make positive growth possible.

STEPS TO GROWTH

No matter where a couple is in their relationship—planning their wedding, just married, or celebrating an anniversary—it is a good time to develop a growing process.

Begin by listing the three things about the relationship that are great; the real strengths that give you the most happiness and satisfaction. Next, list the three things that are pretty good; okay, but could stand improvement. Then, list three things you would like to see changed. You may have a longer list, but three is a good place to begin. Just taking the time to go through this review may make you aware of changes you can make that will improve the relationship immediately.

The next step is to communicate your findings to each other. Realize when you begin to share these feelings that what one person feels contributes to her happiness may not be as significant to him. Also, what one person sees as a weakness may be looked upon as a strength by her mate.

Sid experiences daily pressure from his accounting job. For release, he enjoys an occasional game of racquetball with friends before going home from work. Since Sid is unavailable, Janet has to pick the kids up on her way home which makes her late starting dinner. That, in turn, causes her to be in the kitchen longer than she prefers. Sid looks upon the situation as a strength since it helps him to unwind. He feels he is a much better husband and father if he does not bring the office pressure home with him. On the other hand, Janet resents his coming home late and not taking responsibility for certain family duties. Because they have not talked about this, Sid and Janet are both unaware of the other's feelings on the subject of racquetball.

Correct communication involves attacking the problem, not the person. "I wish you would not be so selfish and that you would think of someone other than yourself," should be changed to, "I'm sure you don't understand how much I need you here after work. I would appreciate it if you could help me more." Work together. Don't drive the other person away by attacking.

Check the list regularly to see if you are attaining your goals and to remind yourself of what already has been done. Even if the spouse thinks the marriage is fine just the way it is and is not interested in a periodic review, one person can still proceed. It will be slower and progress will not be as satisfying, but you will be rewarded by knowing you are giving your best effort.

KEEPING OPPOSITES TOGETHER

While children place a strain on stepfamily marriage relationships, they cannot be blamed for all the problems. It is true that opposite personalities sometimes attract each other, but "What drew us together in the beginning is becoming a major problem in our marriage now." A quiet individual will be attracted to a person with an outgoing personality. A young man who grew up without a mother figure will be drawn to a female who displays motherly affection. The girl who never makes a decision without someone telling her what to do, will be attracted to a forceful, independent male. All of these differences seem fine initially, but later in the marriage the spouse may no longer be able to meet the mate's immediate need, and the marriage relationship will suffer.

Tom's first marriage disintegrated shortly after the birth of his second son. During the two last years of the marriage Tom was not only father to the boys, he took over the mothering responsibilities as well while his wife Susan pursued her career. The divorce proceedings granted Tom custody of the children. He was a responsible, caring person, who was admired by his many friends for his outgoing personality.

Susan grew up the youngest of a large family. Her duties were limited to household chores, and she had no work experience outside the home. Her first marriage was childless and ended in divorce. Susan was a quiet person, content to spend evenings at home with a good book.

Tom and Susan were attracted to one another by their opposites. Tom wanted a good mother for his boys, not someone interested in pursuing a career. And he wanted a mate who would respect him as the family's leader and decision maker. Susan wanted a husband who would give her children, even if they were stepchildren, and Tom's outgoing personality made her feel comfortable in a crowd knowing he would carry the conversation.

As in many relationships, time changed things. Tom quickly discovered his lone paycheck was not adequate to cover all the household expenses and that Susan would need to seek employment. This forced her to give up the joys of motherhood. Shortly after Susan started working outside the home, she began to be less dependent on Tom. She started to resent him when he continued to make major decisions without her.

It wasn't long before Susan grew tired of mothering her stepchildren and began wanting more time of her own. And Tom's winning, outgoing personality, which she found so comforting early in their relationship, began to aggravate her as he continued to dominate conversations at parties.

Time can turn the opposite personal traits into differences that gnaw away at the very foundation of a marriage, often destroying any chance for survival. While these words sound as though they mean similar things, there is a big difference between happiness and comfort. Happiness is defined as, "experiencing great pleasure." To comfort is, "to console." Couples who are attracted by opposites are merely finding temporary comfort in the other person. It is satisfactory for a time, but it will not substitute for genuine happiness.

People need comfort when they are in distress, but eventually the distressful feelings subside and the comfort which was so badly needed is no longer required. Many people could save themselves a lot of hurt and heartache if, in the beginning, they would seek a mate with similar interests who could provide genuine happiness.

WHAT HAPPENS IN A MARRIAGE OF OPPOSITES?

Every marriage relationship goes through cycles. During the first stage, couples are eager to please one another. "Whatever you want honey, if it makes you happy." The new bride and groom believe that a little extra giving will make for a stronger foundation. It's this stage in the stepfamily where the parent makes promises to the new stepparent. "The kids will not interfere with our relationship. I would never let anything come between us." Or the stepparent comes with a promise of his own, "It doesn't matter how the kids behave, I'll love them."

One basic rule for a couple embarking on a new stepfamily marriage: Do not make a commitment to something that is beyond your understanding at the time. A good marriage is built on trust and credibility. You *do not really know* how you will feel about the kids.

Some call the second stage of the marriage the "wearing off" stage. "He's not everything I thought he was." Or, "Boy, was I ever fooled?" When the high hopes and great expectations wear off, each partner becomes aware of a desire to preserve his or her own being, and a noticeable change in behavior takes place. "I'm tired of trying to satisfy him all the time. It's time to think of myself and some of the things I want."

This stage might begin after a few months or not until after several years of marriage. Opposites no longer attract, but begin to repel. His love for country music is no longer macho, it's unbearable.

The future of the marriage now depends upon the couple's ability to develop a friendship with each other. Buck and Mary have been married for sixty-two years and Buck sums it up by saying, "Mary's my best friend." She nods in agreement. In his book, *Friends* (Coward, McCann, and Geoghegan, New York, 1976) Jerry Giles says, "A sense of balance is thus of prime importance in friendship. A feeling that both are gaining from the relationship and that the friendship is of equal importance to both individuals." According to experts, couples who realize their differences and learn to balance them will work to preserve the relationship and often fall in love again.

Vickie and Alex are one couple who showed this could work. "When we first started dating all of our friends said we were complete opposites," confessed Alex. "I was pretty tight with money, and the desk in my office resembled the disorganized chaos of my apartment. One of my stronger points was that I had confidence in myself as a person. Also, I felt good about money decisions I had made."

Vickie was a career woman who enjoyed the freedom to spend her own salary as she wished. She was looked upon by peers as "Miss Organization." Both her work space and her home reflected her meticulousness in every way. However, there was one aspect of her personality that revealed weakness; her relative lack of self confidence.

Problems developed almost immediately after the marriage. Alex complained to Vickie about her spending too much money, and she attacked him for his messiness and disorganization. Though Alex was conservative with money his investments were good, but Vickie wanted to spend now and worry about the future later.

On their twenty-fifth wedding anniversary Alex said, "We had to work at our differences right from the start and to stop attacking one another. Each of us had brought something into the marriage and we could either resent one another for being different or learn from the other and expand our horizons. We're glad we chose to learn."

Experts say that balancing the differences during a long-lasting relationship requires a lot of give and take by both parties. He's strict with the children, she's more lenient. He's not good at keeping records, she writes all the checks. Learn to take advantage of a spouse's strong points and add strength to the foundation of the marriage. There may be upset and dissent on occasion, but if both are growing and strengthening their relationship through the marriage, the differences are not disruptive.

But if the fighting continues and the learning stops, the marriage becomes a battleground. The questions of who's right and who's wrong dominate ... and can often destroy the marriage.

BRING THE DIFFERENCES TOGETHER

If the differences can be brought into a balanced perspective, all is not necessarily lost. Couples should begin by changing their way of thinking. You criticize, he defends. He withdraws and you pursue. If someone is blaming then another is defending. They need to see the problem as interactional, and both must accept that they are part of it. It doesn't matter who initiated the confrontation. A couple's relationship, good or bad, is based on their responses to each other.

Laura resents Paul always going out with the fellows. Instead of complaining about the night at home alone, she arranged a night out with some friends. The evening might end with a relaxed conversation about the two outings instead of the usual argument. Laura may not feel she has accomplished all that much, but she did achieve an evening without a battle. Paul has felt a release from pressure and is now more able to cooperate.

Too often, one partner changes behavior in the hope of changing the other. It seldom works. Counselors advise against any partner practicing a behavior that is not sincere or authentic. The idea is to forget about what the other partner is or isn't doing and concentrate on self. A partner who is working alone to improve the relationship is hindered in that effort, but the possibility of realizing even a little improvement makes the effort worth it.

EXPANDING THE LIMITS

The opposites attracted but did very little to stabilize the relationship. Couples who are more alike in personalities, goals, ambitions, and dreams see a more continuing relationship because they are working and growing together. But opposites cannot change over night. Pick one of his or her traits that you don't share and deliberately try to develop it in yourself.

Suppose one partner is relaxed and the other more hard working. If they would select a project and work hard at it together over the next few weeks, a positive change could develop in the relationship. The relaxed person would begin to understand tiredness and anxiety, while the hard working partner admired the change in—and the effort made by --the spouse. The marriage is enriched as each person becomes more flexible.

EXPERIMENT TOGETHER

Never fail to communicate. A husband and wife may already know the likes and dislikes of their spouses, but reach further. Experiment to find mutual interests in which neither has been involved before.

One couple said, "We found some lost treasure at a local garage sale and learned that we enjoyed refinishing furniture." Another recalled, "I never thought we'd enjoy the outdoors so much until we tried camping one weekend. Now we look forward to the time to get away, all the kids included." Couples must be creative and willing to cooperate in exploring new ventures.

It was by rediscovering that sense of mutual enjoyment that Vickie and Alex also found their love for one another. "It took some time after our rough start, but now I just want to tell him how much I love him," says Vickie. "We found something in each other and felt we couldn't be together enough. We still have differences, but now we've learned to lift each other up and our lives have taken on a new meaning."

In a stepfamily, both parent and stepparent feel they are alone in their struggle. The parent carries the burden of having the children, feeling the added strain they bring to the marriage, and needs the support of the stepparent. The stepparent feels ignorant of the demands of parenthood and needs the parent's encouragement. Both wonder what it would be like not to have the children, but they realize that is not an option. They can work to make the relationship survive, or they can let it drift and risk the chance of failure.

TEN SECRETS TO A HAPPY MARRIAGE

1. The couple are best friends. Good marriages endure for the simplest of reasons: The pleasure these partners take in each other is like being the only members of a very exclusive club. They share secrets, work, play, and hang out together. Most of all, they laugh a lot. Given the choice of spending their time with anyone in the world, these people would choose their spouses. They treasure their time together.

2. They listen to and confide in each other. The couples are in constant contact, discussing and debating everything from the boss to the baby, the weather to foreign affairs. While much of their everyday conversation is simple and small talk, over time they delve much more deeply, daring to risk the vulnerability that comes from revealing their innermost feelings and fears to each other. Studies confirm that free-flowing communication is crucial to a relationship.

3. The couples know how to handle conflict. Married couples will argue, but those in happy marriages are skilled at handling conflict.

They have learned how to fight properly. They focus on the issue, deal only with the current problem. They avoid rehashing past grievances and each criticizes only the spouse's actions, not the spouse. While they argue to clear the air, they choose times of calm to sit down and actually work through a disagreement.

Wrong fighting is fighting to win at any cost, bringing up past wrongs and opening old wounds. Those in a happier union are more likely to admit they are at least part responsible for the disagreement.

4. The couples can deal with negative emotions. All spouses at one time or another experience the quick stab of jealousy or the slow burn of resentment. Satisfied couples, however, find ways of defusing such potential explosive feelings before they get out of control. One way is by alternating the peace-keeping role in different situations. When tensions are low, the husband generally deflects negative feelings by rationally accepting something he may or may not have done wrong. When emotions heat up, the wife assumes the conciliatory role. Rather than responding to her husband's intense feelings with a counterattack, she stays calm and deescalates the conflict. It is interesting that both happy and unhappy wives are better at finding ways to end a fight than their husbands, but only those in good marriages seem willing to call a cease-fire.

5. The couples trust each other. You can open up to a friend and not be hurt. In a good marriage there is so much trust that each partner can show weakness and know that he or she still will be loved.

6. The couples share interests. The activities and friendships people develop as a couple are much more meaningful than the things they may have enjoyed independently before. Couples do not have to have identical likes and dislikes, but they need a core of similar interests and pleasures so they can find joy in being together.

7. They are committed to making the marriage work. Many long-time spouses have considered divorce during their roughest times, but in the end they decided to stick it out. Those couples obligated themselves to a lifetime partnership. However flawed or frustrating it might be at times, they felt it was worth the time, energy, and effort to make the marriage work.

8. The couple is less than brutally honest. Partners in close loving relationships follow the cardinal rule of diplomacy. They think before they talk. They express their feelings clearly and directly, but do not believe in letting it all hang out without any regard for the other person. Even in heated arguments, thoughtful spouses edit their remarks so words do not leave scars on their mates.

9. The couples are flexible enough to change and to tolerate change. The moment the ceremony ends change begins to take place. Happy couples go through just as many moves, moods, triumphs and transitions, setbacks and successes as unhappy ones. But they are able to adapt so well that their marriages endure and improve; not despite the changes and challenges, but because of them.

10. Concentrate on the positive rather than the negative about your spouse. Rather than thinking about the things the partner is or isn't doing for the relationship, focus attention on what you can do for it. Check your communication skills. See if you are listening to the things your spouse considers important or tuning them out. Does your spouse know what's important to you?

IT'S WORTH IT!

A good marriage produces a happy home and a happy home produces satisfied and contented children and stepchildren. Contented children lead to happy parents and stepparents, completing a complex cycle. Often the problem is not that the stepchildren are so bad, but that a poor husband-wife relationship with the spouse makes it difficult to see the good. Clearly the benefits of a positive marriage relationship will extend beyond the couple and influence other relationships.

CHAPTER 14

Living Together Out of Wedlock

Never before have children been more confused by this question than they are in many homes today. In most new blended families the man and woman have married, creating a child-stepparent relationship. However, many couples are choosing to live together without marrying. Without adequate care and attention, this kind of arrangement can have a devastating effect on the lives of children, destroying any hopes they might have for positive relationships in the future.

"DO WE CALL HIM DADDY?"

Before deciding how to deal with the children in a "living together" situation, the parent must first define his or her reasons for the arrangement. In some situations, the circumstances might dictate it's best that a child not be pushed into a close child-adult relationship with the nonparent partner. There will be other situations in which it will be necessary for him or her to become completely involved.

IDENTIFYING THE MOTIVE

In general, two basic motives form the basis for a living together" arrangement: Convenience and sincerity.

Convenience could include a long list of possibilities, including no desire for a future commitment. It is not uncommon for a male and female to live together for financial reasons; dividing living expenses equally, with no romantic involvement; Tax credits offered to single parents and the loss of alimony support being paid by an ex-husband, might cause a person to have second thoughts about committing to a new marriage. With many people taking the "if it feels good, do it" approach to life, two people may live together for sexual relationship with no future plans for marriage. If a couple wants to they can easily find a justifiable reason to move in together.

On the other hand, *sincerity* could be the motive for such an arrangement; a couple's earnest attempt at building a successful relationship before making a commitment to marriage. "We have both experienced failure in marriage and want to make sure this one will work."

Living together for a short time—or for an extended period—before marrying will not eliminate all the problems that may occur in a marriage relationship. statistics prove that the increase in common law relationships has had little effect on the nation's divorce rate. A marriage rate of 9.7 per 1,000 persons and a divorce rate of 4.8 per 1,000 persons confirm that one out of two marriages ends in divorce.

Notwithstanding the statistics, the important consideration is how the motive behind the arrangement will affect the lives of the children involved.

CONVENIENCE

When a man and woman decide to live together for reasons of convenience the parent should be completely honest with the kids. Let them know up front what the arrangement is and that it is not expected to last forever. Children of divorce are already confused and searching for renewed stability. One parent has left the home for some reason. Even if the marriage was a failure, the differences between the spouses irreconcilable, the child has suffered a great loss.

A live-in partner who has not made any commitment is only a temporary house guest. At some point, it's likely the partner will move on. The greater the bond that has developed between child and adult, the greater despair the child will experience once the relationship has ended. A parent must keep in mind the effect this will have on the child.

Don't confuse a child more by giving a partner unrealistic labels. Children automatically attach different meanings to different names. "Daddy Bill" or "Papa Ted" gives a child the impression that even though he is not my real father, mom is going to marry him someday. The relationship is for keeps. An "Uncle Cliff" might be thought of as a relative who will always be there for them. A younger child who has lost a parent recently often will draw close to a relative in search of renewed stability. What happens when the surrogate leaves?

Protect the child from further hurt. A temporary live-in partner should be nothing more to the children than a temporary guest. He or she should have no discipline authority other than that a baby sitter has when the parent is out of the home. When the live-in partner becomes an authority figure the child's interpretation may be this is someone who is here to stay.

"I know Steve is not my husband, but he will be a good friend to you while he's here." The statement is direct and without ambiguity. Steve's presence in the home will be temporary. Even though most aspects of a non-committed relationship have negative implications for the children, some positive effects can be realized.

Children do need adult role models as they grow up. A non-committed male cannot be an example of how a husband should be faithful to his wife, or how a good father should care for his children, but he can do "man things" with a boy, or take him places where a single mother might feel uncomfortable. Big Brother organizations across the nation have done a lot to fill this great need. Even though the boy knows the relationship is temporary, a secure bond develops between man and boy.

SINCERITY

When a man and woman choose to live together before marriage to see if the relationship will work, they must make an all-out effort. The man doesn't come home only on the nights he wants, he comes home regularly and does all the things a husband and father will do in all circumstances. After the marriage he will become a stepparent instantly. There is no way he can know how he will function as a stepparent if he has not first acted in that capacity.

A word of warning. Just because a man or woman reacts positively to the children and everyone gets along well before the marriage, there is no guarantee it will be that way later. "I don't understand it," cried Marilyn, "Chuck was so good with the children before the marriage and now it seems as if he hates them." Before the wedding, even if Chuck's honest intention was to marry, he felt no pressure. He had an *escape clause*. "If it doesn't work, I can still get out."

After the ceremony, everything changes; This is for keeps. He is no longer a single male. Even though they will be shared with a wife, the bills are *his* responsibility. The children are *his* stepchildren, not just his girlfriend's.

PROCEED WITH CAUTION

Children are vulnerable. A child of divorce is looking for someone to replace his or her lost parent. They do not need to be hurt again. Communicate your intentions. "Daren and I love each other and we want to get married one day. You know it didn't work out for me and your father and we just want to make sure this time." The child should realize from the outset that it might not work this time either. Being honest will not alleviate the hurt which may occur when the relationship breaks up, but at least you have let the child know there are no guarantees.

DISCIPLINE

If a stepparent is to function properly in the blended family, he or she must be given the right to discipline. Even in a living together arrangement, the partner must have some leadership role. Without it, he or she will not be able to understand fully all the responsibilities that come with the marriage. Granting a live-in partner shared responsibility for discipline must be handled carefully. Children are apt to resent a non-parent's instruction. "I don't know why I have to do what he tells me. You're not even married to him!" Don't push too hard, but communicate your intentions clearly. "I know you might not understand, but Bryan and I plan to marry one day. He is an important part of my life and I want him to be an important part of our home."

While there are still no promises, the child is informed that plans are in the making. Using the words *our home* assures the child that he or she will not be neglected.

Build confidence in the arrangement. As the relationship between parent and non-parent strengthens, share that information with the child. Point out the good things that are happening the child may not see. "It's really good to have Ken living with us. I feel secure with him in the home and I really believe things are going to work out fine." Even a child who resents a live-in partner will begin to be appreciative when he or she sees the benefits the person is making in the home.

As the relationship builds and the wedding date nears, the non-parent should move with more authority and involvement into the step-parent role.

CHAPTER 15

Traits of a Preschool Child

Each stage in a child's life represents a momentous occasion for the biological parent. He or she grows through each step, learning just enough at one level to advance to the next. But it's altogether different for a stepparent. The next stage is either a frightening new experience, with the stepparent unaware of what will happen next, or it's a repeat of the stage a child passed through in a previous marriage. In either case, it probably will not be a joyous occasion.

The next three chapters will summarize three stages of a youngster's life: preschool; childhood, ages six through eleven; and adolescence. A better knowledge of what normally can be anticipated can help the stepparent prepare for the experiences to come.

Preschool children are extremely active. During the first four months of a child's life, a baby pretty much stays where it is put. But from four months on, the action and motion rarely stop.

INFANT

During infancy the baby develops the foundations of faith; in himself, in others, and in life itself. What happens during the first few weeks and months of his life prepares the child, for better or for worse, for the years ahead. The way his parents handle him should give him confidence in other people. A baby's introduction to the world around him will have a lot to do with his future feelings about it.

"When Jackie and I married, her son was only eleven-months-old," recalled Dan. "We started dating shortly after the child was born and I knew that I would be the only father he would ever know. But it scared the wits out of me, being an instant dad to such a young son." The faith a person has in himself as a parent cultivates early in the baby's life. It is then he gains confidence in his ability to be a good parent. If, because of early difficulties, the caretaker withdraws from meeting the infant's needs it will be harder to participate constructively later.

DIAPERING

There are always going to be certain tasks one would like to give someone else to do. A stepparent can choose how involved he wants to be with the child. Saying "Your kid needs changing" or "Your daughter has finished" is taking the path of least resistance. Any signs of not caring or not wanting to be bothered will be detected quickly by the child, no matter what his or her age.

Don't make changing a diaper a big issue. She may not be your "biological child," but she is your stepchild. Whether she is a weekend visitor or lives in the same household, your response to her needs determines what type of stepfamily you will have. Most of what goes enters the baby's body will leave it. Until she is ready for toilet training, she will need help.

BEGINNING THE DEVELOPMENT PROCESS

Watching an infant develop is a fascinating experience. The newborn has a big head, a little body, and small bowed legs. He usually is red and wrinkled; not much to look at except in the eyes of his loving parents and bragging grandparents who think he's the most adorable baby in the nursery.

He develops more in the first few months and years of his life than he ever will again. What makes this early period so significant is that by the end of the first four years he already has achieved 50% of his intelligence. Another 30% is reached by the time he is eight, and the remaining 20% by the time he is seventeen. What happens to a child in the first few years of his life determines how much of his innate capacity he is likely to develop.

Each baby grows, changes, and develops independently. As he does, he seeks new and different kinds of satisfaction. Impulsiveness and "pure" egocentricity do not last forever. And as changes takes place, he will act in different ways.

The baby learns through his senses—taste, sight, hearing, smell, and touch—and the way he feels about what he experiences. He discovers his hands and what he can do with them early. He soon finds that he can grab small objects and shake and hit things. Loving him and letting him know it, as he achieves these different things, cultivates a loving and happy child.

"Why does he act that way? Do all little kids do those things?" Babbling is a production of meaningless vocal sounds characteristic of infants from about the sixth week. He amuses himself with sounds and often uses them to talk back to adults who are trying to communicate with him. At some point early in the second year, the baby seems to be speaking full paragraphs of babble. The parent will be excited about the child's achievements, but the inexperienced stepparent feels helpless and "out of it" and does not know what to do.

No matter what a person thinks, every child—and every caretaker —will go through the "Terrible Twos" and will survive. At the age of two, the baby is beginning to explore his world. He's on his own two feet now and could be found anywhere. He's waving bye-bye, learning new words, and even putting two words together at times. "All gone." "Baby go."

Curiosity builds up within the young child, and he wants to know everything. Children become fascinated with the many simple elements of their surroundings, but their interest in a toy or a person may fade as quickly as it developed. When a caretaker frustrates a child's curiosity it causes him to withdraw and hold back from the new and the unexplored. Keep him under a watchful eye, but encourage the child to explore and check out his surroundings.

"I want to help with my new stepchild, but I'm not sure what he needs." Babies will try new things at different ages. No one can predict a baby's first step, his first recognizable word, when he'll complete potty-training, or any of the other normal steps they take in their early lives.

They will all happen in their own time and outside persuasion or assistance will not have any effect on their outcome. A child will walk when his legs and body are physically ready. A caretaker can put things in a child's environment to encourage and aid his motor skills, but his physical development will take its own natural course.

PROGRAM OF TRAINING

Some of the youngster's hardest lessons center around toilet training. Not that the child has to learn to urinate or defecate. He is capable of doing both efficiently from the time he is born. When he has to learn when "not" to urinate and when "not" to defecate, it's hard because that control fights against his natural instincts and abilities.

"Why can't you get your kid to wait?" A wet sleeve or an unpleasant odor in an inappropriate place can embarrass or humiliate an inexperienced adult. The child must learn to hold back until the time and place are right. He also must learn the many verbal rituals that accompany his toilet training; the correct words to say, when to say them, how loudly to say them, and to whom they should be said.

In the training period the child needs to learn what is "off limits." Nobody has to teach him how to touch, but what not to touch, what not to take, and what not to use. This can be a frightening experience for the inexperienced stepparent.

At about two years of age the child begins to develop a strong sense of possessiveness. He owns something and it is his. But he must learn sharing with other people, and also must learn that other children's things are not his. These are difficult lessons for a toddler and can be complicated for the stepparent as well.

AVOID UNNECESSARY FEARS

Children pick up many of the habits and fears of the other people who live in their little world. If a child notices a parent is badly frightened by a thunder storm, he is likely to react in the same way. Being afraid of the dark is common in early childhood. A child cannot be talked out of it. You can turn on the light, prove there is nothing in the room, and turn the light off, expecting everything to be all right. But the dark is still there and that's what frightens him. "I can't get used to leaving the light on for the kids," said Bill. "I don't remember being scared when I was little."

Just because an adult doesn't remember being afraid of the dark is no reason to believe the child will not be. No two children are alike. One may not fear the dark, but if the other does, don't ridicule him for something that is natural.

DEALING WITH A TEMPER TANTRUM

Temper tantrums are always annoying and unrealistic, especially to a stepparent who doesn't understand their cause or how to cope with them. A temper tantrum usually is a toddler's reaction to frustrating interference. It includes kicking, screaming, crying, hitting, and banging anything within reach—even his own body—against the floor. The child is so irrational at this point that appeals to reason are useless.

The best thing a caretaker can do for the toddler is to display self-control. When discipline is calm and consistent the child learns in time what he may or may not do. He will acquire some of the self-control he needs to eliminate the tantrums. But try to be patient. Children become frustrated easily, and it may take more time than you would like for them to acquire the self-control they need.

When you are dealing with a tantrum, isolate the child and put him in a safe place to work out his frustrations. Giving him too much attention for the tantrum only gives him what he wants. If he learns he can upset his caretaker and get a lot of attention by getting mad, that teaches the child he can be in control. Hitting him to get him out of it may simply teach him that it is all right to hit.

When a caretaker reacts to the unpleasantness calmly, and pays as little attention as possible to it, the child learns it is not working and he gets over it—usually fairly quickly. Temper tantrums are going to happen, but quick and intelligent parental reaction should minimize their frequency and teach the child how unproductive this kind of activity is.

I AM SOMEONE

By the third birthday, a little earlier for some and a little later for others, the healthy youngster knows she is *someone*. She knows she has power and rarely feels the need to make a public show of it. The youngster slowly begins to think and feel like a different person. She is always looking for new and different kinds of satisfaction, and judges the experiences of her life by a different kind of standard.

The child's new way of looking at herself and the people around her is a way of affirming all the growth she has realized. In the first three years muscular development and coordination were the main focus. Three, four, and five-year-olds are into perfecting some of the finer points of movement. From three on, his brain is in high gear. The child is not as easily distracted. Her capacity to pay attention has lengthened and she will look a little before leaping.

DEVELOPMENTAL TASKS FOR THE TWO-TO FOUR-YEAR-OLD

These are the major developmental tasks required of youngsters going through this period of their lives:

1. Getting into a healthful daily routine of rest and activity.

2. Mastering good eating habits.

3. Learning the basics of toilet training.

4. Developing appropriate physical and motor skills.

5. Becoming a participating member of the family.

6. Learning to communicate with others.

7. Adapting to others' expectations.

8. Beginning to understand what life means, to himself and the other members of his family.

9. Developing initiative and a sense of self.

When a stepparent sees how much a young child is expected to accomplish in such a short time, he will begin to understand some of the frustrations and disappointments the youngster will encounter. To the child these are high hurdles to jump and tall mountains to climb. He may look at adults and wonder, "Why are they so upset. They don't have nearly as much to worry about as I do?"

For the preschool child, imagination grows beyond measure.

Children play house, have tea parties, do the laundry, feed the baby, and act out the parent's role as disciplinarian. They play fireman, postman, policeman, and rescue squad. They play church, school, and hospital. Each of these imaginary enactments are likely to follow some new idea that a child has experienced in the home. A television program or a trip taken will inspire a host of new ideas. One mother said, "Julie lines her dolls up and teaches them the things she learned at day nursery."

When parents and stepparents become aware of small children's need for experiences to stimulate their imagination, they see reasons to take them along on errands and trips. Less caring adults unwittingly discourage the child's curiosity and imagination by being too busy, not wanting to be bothered by a youngster tagging along.

Don't discredit a child's imaginary companion. Don't ridicule her fantasy, and respect the new make-believe family member by not sitting in her chair. A new stepparent might not be accustomed to a child's need for such a playmate, but they are usually there because the child needs them for company, as a model, a scapegoat, or someone to talk with when communication is needed.

The stepparent should not just be a spectator as the child passes through these critical developmental phases, but should become an active part of the child's life as quickly as possible. A stepparent will never catch up to the biological parent who has been with the child from birth, but he can begin to develop himself ... as a step*parent*.

CHAPTER 16

The Stepparent and the Young Child

It's difficult to say if any one stage is more upsetting to the stepparent than another. The "degree of difficulty" is determined not only by the age of the child, but how the stepparent reacts. Some adults will do better with preschool children, where others might be more comfortable with a school age child. Then there are those who seem to have a special knack with teenagers.

Just as there are adults who seem to function better with one age group, it is not uncommon for those same adults to do poorly with younger or older children. Everyone is different, and no one should be critical of a person's human nature. Nor should a stepparent feel inadequate because he or she interrelates well with one age group, less well with another. The issue is not how well or poorly a person has performed, but the effort he or she is making.

Children from six to eleven are different from all other age groups. During this time, the child more fully develops his own identity, and becomes a more actively participating member of his world. People outside the family become increasingly important to him. As the child arrives at school age, he has a whole lot to learn and many new adjustments to make—all in very little time.

In the early part of this period, the children will acquire new capacities, physical and mental, which allow them to develop new skills and to reach a deeper understanding of themselves and others. A child will enter this period rather dependent on a caretaker, with few interests outside the home. He will emerge having experienced physical growth and change, intellectual development, and countless experiences with people, places, and things. He develops a strong desire to be independent of a parent's authority.

These years can be frustrating for a parent and stepparent, but they are good years for the child. Children seem to be more free of illness during this time span than in other periods in their lives. Their physical strength and endurance enables them to be involved in energetic play for hours at a time without noticeable exhaustion. It is the time children begin to sort out their world, but it is also the time they become frustrated at how little they can do.

The time of middle childhood (called the latency period by experts) has been the subject of less study and research than any other stage of a youngster's development. Some call it the quiet before the storm of adolescence, but most parents and stepparents will attest they are not quiet years at all. Though they are good years for the child, his behavior swings from one extreme to another.

Two distinctively different characteristics will be noticed in the six-year period. First, in grades one through three, the child will show developing signs of "individualism." In grades four through six, the emphasis is on "coordinated group activity." There is no specific age at which a child should present a picture of rounded social behavior. When that begins to develop, it is just evidence of growth, not an indication of completion of growth. Experts agree that problems incurred during the latency period are influenced by the parent-child relationship during early childhood and infancy.

All this adds to a complex situation for stepparents. They are apt to be personally unfamiliar with the child's background and do not know what to expect. They only know the child is changing rapidly and they feel helpless.

THE SIX-YEAR-OLD

"I can't believe it's the same kid!" Caretakers are in for a frightening awakening when the five-year-old begins to lose his halo. "I don't know what to do with him!" At five he was a well-organized child, at home with himself, and content with his own little world. But as early as the later half of the fifth year a behavior change can be expected. The visiting stepchild, especially one who comes only on occasion, may seem like a completely different child.

The sixth year brings fundamental changes, both physical and psychological. It is a transition period. The baby teeth are coming out and the first permanent molars are emerging. Even the child's own body chemistry is undergoing subtle change, resulting in increased susceptibility to infectious disease. One thought to remember; the six-year-old will not be a bigger or better five-year-old, he will be a different child because he is a changing child. Each stage of his life is complex. Some stages evolve smoothly into the next, but that is not true for the six-year-old. It's like closing one door and opening another.

It seems that the six-year-old is trying to grow in stature and understanding as fast as she can so she may make herself ready for adolescence. No matter what the child does, it seems that her inner world is strictly private. She tends to jump from one extreme to the other. A decision which was easy at five, becomes complicated at six. "Will you have vanilla or chocolate ice cream?" Even after choosing chocolate, she has not ruled out vanilla. What may confuse and frustrate an adult is an indication the child is thinking ... maturing.

The play life of a child between the ages of six and eight tend to mirror his inner life. At play he reveals his thinking and feeling processes, tackles difficulties of relationships and tries to solve them. Children who cannot or do not play find it more difficult to make adjustments to their friends, family, school, and to their world overall.

At six, his sense of privacy keeps him from playing freely in front of adults. He does not want to expose his feelings and insecurities in front of his parents and teachers. If an adult or caretaker is to learn of his private world she is forced to snoop or eavesdrop—a complete change from the chatty preschooler who wanted to share every new experience.

The inconsistencies of a six-year-old's conduct—running out of the room, slamming doors, being verbally aggressive, concentrating intensely, and exploding emotionally—are all from the same pattern. With the help of correct guidance, the child can become more stable.

At the age of five, awareness and capabilities were in better balance. However, the six-year-old is aware of more than he can manage. He wants to be first and always wants to win. At home there was no competition and that was not a problem. At school, however, everyone cannot be a winner, and that realization makes him quarrelsome and accusative on the playground and in the classroom. At Christmas (another aspect of the same syndrome), he wants many big presents but does not know what they should be.

For an adult, it's hard to remember that the six-year-old has expanded his horizons to include two worlds: the warm assuring world of home, and the new challenging world of school.

THE SEVEN-YEAR-OLD

At seven the child tends to be relaxing, beginning a more quiet period. After bursts of activity at six, seven goes into lengthening periods of calmness and self-absorption. He works things over in his mind, oblivious to the outside world. He becomes a good listener and likes to hear the same things over again. For the child, seven seems a more pleasant age than the disruptive year that preceded it. One might say, "He's a much better child now." Basically he is the same child, just into a new stage.

The seven-year-old still has a lot to learn in his new world; not so much factual knowledge, but in comprehending the life situations which confront him at home and at school.

He is able to take in more than he gives out. His new awareness is not only of himself, but of others. During this stage the second grader is likely to have a more personal attachment to his teacher. At home he is known to renew a more companionable relationship with his mother and father than he had at age six.

With behavior jumping from one extreme to another, the seven-year-old believes she is now ready to take on some of the responsibilities around the household and should be permitted to do so. Sevens like to help with routine chores such as raking the yard or making their bed, but often, as quickly as she begins a project, they will just as quickly tire and want to shift to another. Money for her labors may not be the motivator at seven as much as it will be at eight, but parents do speak of their seven-year-old as being easier to control. The six-year-old freshness has changed to a mode of polite and sympathetic cooperation, with less resistant behavior and less stubbornness than before.

In expanding his world, the seven-year-old may begin to ask for his own room if he has been sharing with another sibling. Yet he usually is fond of a younger sibling, especially if he is a baby. Because of the nature of the developmental process in progress, it is natural for a seven-year-old to be passive one time and assertive another. He is not so organized that he can function at one well-sustained level. There will be great variations in his performance, not only from day to day but within the same day.

Home and school for sevens become even more separated. The child may begin asking to walk to school alone, trying not to be seen with his mother's assistance. In turn he collects numerous items, papers, rocks, trinkets, or a favorite toy series, and his mechanical ability persuades him to attempt to insert one object into another with such force as to break it.

During these years, the natural parent learns to accept the extremes as growth, but confused stepparents look upon radical changes as uncontrollable and begin to wonder what they have gotten themselves into.

THE EIGHT-YEAR-OLD

The stages come so quickly it makes a person wonder how many different stages a child will go through before repeating himself. Remember the four-year-old; the eight-year-old is merely a modified version. He is faster, more expansive, and more analytical than he was earlier. At eight, he begins to look more mature and he generally is healthier and less apt to tire as quickly than at seven. Rough and tumble play is more sport now and he will walk, talk, read, and write in high gear. He devours his food—then more of it—and is ready to bolt out of the house in search of more activity. In the morning a caretaker had better slow him down or he will be out of the house with his shirt out and only half ready for the day.

The body movements of an eight-year-old are often more graceful and poised, and his sport interest has turned from individual to team effort. He is more receptive to learning new techniques, but he frequently goes back to his own way after he has tried something different.

He may be seen as being easier to handle in the home, but his best behavior usually occurs when he is somewhere else. Volunteering around the house is now a thing of the past. He just is not the helper he was at seven. What he does or doesn't do now depends upon his moods. Though he dislikes many of his old jobs, there are certain new tasks he attacks with real enthusiasm.

The mess he leaves behind is not intentional, but a result of expansive high speed activity. He really spreads himself too thin. Unlike the six-and-seven-year-old, he wants money for what he does. He won't save much of it, but it now motivates him.

The group is important to him. At eight he finds school more enjoyable than ever. When he is absent for a day he is home thinking about the group at school and wants his homework sent to him so he can keep up with his friends.

Every stage has its peculiarities and to the unsuspecting stepparent they seem far out. Without prior experience it's hard to understand how a child can behave one way in one stage and totally different in the next.

THE NINE-YEAR-OLD

The age of nine represents the middle zone which lies between kindergarten and junior high school. The big difference is that he is no longer a child, but he is frustrated that he is not a youth. Behavior trends of the eight-year-old become clearer at nine. The child gets a better hold on himself and acquires new forms of self-dependence which greatly enhances relations with his family, teachers, and classmates.

Nine works hard and plays hard. He is more skillful than in the earlier stages and wants to display it. His interest has now turned to competitive sports and he wants to be the best on the team. Boys at nine are quick to take up a fighting stance and they will strike out at each other with little cause. He has difficulty calming down after recess or after a strenuous activity and he may play or work too hard until he is completely exhausted.

The child at nine becomes so busy with his own life that he makes fewer demands upon the adults in his home. Yet when his parents make demands upon him he usually will respond positively and may even interrupt what he is doing without resentment. The only obstacle to responding to a command would be not hearing it, because he is so absorbed in his own activity. And his self-involvement may create the need for a lot of reminding. "Did you remember to wash your hands before coming to the table?" He leaves his clothes out and fails to brush his teeth. He will accept the reminders willingly and usually respond at once.

At eight money was important, but a year later it has lost its ability to motivate. At nine the child is happy to run an errand, especially if it's a boy doing something for his mother. At times he will even try to protect her from certain unpleasant tasks. In a stepfamily, the nine-year-old who became "the man around the house" while mom was a single parent is more defensive with someone he may consider an intruder, the stepfather. He is not nearly as willing to relinquish the responsibility as he would have been at eight.

At nine discipline is not as difficult to administer. A serious look will often suffice. If more is required, a short period of isolation from other children will do. The peer group is beginning to influence him, sometimes negatively but a brief separation should restore his normal behavior. While the group is becoming important to him, a special friend of the same sex becomes a necessity.

Boy and girl attractions will persist, but there is not much playing together. The girls will talk more about boys than the boys will about girls. Nines will talk among themselves about everything that interests them.

THE TEN-YEAR-OLD

When a child reaches the magical age of ten he has become an adult in the making. His individuality is now so well defined and his insights are so much more mature he can be regarded as a pre-adult, or at least as a pre-adolescent. Distinctive characteristics of the ten-year-old are best described as maturity traits. He is more relaxed and casual, yet also more alert. The capability to budget his time and energy is more evident. However, adults often fail to accept his intelligence and awareness of world situations as anything more than imaginations. At this age a wise caretaker could take advantage of the opportunity to plant valid ideas and to stimulate adult conversation.

The peer influence which began at nine becomes pressure at ten. Ten wants the acceptance of the group. But parents and stepparents seem content to wait until the pressure reaches a danger point, usually during the teen years, before they take any steps to combat it. It is difficult to put the pieces of a life back together if they have been shattered over a four- or five-year period.

The small seed of group conformity which was planted at eight and nine was overlooked at the time, but it is now beginning to blossom. A ten-year-old will esteem his gang and peers more than he will his family. Much of his self-esteem comes from his peer experiences and relationships.

Boys and girls will have different characteristics at different ages. At ten the girls become more aware than boys of interpersonal relationships. They are more aware of their clothes and appearances, while boys are trying to look like their peers. Even though girls show an awareness of their own persons, boys at ten give more evidence of approaching adolescence. If a person wonders what the child will be like as an adult, a fair evaluation can be made now.

THE ELEVEN-YEAR-OLD

The eleventh year marks the end of an era. Caretakers began saying at eight and nine that their little boy or little girl was no longer a child, but those were only signs. At eleven, childhood clearly surrenders to the beginning of adolescence. The settled ten-year-old now displays elements of self-assertion, curiosity, and of sociability. He is simultaneously restive, talkative, and investigative. He's not ill at ease, but he likes to be on the go. His appetite for food is matched by his hunger for experience.

Eleven's emotional life features peaks of intensity. He can fly into rage on short notice and is subject to bursts of laughter and to variable moods. One moment he is bright and cheerful, the next grumpy or dissatisfied. His emotions rise and fall unpredictably, but behavior which seems so strange and variable actually reflects new emotional developments, now in the beginning stages.

The bodily activity and expenditure of energy are the outward manifestations of the inner changes he is undergoing. As he grows restless he stands, stretches, moves from chair to chair, and often sits with his knees wide apart and hits them together. The eleven-year-old knows how he feels, but rarely knows why.

The rush to adolescence brings about a sense of leaving the once-adored parents. It uncovers some disagreement with the once-so-close mother, and the child develops the opinion that mom doesn't know as much as I thought she did. At this time—perhaps like no other time—the child gets along poorly with other siblings in the home. He may control physical expression of his anger, but his attitude is clearly saying "I'd like to hit him with a club."

In spite of all the frustrations eleven has with his siblings, he or she will be a staunch supporter if a sibling gets into trouble. The eleven-year-old looks upon himself almost as a parent to a younger brother or sister. The eleven-year-old is quick to defend a blood sibling in the household quarrels, but just as quick to support a stepsibling when the assault is outside the home.

With all the helpful knowledge available in books and magazines, all the expert advice therein for parents and stepparents, the fact remains that no two children are alike and not two children develop at the same pace. The middle period of a child's life, ages five to eleven, is just one step along the way from birth to adulthood. With each step will come changes inside which will result in frustrations and lead to behavior changes on the outside.

Everything is instant, new, and frightening to the stepparent. A child who behaved one way six months before the wedding may behave in completely different ways after the wedding. The changes may or may not have been brought about by the re-marriage or the presence of the stepparent in the home and family. It might just reflect the child's advance to the next stage of her development. It may not make step-parenting any easier, but it's helpful to know that complicated behavior is part of the child's growing toward maturity.

CHAPTER 17

The Frustration of Adolescence

All parents and stepparents want to believe their situation is worse than everyone else's. The stepparent with a preschool child says "You have no idea how bad it is to have a squalling youngster around the house." And the stepparent with a young school age child complains, "He's ten going on twenty, and thinks he knows everything." Then the stepparent seeking instant martyrdom speaks out, "If you think you have it bad, you should have to live in the same house with a teenage stepdaughter."

In adolescence the child experiences a series of events; initiated by his own body, some by the people who surround him, and some by his own self-esteem. In *Coming of Age in America* (Random House, 1965), Friedenberg says "The plight of the adolescent is basically similar to that of an emigrant, in that he cannot say what he was nor ever fully becomes what he started out to be." Adolescence sees the child in opposition to his parents, a threat to his leaders, and in competition with his peers.

This chapter will not cover every minute detail of adolescence. Many comprehensive works by qualified writers are available on the subject. The intentions here are to summarize as much significant information as possible to help struggling stepparents survive this difficult and evolving period.

Learning that a certain behavior is normal does not make it less frustrating, but it does help the stepparent understand that it's part of growing up and that other stepparents are going through similar experiences. Without this knowledge, a stepparent might tend to think his stepchild's behavior is abnormal and out of context with the behavior of his or her peers.

The adolescent is not a static individual. He's in motion; dynamic and constantly changing. He won't stand still for measurement, study, or for comparisons. He may be viewed as an individual, as the member of a group, or as a part of society. Regardless of how he is looked upon, he is always changing—in part because he is under fairly constant scrutiny. He knows people are watching him and their reactions concern him.

"When my husband's fourteen-year-old son asked what was for dinner, he was upset that we weren't ready to eat right then." The term "now" is vital to the adolescent and frustrating to the adults in the home. Whatever he wants, it must be now. Whatever he likes, he likes it now. His concept of value is simple: Is it of value to *me* right now? Everything that offers pleasure and satisfaction is not highly valued unless it offers pleasure and satisfaction now.

According to experts, there are four tasks the adolescent must accomplish as he or she moves toward adulthood: establish heterosexual identity, decide on a vocation, separate himself or herself from the parents, and make a commitment to responsible adulthood. The problem is that the youngsters know these things must be accomplished, and they think it must be done NOW.

Adult attitudes toward adolescence range from admiration to apprehension, dismay, and condemnation. Any of these might be directed toward one particular adolescent or a group. All of them are likely to be manifested to any youngster at different times as he progresses through the adolescence. More often than not, an adult's attitude is negative and critical, reflecting the feeling that adolescents pose a threat to the existing order. No matter what the adult's age is, he or she is quick to forget their own adolescent experiences.

In order to understand the outward behavior of adolescents it is necessary to know more about what inner developments are taking place. According to professionals who have studied this prolonged rite of passage, adolescence is a psychological, social, and maturational process initiated by puberty.

PUBERTY

Puberty is characterized by the onset of hormonal activity, under the influence of the central nervous system. Tests suggest that psychological events may influence the time and the sequence of pubertal changes. Physical growth and sexual maturation in both sexes may be hastened or retarded by emotional difficulties. The budding of breasts and the beginning growth of pubic hair occur in girls at the age of ten or eleven years. Menstruation typically begins between the ages of eleven to thirteen.

For boys, the beginning of pubic hair growth and of testicle enlargement typically occur during the twelve to sixteen period. Penis enlargement and ejaculation begin to take place between the ages of thirteen to seventeen.

The most distinctive sign of the transition into adolescence is the physical maturation brought on by increases in hormonal activity during puberty. The bodily changes are, of course, noticeable to others. They are astonishing to the youngster. In early adolescence the youngster begins to show marked increase in modesty and will usually for bid father or mother being in the room when he or she dresses. Jokes with sexual overtones are both offensive to them. The youngster may at any time erupt for no reason and become difficult to live with. An early adolescent's ego responds to the surge of sexual and aggressive energies as though they were both assets and liabilities.

The emotional turmoil is difficult for the youngster, and the withdrawal from parents typically causes a kind of depression comparable to what is experienced at the loss of a loved one. Unable to maintain a close dependency upon the parent, and considerably upset emotionally, the adolescent sometimes reacts to the resulting internal confusion with fear that he or she is going crazy. The desperate need for supportive relationships lead youngsters in early adolescence to reach outside the immediate family for guidance and identification.

With the youngster searching for answers during this transition period into adulthood, the peer group becomes more important in his life. The peer group provides the sense of belonging and feeling of strength and power that is so badly needed. In order to gain acceptance the early adolescent often tends to conform to the dress code, hair style, musical taste, and peer group mannerisms. It's not easy for any adult to understand the confused youth, especially stepparents who are having difficulty making their own adjustments.

TRAITS OF THE TWELVE-YEAR-OLD

The bursting, talkative energy so evident at eleven is finally beginning to calm at twelve. Even though they express frustrations often, youngsters at this age are more capable of organizing their energies. Boys of twelve develop an enthusiasm for sports, while girls often become equally interested in caring for young children.

Girls also take their most significant steps toward womanhood at twelve. It usually is the time of the most rapid growth, in both height and weight, her interest is now focused on menstruation. Some have difficulty becoming emotionally ready for this new biological event— one they have been told so much about—just as friends are experiencing it for their first time.

Many girls see it more as a disruption in their lives than an advance toward womanhood. Though they are *intellectually aware* of what is coming, the impact of the first menstrual cycle may produce some tears and vomiting. After the first hurdle has been crossed, a change of attitude and a more positive attitude about growing up begins to develop.

The physical development of twelve-year-old boys produces a wide range of results. Some will show little change from the development they had attained by eleven, while those who do begin to mature will advance significantly. At this age boys are becoming more interested in sex than before, and some interest in girls is almost inevitable. Yet their knowledge is extremely limited. Lacking a good source of information on the subject, a twelve-year-old might seek out material elsewhere—magazines, newspapers, and dictionaries, and often swapping stories with pals.

Erections occur often in twelve-year-olds, both spontaneously, without apparent external cause, and because of various kinds of stimulation. Caretakers are now apt to find pictures of nude girls hidden in the boy's room.

In spite of the extreme differences in physical development and sexual curiosity, twelve typically smoothed a lot of the rough edges of eleven. He may be spirited and impatient, but on the whole he is good natured, pleasant, and willing to listen to reason. Though he recognizes that growth brings more responsibilities, he also feels a bit fearful. Anger is not yet under control at twelve, but it is moving in that direction.

THIRTEEN AND GROWING

Each year of adolescence brings increasing maturity. Thirteen is quite a complex year. The youngster's trip through adolescence is now well under way, and many new phases of behavior will continue to emerge. At home the youth may lapse into spells of silence, but at school behave differently. She responds with interest to class assignments and discussions, and shows a great capacity to gain knowledge through reading, listening, and looking.

So much is happening for the first time to thirteen, it can be overwhelming. But outside events and experiences do not always show their effects instantly. He will withdraw into himself from time to time, trying to catch up with his world. The brief intervals of self-absorption and rumination are times when he reviews and releases some of his inner feelings, tensions, and attitudes.

A thirteen-year-old's relationship with his family also is undergoing radical changes. He cuts them off with short answers and is apt to be touchy and go off by himself. He's not sure why he treats the family as he does, it just happens. He does know that he's nicer to his friends than his parents. Caretakers look upon these behavior changes as being rude and disrespectful, and have a hard time understanding why their child can care more for an outsider than for a loving, caring parent.

The thirteen-year-old knows her mother cares about her and her welfare, but she will not ask personal questions about aspects of growing up that bother or confuse her. Somebody else always knows more. The mother who always was present to nurture the youngster now finds the child embarrassed by her presence, especially when she is in the company of friends or some place where people might recognize her. If she is some place where she does not fear recognition, she will get along very well with her.

Thirteens also become critical of their parents, not to their friends, but in the intimacy of the home. If it's not her hair, it's her make-up. If it's not her clothes, it's the way she keeps house.

A new stepmother, trying her best to love her husband and his children, finds it's hard when all she sees are radical behavior changes and all she hears are disrespectful remarks. A stepfather who just moved in with his new bride and her children hears nothing but criticism. The wife/mother has spent many sleepless nights worrying about their welfare, especially since their father left, and this treatment of the new husband/father is the thanks she gets.

He wonders how even she can love them. When such feelings exist, just studying and trying to understand biological development in adolescents will do little to change a stepparent's attitude. It is best to wait before speaking and, more often than not, let the natural parent handle communications.

The only thing a stepparent has on their side is time. The age of inward absorption, withdrawing, thinking things over, being disrespectful to parents, changing attitudes, and having periods of inner concentration may actually produce a kind of social deafness. A thirteen-year-old is not as defiant as he is just not hearing the parent. Once the parent gets his attention, they are able to work together.

THE FOURTEEN-YEAR-OLD

At fourteen the child's emotional make-up undergoes a drastic change. The shyness, touchiness, and whims of thirteen give way to a more robust and vigorous personality. There is more free expressions, more laughter and noise. The withdrawal symptoms so evident at thirteen are now gone, contributing to a more relaxed and contented household.

This year finds the young person more aware of himself and of his interpersonal environment. The rush to maturity which began at twelve is stabilizing, and he feels he finally is coming into his own. He is developing self-assurance, and really beginning to enjoy life. The relationships both at home and away tend to be friendly and outgoing. There is a more mature attitude towards adults in general and to his family in particular. Fourteen is developing a capacity to perceive how others feel, and to see himself as others see him.

Not only is the household more at ease with the youngster's relaxed feeling, but she also gets along better with younger siblings. More so if they are five and under: not so helpful with eleven-year-olds, since they are in an earlier stage of the same transition. Stepfamilies often put children closer to the same age in the same household, adding to their adolescent frustrations. Jeff is fifteen and now he has a stepbrother in the home just six months his junior.

Although there are still differences in growth rate, the fourteen-year-old girl's body shape seems to be more like that of a young woman than that of a child. Very few girls have not menstruated by their fourteenth year, and they are becoming more accustomed to the premenstrual symptoms which occur a day or two ahead of their period. By this time girls may also begin to feel an actual physical involvement in their response to boys. These feelings may be confusing and troublesome to her, sometimes increasing her feeling of vulnerability.

At fourteen boys still are far from mature in total development, but they seemed to have crossed the line from boyhood to manhood. It may be earlier or later, but this crossover usually occurs in the period between the fourteenth and fifteenth birthdays.

The larger physical physique at fourteen gives a strong impression of adolescent masculinity. And they are now trying to find their own way, to clarify for themselves how they feel, and to decide what paths are best for them. Unfortunately many youngsters are left alone to make important decisions when they are not adequately prepared to do so. A fourteen-year-old girl, with her increasing sexuality and preference for older boys, may be rather vulnerable in some situations. If someone takes advantage of that vulnerability, pregnancy could be the result.

Without proper parental guidance, many fourteens do not know how to establish controls or understand why they need them. With the freedom in dating fourteens have today, adults at least need to arm them with knowledge they need to behave morally, intelligently, and with restraint.

Boys at fourteen have a really good time together. They especially enjoy each other's sense of humor. Often, one will stand out as a comedian whose every word is considered funny by both his friends and himself. The expanding social interests of fourteen include a real drive toward the opposite sex. Most boys now consider girls more fun than nuisance. They date mostly younger girls and dates are often party-oriented.

A girl's first date often is at a party with older boys. They know that if they are with boys of their own age, the party will turn into horsing around and sometimes throwing things such as food. Activities in dating vary from the more usual parties at home, to a movie, a sports event, or school activity. Double dates are common as well as going out in larger groups.

Proper discipline from the home is especially important because of the extra guidance youngsters need to cope with their changing world. All of the new experiences tend to bewilder a young person. The goals which growing boys and girls strive to reach during these years are many and varied. Whether it is an unsuspected burst of energy or complete withdrawal, fourteen knows no better than the adult what initiates this behavior change. As biological development brings new impulses into action and strengthens old ones, the whole structure of inner controls expands and changes.

MATURITY TRAITS OF A FIFTEEN-YEAR-OLD

Each year of change is more confusing and frustrating than the one that just passed. The fifteenth year is no different. The maturity changes typical of this year are so complex they are difficult to summarize. Fourteen has so many facets and phases that young adults at times seem confused. Though those around them are baffled by this, the youngsters keenly wish to understand themselves and be understood by others.

The transition from fourteen to fifteen is not something a person would recognize overnight, yet the change can be striking. At fourteen there were signs of his coming into his own. He was happy, independent, energetic, and fairly stable emotionally, showing signs of being ready to meet the demands made upon him.

It would be reasonable for one to expect that fifteen would be a year of completing or following up those changes, but it does not happen that way. Instead, the child becomes indifferent frequently and speaks with a soft voice. The outgoing style of fourteen has changed. Adults will consider him lazy or at least tired most of the time. He looks and acts apathetic.

One of the more distinctive signs of maturity at fifteen is a more keen awareness of how he thinks the world should be. He tends to be more of a stickler for precision, almost a perfectionist at times. This feeling expresses itself in sensitivity, moods of irritability, acts of resistance, and suspiciousness—all of which become part of his behavior. Fifteen reaches into intellectual, philosophic, and aesthetic realms, revealing a new thoughtful, quiet, and serious side that is quite different from the enthusiasm of fourteen.

Janet questioned her fifteen-year-old son's attitude when he said, "I'm just not going to tell it all." She said, "He's never been like this before. He always has been so agreeable and cooperative."

Because of the many things that are going on with the fifteen-year-old, acting on a grudge, taking revenge, even acts of violence may show up in his conduct. At fifteen, whatever maturity has been achieved is still very vulnerable. The urge for independence is rising, but because it is immature it is expressed in crude, naive, and frustrating ways. These expressions can be misleading. Adults may think he's drifting away from the family when actually his thoughts are more toward the family he will have later.

At fifteen, the search for self becomes a very serious matter. The young adult is finding out that fulfilling his destiny depends pretty much on his own actions. That may explain why at times he faces life with such indifference, even apathy. There is no one more eager to find out about himself, to learn why he feels and acts the way he does, than fifteen. Independence and liberty are his constant quest, and he doesn't like to be held down or to have questions asked about his whereabouts or plans. He can stall an adult and tell that person nothing.

The family becomes puzzled just watching him. He can sit in a room crowded with people without showing any sign he knows they exist.

Fifteen can turn out to be her own worst enemy. She is so afraid that others will think her childish she can be over-protective of her actions. In the confines of her home a fifteen-year-old may be discovered playing with a younger sibling's toys and enjoying herself. But if anyone in her group were caught doing such a thing, that person would be ridiculed by her.

Fifteens are also beginning to think seriously about themselves. College is ahead and they are thinking in terms of what they would like to accomplish. They may set their sights too high, just to feel successful about themselves.

The boy at fifteen may not know what he wants in a career, but he is starting to give it some thought. He was carefree at fourteen, but now the future seems closer and it troubles him somewhat. Though he may not be sure of what he wants, he knows pretty well what he doesn't want and all the advice in the world will not change his mind.

More girls than ever are planning to work outside the home, as many of their mothers do. Many would like meaningful careers and virtually all of them see the necessity for a second income in the family. In an earlier generation, a girl might plan to work until marriage, giving it up to raise a family. Now wants and needs have changed. Some are looking for personal fulfillment; virtually all would like to be able to afford a better way of life.

It would not be uncommon to hear, "I don't want to be an old maid." Girls at fifteen begin contemplating marriage and nothing will stop their quest. It's not that homemaking as a full-time job is so appealing, but they want to have a husband with whom they can enjoy life; someone to discuss their problems with, who will agree with them more often than not. Parents are parents and they tend to offer their parental advice freely, rather than agreeing at all times.

The family ties are loosening. Boys want to be free of home and family and begin to want to get away. Sitting on the hood of a car in some parking lot until all hours of the night is more gratifying than spending an evening at home with the family. If there were no limits imposed by the parents, some boys would go out every night of the week. Where they go is not as important as the going itself.

Parents, especially stepparents, want to know if this is normal behavior. It is. It's fifteen. The parental frustration and concern increase when the son or daughter is vague about the evening's plans. Sometimes they are not sure themselves. Other times they know what they are planning is likely to be something to which the parents would object.

Dating changes at fifteen. The "going steady" urgency now relaxes, and a more "take them or leave them" attitude becomes more typical. For girls, one-to-one dating which was important at fourteen has now moved toward group intermingling. This doesn't mean there will not be exceptions, but on the whole fifteen-year-old girls find group dating more interesting. Much of the dating that takes place is done more for something to do than to be with a particular person or group; another manifestation of the "anything to get out of the house" syndrome.

Fifteen is an age when demands often are too much to cope with, and some give up the struggle and become discouraged. School becomes a prison to them and many develop the feeling "I've got to get out of here." It's no wonder the dropout rate is high at this age. Youngsters are confused. If they are not part of a stable home life, they can easily drift out of the mainstream.

Stepfamilies can add to the complexities of adolescents life, when stepmothers and stepfathers refuse to take the hand of their stepchildren and give them the support they so badly need.

SIXTEEN-YEAR-OLD

If the sixteen-year-old figuratively stands on tip toes, he or she can almost see the beginning of adulthood. They finally are reaching the exciting pre-adult stage. Fifteen laid the foundation and prepared the way for the more balanced behavior of sixteen. Wholesome self-assurance is in place and independence is so taken for granted that adults in the home accept it too. A most important year, sixteen has far-reaching implications for all girls and boys.

The ease and smoothness at sixteen is so evident after the restlessness of fifteen that one can hardly believe it. The physical development for girls is not changed much from the year before, although she will have assumed more adult feelings toward her biological functions. Cramps are more common and the menstrual cycle has been accepted as routine.

For boys, it's a continuation of growth and maturity. There is a firming of physique, and height typically is 98% of what it will be ultimately. Boys who have shown an interest in girls are now more interested than ever. Some who find it difficult to control their sex impulses masturbate frequently.

The ending of adolescence and the beginning of adulthood does not come in a particular month or year of a child's life. Just as when the youngster *became* an adolescent, there is an "estimated" time frame during which he or she will *become* an adult. In the later stages of adolescence and pre-adulthood, the young person will become employable. Financial dependence upon the parents will lessen and, in some cases, end.

After he obtains his driver's license, a car is prized by the boy; not only as a means of transportation, but as a symbol of independence from parents and adult supervision, of defiance and escape, of freedom from restraint, and of a newfound power.

The ending of the adolescent stage is characterized by five indicators: (1) the completion of separation and independence from parents; (2) a commitment to work; (3) the capacity for a lasting love relationship with a mate; (4) a newfound relationship with parents based upon relative equality; (5) and the development of a personal moral value system.

The big step is when the adolescent joins the adult world with an ability and motivation to come to terms with it. He may have his own values, not always accepting the values endorsed by preceding generations. No matter what confusion and disturbance the adolescent has encountered, once the conflicts are resolved, adolescence has come to an end.

Learning what is normal during the various stages of a child's life is frustrating to parents, stepparents, and to the children themselves. Simply because one child makes the transition from adolescence to adulthood during a certain month or year of his or her life does not mean another child—even in the same family—will achieve the same result at the same age. It may be faster or it may be delayed. The important thing to know is that it will happen, and caretakers cannot do anything about it except to love and support him or her through it.

Unexpected interferences can have a significant effect on the child's developmental process. Such events as the loss of a loved one, the family split by separation or divorce, mother leaving the home to seek employment, changing schools, or changing residence are capable of pushing a child hurriedly into the next stage, delaying the move from one stage to the next, or even forcing the child to take a backward step—if only temporarily.

A stepchild has experienced some of these setbacks as he or she went through the break up of the traditional family. Adults—parents and stepparents alike—are prone to become angry with their kids, but they must ask themselves if they would have behaved any differently had they been the stepchild.

The best advice is to roll with the punches, learn as much as possible about what the child is going through at each stage, and be there for the child when you are needed.

CHAPTER 18

What's in a Name?

Squabbles can erupt in a stepfamily over the simplest disagreements. One subject which should produce little conflict often becomes complex and argumentative. That is deciding what name is appropriate for the new step-relatives. How should the children address the new stepparent, and what is appropriate for the stepparent to call his or her stepchild. Then there are the stepgrandparents, the stepaunts and stepuncles, and finally the stepcousins.

The words "stepparent" and "stepchild" normally carry such negative baggage that many people choose not to use them. Experts fail to agree on any one policy, leaving the decision where it should be—in the hands of the parties involved. Some professionals lean toward terminology like "New mother" or "New father" in place of stepparent. Others believe the term "step" is more accurate but realize the word still has negative implications. While stepfamilies find themselves pondering the subject in search of an agreeable solution, they usually fall back on the use of stepmother, stepfather, stepson, and stepdaughter.

PARENTAL PERSUASION

Whatever titles are chosen, it's the basic relationship between stepparent and stepchild that is important, not the names they use to address one another. Though names can be important to some, a child should not be forced to use a name with which he or she is not comfortable. Often it's done to create an appearance of closeness and intimacy for a relationship that lacks both those ingredients. Such artificial pressure usually makes the relationship worse.

The dilemma in choosing something as relatively unimportant as a suitable name symbolizes how the stepparent often is torn in two directions. The options here seem to be pretending on one hand, offending the child on the other. It is wrong to be false and wrong to hurt the child. Some children are particularly sensitive to any reminder of their *different* status.

One problem in dropping the "step" title is this. When the actual make-up of the blended family becomes known, as it almost always does, it gives the impression that the "step" relation is something to be hidden. The stepparent's intention might have been genuine, an effort to show a close relationship with the child, but in other cases avoiding the "step" connotation is used as a cover-up.

The fact that stepparents feel alone in their world has been discussed earlier. They are ashamed of past failure. They don't want to talk about their present problems because they fear a second failure. They do not want to hear "I told you so." The fact must be accepted that one marriage has ended, either by death or divorce, and another family—the stepfamily—has been formed. People should face that reality immediately and not try to live a lie.

Charlene told her two boys to start calling their new stepfather Dad. The boys were very young so it did not matter to them one way or the other. The stepfather was not so keen on the idea, but he did not refuse. Charlene admitted later, "I only used it as a weapon to get revenge on my first husband." First of all, Charlene's first husband divorced her, not his children. Though he did leave them he can still love them and want to have a father-children relationship with them. Second, the children should never be used as weapons or bargaining chips in or after divorce settlements.

In the earlier stages of the stepfamily tension affects all its members. The urgency to be accepted and loved by all keeps everyone on edge. "How do you like your new dad?" was asked of a fourteen-year-old by the mother of her best friend. "He's not my dad," the girl shouted. "I already have a father." Position, acceptance, respect, love, and the absent natural parent should all be considered in the name given to new steprelatives.

It will release some of the tension if family members can decide ahead of time, before the wedding if possible, what names are to be used. Sometimes facing what could be a problem early will prepare the child for the transition later. Talking it over with the child lets him or her include their feelings in the matter. Serious consideration should be given to their suggestions before the final decision is made.

When the natural parent is still living and involved in the child's life, the child may be concerned that calling the stepparent Mom or Dad would be considered a sign of rejection by the natural parent. One fifteen-year-old refused his stepmother's help in any way, thinking "If I call my stepmother Mom, it will hurt my real mother."

Children sometimes are placed in tough situations, especially when they like the stepparent and don't want to offend the natural parent. This young man solved his problem by addressing his stepmother by her given name and introducing her to his friends as his stepmother. Not all answers will be that direct and satisfactory to both parties, but, with a little creative forethought, a solution usually can be found.

CONFUSION BROUGHT ON BY NAMES

When a child uses the term Mom or Dad in speaking of his stepparent, the person to whom the child is speaking may not know if he or she is referring to the natural parent or to the stepparent. If the natural parent has anything close to a good relationship with the child, he or she will generally resent the child using those terms in referring to the stepparent. No matter how hard the stepchild and stepparent work at building a relationship, however, that relationship rarely reach the level that typically exists between a child and his or her natural parent.

"My husband has three children who only get to visit on occasion since they live so far away," recalled Evelyn. "Normally my girls address their stepdad by his given name, but by the end of his kids' visit they have picked up their terminology and will call him Dad. It only lasts for a short time and neither of us make a big deal out of it as long as they feel good. But we did chuckle the other evening when my four-year-old, referring to his natural father, called him by his first name."

Though they seem insignificant, names can be important to a hurting child. When the youngster's relationship with the natural parent is impaired or deficient and the child has a genuine desire to use the term Mom or Dad when referring to the stepparent he should be permitted to do so. The unsatisfactory relationship with the natural parent might be the result of abandonment, or child abuse when the parent was living in the home, or it might just reflect the fact the natural parent is deceased. Any time a child prefers to call a stepparent "Mom" or "Dad," he usually has a good reason for doing so. It is a positive sign, reaching out to recover a lost sense of security.

The stepparent's biological children must also be considered in the decision. "Why does he call you Dad? He's not your child." Or, "Do you like her as much as you do us? Is that why she calls you Mom?" A girl may not want a stepsister or stepbrother calling her parent Mom or Dad.

Not all problems in the stepfamily will be easy to resolve, this one included. But in this case, a good stepsibling relationship, along with the assurance that the natural child still has her important place in the family, usually will satisfy everyone.

MAKING THE DECISION

A lot of talking will be done and all the options will be explored, including inputs from the kids, but the time will come when decisions have to be made. How will the children address their stepparent? Will it be a version of mom or dad, the stepparent's given name, or a special nickname? And are the children going to use "step" words in introductions and conversations? If the kids stay with their mother in her new marriage, will they keep their father's last name or will they choose to use their stepfather's?

For many stepfamilies, and for various reasons, the choice is to use the stepparent's given name. "When Shirley and I married," said Paul. "She asked me how I wanted the children to address me, Dad, Daddy two, or Paul. She went on to name a number of other alternatives. I had already given it some thought, so I told her Paul would do fine. The children's father is still alive and very close to them. He pays their child support and I believe he deserves the privilege to be called their dad. I have my own children and I appreciate the things their stepfather does for them, but I hope they'll always call me dad."

The general opinion is that a stepchild may choose not to call his stepparent "Mother" or "Father" out of loyalty to his own parent. This should not be looked upon as failure by the stepparent.

An opposing view on the subject is that a stepparent's authority in the home may be weakened if the stepchild does not call him or her a paternal or maternal name. Whether this view carries any weight is up to the individual stepparent. As a matter of proper discipline, a child should respect those in authority no matter what the name or title.

If the stepparent asked to be addressed as "Mother" or "Father" and the child refused for no good reason, parental authority would be tested and possibly damaged. But if the child uses a name agreed to with the stepparent, there should not be a problem in this area.

Adding a paternal modification to a given name may be an alternative to consider. The mother of Julie, age ten, had married three times. Julie solved her dilemma by selecting a special name for each of her mother's husbands. She called her father, her mother's first husband, Dad. The others she called Daddy Chuck and Daddy Bill.

Names and nicknames are part of our heritage and personal choices no one outside the family should criticize. The name a person chooses will generally come out of the relationship. "Why shouldn't my stepkids call me Fred? They call their grandparents, 'Mee Maw' and 'Paw Paw' and they love them very much."

A child will have two sets of grandparents; one from his mother's side of the family, and one from the father's side. There may even be great-grandparents still living. The grandparent and grandchild usually discover an appropriate name for their relationship. If a grandparent wishes to be addressed as "Grandfather" it would be disrespectful for the child to call him "Gramps." But if "Gramps" is satisfactory to the grandparent, who should criticize that form of address?

WHAT ABOUT LAST NAMES

Special and affectionate names show the relationships that exist between family members, but the last name tells the world who a person is. Even more so, it tells who the father is. For the woman and her new husband, the different last name of the children is public admission that she has had another husband. The fact that many couples, and step-children, want to hide the former name is a sign that society is not as relaxed and accepting of divorce as they want to believe.

But getting the natural father's permission to surrender his children's use of his last name is another matter. He may allow another man to raise his kids, take them places, and even pay some of their bills, but when it comes down to adoption or changing the last name, the father firmly puts his foot down and says "No."

When the stepfamily is content with the situation, two last names are no problem. One minister jokingly said, "My four-year-old step-son told his Sunday School teacher, 'I sure hope my daddy quits drinking beer and smoking cigarettes, it makes him stink.' It's no secret that I'm divorced and remarried, but sometimes people forget. I'm glad that teacher didn't."

Everyone knows that children do not want to be different. They often choose their stepfather's name to be like others in the household. Harriet's first husband died in an auto accident and she remarried three years later. "The girls wanted to keep their father's last name and we all agreed. A few weeks into the new school year and I noticed on some of their papers the name Morris, my new husband's last name."

Although the big question seems to be how will the child address the stepparent, there may also be some anguish and concern on the other side of the equation. How will stepparents address their stepchildren? She's my husband's daughter. They're our kids. Or a straightforward "He's my stepson." For many of the same reasons children have, many adults will go to great lengths to avoid putting the "step" label on the child. A stepmother may want to confirm that so much love exists between her stepdaughter and herself, or she may not want to admit a past marriage and divorce.

It would be better if terminology had no effect on the children or the adults, but old wounds remain. The general feeling is that the term "step" is less painful on the child when the parents are divorced and the natural mother or father is available. One stepmother rudely stated, "I'm glad to call him stepson. I wouldn't want anyone to think I raised a child to look like that!" But children can be just as vindicated in their equally direct remarks. If they had been involved in the selection, many stepparents would not have been chosen.

Children and adults should be assured that it's not what you call a person, but how you feel about that person that counts. Lori, seventeen said, "I'm sorry dad and mom couldn't make it together and I still love them both. But my stepmom's been good to me and my dad and I've grown to love her very much too." Respect, acceptance, and love can exist even when parental terms are not used.

CHAPTER 19

Rewards of a Stepparent

The stepparent is very seldom the beneficiary of much appreciation, especially during the early stages of the new marriage. Instead of holding him or her in high esteem, everyone seems to be down on the new arrival, thinking that person was in some way instrumental in the break-up of the original family. The children are quick to blame anyone and everyone—except the loving mother and father—for their miserable circumstances. So the stepparent (the home wrecker, the intruder) is the most likely target. "If it weren't for you, my mom and dad would still be together and we'd be happy." It may be years before the hard-working, hard-trying stepparent is accepted, appreciated, or loved by the new stepchildren. It may never happen.

THE WEEKEND ARRIVAL

Weekend stepparents complain of not being appreciated by their visiting children. "I start getting ready for them on Thursday evening,"said Betty, "Our house is small so I have to make room for cots and mats for extra sleeping arrangements. Usually it's my kids who end up on the floor. Not that they mind, it's just that I wonder why his kids can't sleep there some time. I buy extra food, snacks and treats I don't normally purchase, but his kids expect them to be there. And then all weekend it's want, want, want, and never a word of thanks, from the time they walk in until he leaves to take them home."

From a stepmother's point of view, the children are guests, should be polite, and should show good manners by appreciating what is done for them. The child sees it from a different perspective. He's been told from the beginning that he now has two homes, even though one may be part-time; one with his mother and one where his father lives. He is doing his best to involve himself in both households. The problem is not that he doesn't appreciate his stepmother's labor; most children just do not show the same respect to a stepparent as they do to their natural parent.

A divorce and remarriage may change the parents, but it does not change a "programmed" child. From birth, right or wrong, she has taken her mother for granted, and feels little motivation to show thankfulness to a stepmother she did not ask for in the first place. The fairly unyielding attitudes of stepmother and stepdaughter offer the situation little hope of recovery. The stepmother expects signs of appreciation for all the efforts she has put into her visit. If the stepdaughter cannot show her respect and gratitude, she feels no obligation to keep on giving. The girl is not likely to change or respond. After a few such impasses, the stepmother's smiles are forced and her welcome much cooler, revealing her basic desire that the kids won't come at all.

HURT BY CONFLICT

Rewards or thanks to the stepparent also can be delayed or eliminated by the loyalty conflicts within the new stepfamily. Where conflicts exist between a stepmother and her stepchildren, the father's loyalty to both sides is continually being tested. In situations where the differences involve stepfather and stepchildren, the mother's loyalty is put on trial.

Although he may understand his new wife's work load, the father feels rejected by her lack of attention. When the stepmother turns her attention toward her husband, the children become jealous and irritable. Any criticism from the stepparent to the parent only exacerbates an already shaky situation. "I think you are too hard on your daughter." And then when the stepfather is caught reprimanding her children and not his own, it worsens the chill between the two. These conflicts in the home disrupt relationships, and postpone or stifle entirely any chances for expressions of gratitude from the children.

Everyone *should* be thankful for what he has and for the things other people do for him whether it be a friend or relative. At the same time, favors should not be done only in expectation of a reward. As in most situations, it is two-sided and both parties need to improve in their giving and receiving. These problems develop and fester because communications between the two sides tend not to reflect proper thought and consideration.

GRANDPARENTS AND IN-LAWS

The grandparents, better known as the new in-laws, rarely greet a new stepparent into the family without some sign of suspicion. The husband-to-be painted a different picture than what his new bride discovered when he said, "Mom and Dad will be delighted to have you as their daughter-in-law." Actually Mom and Dad have the same suspicions as the children, and wonder what part she had in breaking up their son's first marriage.

The husband-to-be's illusion that they will appreciate her for what she's doing for their son and his children will soon vanish, when they compare her to his first wife, the kids' *real* mother.

"I married Barbara, who was divorced with two young girls," recalled Arthur. "Her income, including child support, was insufficient to meet her monthly obligations. Even while we dated I helped with her car payment and paid part of her utility bills. We did not live together. Her father and mother were in no financial shape to help her and there was no one else she could turn to. We've been married six years now and with our combined income and wise investments we have done very well for ourselves. The past two years we have helped her parents through some hard times, mostly at my suggestion. But still they refuse to include me as part of their family. They call Barbara and invite her and the girls to visit, but do not ask me to come along. I don't want any medals for what I did for Barbara. I love her. But I do expect her parents to say thanks for what we are doing for them."

MIXED FEELINGS

It is not uncommon for children to enter the new stepfamily confused, and with mixed feelings. The wedding may or may not have been a happy occasion for them. While that event represented a new beginning, it also put an end to all hopes of the traditional family reuniting. No matter how much time had lapsed since the divorce, the wedding still finds the child feeling abandoned and defeated.

Another adult in the home is someone else with whom to share mom or dad, and the child starts having feelings of being pushed aside. Some children may get upset to the point that they try different ways to break up the new marriage. "If we can only get rid of our new stepmother everything will be all right again."

Instead of the rewards and good feelings he or she might have been anticipating, the stepparent becomes the target for the hostile feelings that have been building up in the children. Poor relationships between the absent parent and the child or frustrations in the relationship with the custodial parent will sometimes be acted out in the relationship between stepparent and stepchild. "I cannot take it out on Dad. He has enough on his shoulders already." So there is only one person left, the stepmother. It's not that the child dislikes the stepparent so much, there just is no one else he or she can dump on to unload their rotten feelings.

Fear of new relationships is felt more strongly by children than adults, and children of divorce are more hesitant to reach out than a child who has an intact home life. Having lost one important adult already, children anticipate a recurrence. They are likely to need time to let their defenses down and accept someone new in their lives. A wise stepparent will take these factors into consideration and work slowly, being grateful for each small move toward recognition and acceptance. Coming on too strong might be too much for the child and drive him even further away.

MISREPRESENTING THE TRUTH

It's easier (as well as sounding better) to say, "She hates me!" than it is to say "I hate her." When describing the situation with his or her stepparent, a child typically will say "I try, but I can't get her to like me. She is so unreasonable to get along with." But the stepmother is a warm, caring person who is frustrated by her failed attempts at stepmotherhood.

Many stepparents suffer from undeserved bad reputations because of the stepchild's misrepresentation of the truth. The child will wrongfully project his or her own hostility onto the stepparent in saying "I don't hate her. She hates me." Because the child needs to keep a positive feeling about his parents, biological parents are not good targets for such hostility. But because the stepparent is looked on only as an unworthy replacement, losing him or her would not be considered all that important.

Though there may not be any love lost between the child and stepparent, not all of the child's hostility is aimed at hurting the stepparent. Some of it is a test to see where the natural parent stands. For example, when a stepmother is brought into an argument by the child, father often is called upon to settle it. In such situations, the child is waiting to see if the father's allegiance lies with his own flesh and blood or with that intruder, his new bride. Once the question has been settled and the child knows where the parent stands, building a relationship with the stepparent can proceed.

A child's standing with the natural parent will have a significant influence on the relationship with the stepparent. For example, if the child feels good about her mother, she will tend to view other adult females, including her stepmother, positively and will anticipate a good relationship.

On the other hand, children who have had bad relationships with their mother, who have been rejected or misunderstood, will expect similar treatment from the stepmother. "I know what you want. You're all alike." It could delay significantly any positive feelings from forming. Certainly the stepparent's own attitude and personality will have some effect on the stepchild, but outside influence can either speed up or slow down the acceptance process.

NO GUARANTEES

Stepparenting offers no guarantees. Time is often a great healer and bad feelings can change, but there is no promise that tomorrow, next year, or even ten years down the road will be any different. After some time has passed, stepparent and child can become more close, as long as each party respects the other. But no one can *make* someone else like or love them.

"All my friends, and even some of Mike's close associates, warned me to beware," exclaimed Janice, a twenty-seven-year-old divorcee and mother of six-year-old Valerie. Mike had two sons living with him from his first marriage, Jack sixteen and Alan fourteen. Every time Mike showed interest in a lady friend, Jack would take off on a drinking spree with some of his friends, sometimes staying away for as long as two days. Alan would just retreat to his room until Mike gave up. Janice's friends scolded her for even exposing Valerie to such rotten behavior.

"I didn't know if I would ever win the boys' affection, but I know how much I loved Mike and I was going to give him my best." Janice's and Mike's case was not as unusual as some might think. When older children are involved, stepmothers and stepfathers often walk into situations as difficult as this one.

Janice recalls "it was shortly after our second wedding anniversary before I learned that I had made any impact on the boys' life. I noticed that Jack had stopped spending so much time out with his friends, but the night of his high school graduation said it all. He came up to me at the end of the program and said, 'Thank you for just being there,' I knew what he meant. His mother had stopped visiting and hadn't even acknowledged his last birthday, his eighteenth."

Jack discovered after some time together that Janice wasn't so bad after all. She was not the wicked stepmother he had visioned in his mind, and she was not responsible for the break-up of his parents' marriage.

IN-LAWS

It's not impossible for the in-laws to change their attitudes after a little time. Once the initial suspicion is overcome, the in-laws begin to take a more serious look at their grandchildren's new stepparent. "It took a long time for Pete's parents to treat me like a member of the family," recalled Sharon. "I tried to make them like me, but it wasn't until after my relationship with their granddaughter proved solid that they began showing any signs of warmth and acceptance towards me."

In-laws have a built in instinct that a second spouse either is out to take advantage of their son or daughter, or it is a fling that will wear itself out with time. Mid-life crisis is blamed for many of today's divorces; men in pursuit of their youth looking for younger women to prove their manhood. Mid-life is an important stage of the life of many, but people should not hasten to blame all divorces on it.

Whatever the circumstances that led to the new marriage and step-family, after a suitable amount of time has passed—sometimes months, sometimes years—the in-laws generally see the new spouse is serious about his or her responsibility and begin to think more positively.

"When I first started dating Paula her mother found out and began calling me on the phone. She accused me of interfering with her daughter's marriage, which I had not done, and then started preaching that I was too old for her daughter. When all else failed, she even criticized her own daughter to me saying, she was only out for a good time and it would soon wear off. Next, Paula's mother even suggested we live together for a while to see if this thing would pass. We disagreed and married anyway without her blessing. Later my age became even more an issue. Her parents felt like they were losing a grip on their daughter because in her first marriage they had always told her what to do and she did it. Now they know Paula will listen to me instead of them. We just celebrated our fifth wedding anniversary, the first with their best wishes."

Rewards are only what people make of them. Tim said, "I didn't expect much from Harriet's parents and not much is what I got. But I didn't marry her parents. As long as she appreciates me that's good enough for me."

Love, care, a good deed, and real concern should not demand rewards. The real motivation must be to make the best home possible, no matter what the circumstances. In a stepfamily home that often can be a real challenge.

"I nagged at my son for two years to tell his stepmother he appreciated the meals," remembered Chad. "Two weeks after I finally gave up, I heard him say, of his own accord 'The meal was good. I enjoyed it.' I guess he's a lot like me. He would rather do it himself, not because he was forced into it."

Most children do not intend to be rude or ungrateful. Usually there is some negative force which causes them to act the way they do. If you attack the source of the problem, not the child, most problems will evaporate.

CHAPTER 20

Yours, Mine, and Ours

The questions most on the minds of stepfamily newlyweds are on the subject of children. Do we want to have children? If so, how many? If we are going to be parents should we start now or wait a few years? If we plan to have more than one, how long should we wait between births?

These are standard questions for most newly married couples, but they take on a different meaning for newly married stepfamily couples. The questions become more complex since there are more complicating factors to consider.

Simply put, a stepfamily is a family in which at least one spouse is not the biological parent to one of the children in the family. It could be that just one spouse has children from a previous marriage or it could be that both husband and wife are parents. The fact that the children live in the home or only visit on occasion has no bearing on the status. The fact remains, it's a stepfamily. The big question then changes from "Do we want to have children?" to, "Do we want to have *more* children?"

THE HUSBAND IS A FATHER

When the husband has children from a former marriage there are two aspects to consider. The new wife also may have children or she may come to the marriage childless. In either situation, both the husband's and the wife's feelings about more children should carry equal weight in determining the final decision.

When the wife has not had children, she has never experienced the joys of childbirth nor the many things which go along with it; the nine months pregnancy, filled with eager anticipation of the baby's arrival, and the momentous days of early infancy. Mothering a child from birth is an experience no one can share vicariously. It is strictly between mother and child. No matter how much it is discussed, until a person goes through it she cannot know what has been involved.

Even though his children may be in the custody of their mother and he sees them only occasionally (they are, inferentially, not much of a burden) a stepfather may not be nearly as excited about having more children as his new wife might be. He already has been through one or more pregnancies, and has experienced the effects on his wife and the home. As wonderful as the new child was, the new arrival changed the couple's social life drastically. He's not sure he wants to go through it again.

It really boils down to one conclusion. The basic parenting desire that is in most people already has been fulfilled in the man who has fathered children. Before the divorce, he had an active part in the child raising and he feels no compelling need to do it again.

If they reflect honestly on the experience, many fathers would admit they were not really able to give their children enough time when they were with them and that fatherhood had not been a very satisfying experience. For the most part, the children were part of a quarrelsome household. At the same time, while these fathers feel they were inadequate in the role, they also are haunted with the guilt of having left their children. "I can't do it do my kids," they might think, feeling that having more family might tell them "I didn't have time for you, but I do now."

His age and the status of his career also will have an important influence on the husband's decision. In a second marriage the husband often is older than his new bride. A man at the peak of his earning power is not apt to see it as a good time to start or increase his family.

THE WIFE IS A MOTHER

The decision to have a child, whether it be in a step-family or a traditional family, should not rest in the hands of one person. There are always the feelings and opinions of two people to consider and neither person should dictate the final outcome. There will be stepfamilies in which the husband has children from a former marriage and the wife does not, and about as many cases where the wife has children and her new husband does not. And of course there will be situations in which both husband and wife bring children to the marriage.

The stepfamily in which the wife has children and the husband does not will have to cope with more or less the same kinds of conflicting desires and interests that confront couples where only the husband has had children. If the wife has been through it all before, she may not share her new husband's urgent desire to be a father to *his own* children. Her basic motherhood needs have been met and she may not want to go through it again.

The wife's age and the age of her children also are important factors to consider. Unless her divorce took place shortly after the birth of her last child, the children will be old enough for her to have moved forward with her life and career. It's not that she feels her children are a burden, but having and raising them has occupied quite a few years of her life.

Having another child will postpone any personal plans she might have and might even cancel them altogether.

Until the need has been satisfied, the basic desire for a child usually will be evident in both male and female. In a stepfamily where one spouse is childless he or she may be able to satisfy *part* of that need by being involved with the stepchildren. Although nothing will replace the genuine thrill of bringing a child into the world, a childless stepmother may become an active part of the children's lives, taking them shopping, buying for them, talking with them, and being available when they need her. The weekend visitor may be a poor substitute for seven days a week and twenty-four hours a day involvement, but when it is not practical to add another child to the family a person may have to make the best of the situation.

A childless husband also can get involved with his wife's youngsters and satisfy some of his parenting needs. The children have needs only a man can fulfill. Girls need a father figure in the home to help them in their growing process and to learn more of what to expect in a husband. The boys need a male role model they can learn from. While it is not the same as biological fatherhood, a childless husband can do a lot more than just sit on the sidelines.

In some situations the extent of involvement may not be determined by the stepparent alone. The natural parent usually will decide, consciously or unconsciously, how much involvement the stepparent can have with his or her children. Many stepparents try to be involved and caring, but then give up saying "I argued over the children in my first marriage. I don't have to do it again." Whatever they agree to do, the couple must communicate openly and respect each other's feelings.

BUT I WANT A CHILD OF OUR OWN

There are many stepfamily spouses who are not willing to have more children, but there probably are equal numbers who want children of their own. However just wanting to have a child does not necessarily mean it is the right thing to do. In a stepfamily, the other children's feelings need to be considered. The children may think that another child by a different father or mother would tend to take their places in the hearts of the parents.

Financial reasons also may stand in the way. Divorce in this country may be easy, but it can be costly. Lawyers' fees are substantial and the husband may be paying alimony if his ex-wife has not remarried. The expenses can impose a very heavy burden on the new marriage. If the wife is not working yet, she may need to in order to help her husband pay off his bills. And it's unlikely she came away from her divorce free of debt. No matter how badly the couple may want a child of *their* own, it may have to be postponed or put off indefinitely.

If the couple is determined to have a child—and do so—financial considerations may force the wife back to work sooner than she would like, forcing her to leave the child and forfeit the pleasure of bonding during early infancy.

FRIENDS AND OTHER RELATIVES

Everyone has an opinion on the subject whether or not their opinions have any value or relevance. Grandparents and in-laws may argue that another child would only cause conflict. Their arguments might have some substance, but they are selfish. They tend to think first (sometimes only) of themselves, not wanting to share their attention with another child. "Everything seems fine the way it is. Why change it?"

Most grandparents look on the new husband or wife as an outsider, and consider a child by an outsider more an invasion than a blessing. Friends will have a lot to say too, even though they might choose differently if they were in the same situation. "Why do you want another child? You two are doing so well." Or, "Do you think it's wise to have another child at your age?" Age should be regarded in the decision, but it is for the couple alone to consider.

Another child will change the life style of a newly married couple, traditional or stepfamily. But it may have more effect on the stepfamily, since it is not the first child, but the second, third, or ... All the opinions and all the evidence in the world cannot make the decision for the couple. They must decide what's best for themselves. If the desire for more children is strong enough they somehow will make whatever sacrifices are necessary.

CHAPTER 21

Rights of a Stepparent

In spite of all it's frustrations, agony, and giving without getting much back, stepparenting still seems to get the "short end of the stick" when it comes to rights. "Recently the mother of two young children in our community was killed in an auto accident," said Harold. "Her husband, the stepfather to the children, was furious when the children's father arrived two hours before the funeral to pick up the kids and their clothes. Doesn't the stepparent have any rights?"

The only law that protects the stepparent is the "law" of common humanity. In most cases, depending upon the stepparent's relationship with the children's natural parent, that law does not count for much.

This chapter will not presume to offer legal advice or attempt in any way to be a substitute for professional legal service. In fact, the discussion of parental rights in any context seems almost irrelevant, in light of such highly-publicized recent events as children suing their parents. "Parental rights" seems almost an anachronistic concept. In custody disputes, the courts routinely are more concerned with the child's welfare than with the rights of the parents.

Where individual rights are involved, most courts choose to resolve each case individually. In decisions dealing with "step" relations the judge often will decide the child's best interest is served by living with the natural parent, not the stepparent. However, the subject of rights for the stepparent is beginning to be examined with more interest.

WHERE DO I STAND?

A stepparent has good reason to be confused about his or her legal position with respect to the children. If stepparents sense they have obligations without rights, they have analyzed their status pretty accurately. In the eyes of the law, stepparent and stepchild are considered strangers. The fact that their relationship might have become close over the years carries no legal weight. The relationship contains no rights and imposes no duties.

As it affects the stepparent, the law is confusing and contradicting, and almost always at the stepparent's disadvantage. The status of the stepparent is classified more as a social relationship than a legal one. Because most stepparents conduct their lives (and relate to their stepchildren) well within the boundaries of the law, whatever legal rights they may have are never challenged.

On the other hand, parental rights are very real. A stepparent is well-advised to familiarize himself with them. The most important right both parents of a legitimate child have is custody, the care and physical possession of the child. When there is a divorce, one parent will surrender his or her physical possession of the child, but will retain visitation rights, among other varying privileges.

The stepparent has none of these rights. No matter how many years the stepparent has lived in the same home with the children, looking after them and caring for them, no parental rights have developed. Frequently a stepparent will refuse to surrender a stepchild, in a struggle with the natural parent for custody, but parental rights are intrinsic to the natural parent only. The only way any parental right can be acquired by a stepparent is by legal process.

Even though such outcomes are very much in the minority, there are cases when a court decides in favor of the stepparent against the natural parent, grandmother, or other blood relative. The grounds for the decision have nothing to do with establishing any form of parental rights for the stepparent; they have to do only with what is best for the child.

Individual states determine their different laws and most decisions still remain in the hands of the judge. Courts may also terminate parental rights in certain situations: for example, instances of child neglect or abuse, or indefinite loss of contact with the natural parent. In instances when the parent who has custody wishes to relinquish it, custody may be reversed. The fact remains that the stepparent's position is weak in any custody battle and parental rights cannot be assumed simply by acting like a parent.

The laws involving stepparent and stepchild depend on the society that makes them. Some of the laws make sense, others do not. Most laws have not caught up with the pace at which new stepfamilies are being created. Perhaps the delays in rewriting old laws and passing new ones reflect the legal system's trying to make sure the changes taking place are both valid and here to stay.

The rapid formation of new stepfamilies in huge numbers is leading society into new areas of sociological and legal consideration. The courts are beginning to explore the legal aspects of step relations. Significant changes are beginning to take place.

Since the law indicates that stepparent and stepchild are strangers, the stepparent has no obligations in common law that obligate him or her to provide financial support for the stepchild. The basis for this is the fact that marriage of the stepparent to the child's parent creates no legal relationship between stepparent and stepchild.

The step relationship is established by law rather than by blood (commonly recognized as a back door relationship). Because someone married a parent, his or her child becomes the person's stepchild. The law seems to offer no more on behalf of the stepchild than it does for the stepparent. Each state makes its own laws on marriage, divorce, custody, and parenthood, but each state tends to ignore the stepchild.

WHO THEN IS RESPONSIBLE FOR THE CHILD?

In stable stepfamilies, bills get paid, allowances are given, and needs are met. It is when there is a breakdown in the stepfamily—economic, physical, or emotional—that law comes into play. While the stepparent and stepchild are classified as strangers in one legal sense, they may not be in another.

As in most laws, there are loopholes here as well. In some states, the stepfather cannot always escape responsibility for the stepchild's bills, especially when the natural father is dead or unwilling to provide support. The implication in such cases is this; if the alternative is that the child go on relief, the stepfather must pay. Other states have no statutory obligation, but the courts still can hold the stepfather responsible, claiming he voluntarily assumed the accountability by taking the child into his home and letting it be known he was the person responsible for the child's care and education. In our country this law is as acceptable as the *in loco parentis* (in the place of the parent) relationship.

Child support is another subject entirely, but a combination of legal and social pressures are working now to compel a natural father to meet his child support responsibility. Some states are even going as far as to allow missed child support payments to be garnisheed from the father's paycheck.

There can be considerations involved in addition to the laws that are enforced. An indirect way to force the stepparent to participate in support of the stepchild is to deprive a mother of welfare benefits when she marries. In some states the amount of the benefits is determined by total household income, whether or not the couple is married. Aid to independent children also is frequently denied to women who have a husband or even a male companion in the home.

STEPPARENTS AND CUSTODY BATTLES

Court decisions on custody reversals are not flooding the system yet, but such reversals are not as uncommon today as in years past. When a man remarries, for example, the new home environment is now a place where he too could effectively raise his children. He tries to modify a custody decree on the grounds that he has a new wife and can now provide the better home for the child. The judge will then take a good look at the stepmother, to determine if she is willing to accept the child as her own. The judge's decision usually is based on the stepparent's appearance and demeanor in court. Many stepmothers have exhibited their most maternal charms to help their new husbands win back their children from ex-wives.

With the changes in the law governing child support payments, children often become bargaining chips in courthouse back rooms. "My greatest fear was losing my children," explained a mother in Florida. "And when my husband took them away just before the settlement, I was willing to agree on anything just to get them back." Courts try hard to protect the child, but many times their hands are tied. Often decisions are influenced by underhanded deals made out of the sight of the courtroom.

INHERITANCE AND THE STEPPARENT

Whatever relationship the stepparent has established with his or her stepchild over the years, all the support, custody considerations, and rights and responsibilities end at the stepparent's death. The law stands firm on this point. Whatever good intentions the stepparent may have had are irrelevant. The stepchild has no right to a stepparent's inheritance, with one insignificant exception; i.e., some states allow an estate to go to a stepchild if there is no other living relative and the alternative is that the estate would pass into public funds.

The stepchild's position in *in loco parentis* is contradicted at the end of a stepparent's life, returning to the basic premise that stepparent and stepchild are as strangers. The stepparent can fight the system by leaving a will, specifying a specific bequest or bequests to the stepchild. When a will is not made during a person's lifetime, the state makes it for them and says the stepchild almost surely inherits nothing.

Earlier in this chapter it was stated that society sets its own laws. Change is moving in the direction of recognizing stepparent-stepchild relationships. Since the way people live eventually influences the laws that regulate our lives, it is reasonable to suggest the modern stepfamily will some day be more involved in the laws of our land.

CHAPTER 22

Stepparents and Adoption

Adoption may not have been on the stepparent's mind during the court-ship or even in the earlier stages of the marriage, but it may tend to come up as the relationship matures. There are many incentives that might encourage a stepparent to seek to formalize a relationship with a step-child through legal adoption. The idea may come to fruition as an emo-tional response to the desire to create a *real* family atmosphere; that is, transforming a stepfamily into a unit that more closely resembles the traditional family. Sometimes different last names become an incon-venience for the stepfamily, and adoption can provide a common sur-name for all family members who reside in the same home.

Adoption may also be considered as a means of making more visi-ble the real commitment of the non-blood-related parent to the child or children of his or her new spouse. "Even though I did the same for Marie's kids as I did for my own," remarked Matt. "The day I told her I wanted to adopt her two children she said, 'Now we can be a real family.' I always thought we were."

As is true of virtually every other aspect of the step-family, dis-cussion of adoption brings forth both negative and positive opinions. One stepfather may be upset at even the mention of the idea, where another stepfather might anxiously be awaiting an opportunity to sign the adoption papers. Stepmothers also approach the subject with mixed feelings. "Adoption is forever. What if something happens to my husband? Will I still want to be responsible for 'his' kids?"

A stepparent must be aware of the responsibilities which accom-pany adoption. The children are no longer yours or mine, they are ours. Stepfamilies often need more of a sense of closeness, but it sometimes is difficult to attain a true family feeling when stepparents know the child is not legally theirs.

ADVANTAGES AND DISADVANTAGES TO ADOPTION

"Why do you want to adopt your stepchild? She lives in the same household as you do, you raise her according to your standards, and you pay most of her support." There actually are many significant details which separate the stepparent from the adopted parent. Many stepparents look upon their role as a duty. Some may like it, and others may not, and those who do not often feel inadequate to the task. Like it or not, however, most feel a sense of obligation to the relationship.

On the other hand, a prospective adoptive parent looks upon her role differently. She may not have experienced the joys of motherhood. And her new husband's two children need a mother. This stepmother sees her responsibility with a different point of view. While stepparents generally marry and more or less accept the children who come with the new spouse, stepparents who want to adopt parents have given the matter serious thought. They have a burning desire to become parents in every possible sense of the word.

A practical side of adoption is the guaranteed right of a stepchild to inherit from the stepparent's estate. A stepchild who has been raised and loved by a stepparent can be left with nothing except memories unless appropriate legal steps are taken to protect him. The adopting stepparent must act cautiously, however. In some states, adoption by a stepparent severs the right of inheritance from the natural parent who has relinquished parental responsibility.

Adoption also gives the stepparent the power to make medical decisions regarding the stepchild in case of emergency, such as when consent must be given for an operation and the legal parent cannot be reached.

Thoughts of adoption might come into focus in a case where the natural parent has totally abandoned the child. It can then be a psychological benefit to the child, lessening his or her feelings of rejection. Or if the child is very young and the natural parent has died, adoption might serve to give the child more assurance about his or her place in life.

Just as adoption may work to the child's psychological advantage, it also might be a complicating actor. Children often retain a basic need for connection to their roots. Giving everyone in the home the same surname may seem important to some family members, but this act might upset the youngster who is giving up the last hold on his or her heritage. The child may have the inner need to feel good about his or her natural parent, and adoption—with the accompanying name change—symbolizes complete abandonment.

Adults should realize that the human relationship which exists between stepchild and stepparent is more important than changing the child's legal name. If the relationship is good, the adoption will just be a "fringe benefit," with little overall effect. But if the relationship is poor, the adoption will do little to improve it. It sometimes will be met with resistance. Custody rights also are affected by adoption. If anything happens to the biological parent, the adoption gives the stepparent legal custody of the child.

Finances also are affected. With child support laws being enforced more consistently, the stepfamily is under less financial pressure than in past years. Many stepparents will think twice before surrendering the financial assistance which comes from the natural parent. Will the few rights gained by an adoption equal or offset the financial support that is lost? In many cases the stepfather who is receiving child support payments in one home is paying child support into another, and the payments may come close to balancing themselves out. But if the decision is made to adopt, the incoming payment is eliminated.

THE NATURAL PARENT'S ROLE IN ADOPTION

Like it or not, the natural parent is the controlling factor in an adoption proceeding. He or she must decide whether or not to permit it. A father facing the decision claims he still loves his daughter and wants to maintain a good relationship with her. But the relationship is impacted because she feels awkward with her peers and in school. She does not have the same last name as her half-siblings, her mother, and stepfather.

If the father is sincere about maintaining a close relationship with his daughter, he should seriously think twice about his decision and perhaps reject the proposed adoption. However, if his expressed desire to stay close is not sincere, and his real objective is to evade responsibility to his daughter, the adoption might benefit all concerned.

If the child's use of the stepfather's last name is the only issue in question, a suitable compromise usually can be worked out. The child could use the stepfather's last name but legally retain the last name of the natural father. Most schools will go along with such an action if the parents request it. Later, when the child is older and more capable of making a reasoned decision, he or she can decide which last name to use. Reverting to the legal name then becomes easier because the youngster is no longer as deeply involved with the stepfamily unit. He or she can legally change the last name to that of the stepfather without being legally adopted.

Finances come into the picture on all sides of adoption. Just as the stepparent may not want to give up the financial aid coming into the home, the absent parent — who has practically no contact with his child—may be receptive to the adoption for financial reasons. Once a person adopts a child he usually assumes all financial responsibility for the remainder of the child's upbringing, even if the new marriage dissolves.

Sharla and Cliff had been married two years when the decision was made that Cliff would adopt Sharla's four-year-old daughter. Shortly after their fifth wedding anniversary, the marriage dissolved. Cliff said, "If I had known it would end like this I never would have gone through with the adoption. Now I'm paying support for a child who is not blood mine."

A stepfather may sense that his new marriage is not as stable as he wishes and thus may be hesitant to adopt. This thought is in his mind: if the marriage breaks up the children's natural father will still be responsible for their upbringing. However, the wife may try very hard to persuade her new husband to adopt the children in the hope of creating greater financial security for them. Lawyers may even complicate the deliberations more by advising such stepfathers not to adopt and encouraging the mothers to do everything possible to move the adoption proceedings forward. Sometimes these activities are not for the benefit of the child, but are merely undertaken for financial gain.

Greg said, "I was excited about the idea of adopting Susan. My marriage with her mother was good at the time and her father had been killed in Viet Nam before her second birthday. She doesn't remember him and I was the only father she knew. Four years later her mother and I divorced and now I'm paying child support. Some people said I was crazy for strapping myself down, but I have a daughter whom I love very much and it's not her fault that the marriage went sour."

SHOULD CHILDREN BE TOLD THEY ARE ADOPTED?

One of the more serious decisions to be made in an adoption has to do with informing the child. Should we tell? And if so, when? The best time to adopt a stepchild is during early infancy. For this to occur there usually has been either a death or total abandonment by the natural parent. For example, a father abandons his child shortly after birth or during the pregnancy. The mother remarries and the new stepfather adopts the infant. The child is brought up with no distinction made between him and his stepsiblings and there is no memory whatsoever of the natural father. The only father he knows is his stepfather. Should the parents feel obligated to tell the child?

There are a number of good reasons to support telling the child the truth about his background, but the decision remains with the parent. Should the truth ever come out about his true origin he could not help but resent his mother and stepfather for their having withheld this vital information. The sudden shock of the delayed disclosure could bring about lifelong distrust between him and his parents.

Others argue that he will never find out, but in such situations there usually are many people who know the story; friends, relatives, and co-workers. The odds are great that, intentionally or otherwise, the truth will be divulged. Not only is it almost impossible to depend upon dozens of people to maintain secrecy about something so important, it is stressful to live with the constant fear the child will discover the secret.

No matter how hard a stepfather or stepmother tries to conceal true feelings, they find it exceedingly difficult to treat an adopted child as they do a biological child. In situations where there are no other siblings in the home, an adopted child may be treated as if she were a natural child. But even though the child may have been adopted early in its life, she is still someone else's baby. The stepmother did not carry the child inside her for nine months or suffer the pain of delivery. The psychological bond formed by such experiences is deep. When that bond is not there, the mother inevitably does not treat the adopted child in the same ways she treats her natural child. As the child gets older, she comes to recognize this, and no matter how hard parents try to conceal the fact, "mother" or "father" are not really who they say they are.

For the child who is adopted early in life, the same patterns are seen. The youngster has the same drive to acquire information about the departed parent and to express his or her feelings and concerns openly with the parents. Preoccupation about the absent parent can become quite intense, especially during the adolescent years and if the parent is the same sex as the child. Presently there are more people who were adopted as children (by both relative and non-relative) seeking their natural parents than ever before. This is partially due to the increase in adoptions in recent years and to the greater assistance which is available to help adopted individuals trace their roots.

Also, people who have given up children for adoption are seeking information about the children. Organizations have been set up which actively seek to help such parents and children find one another. The belief that there will never be any contact between the natural parent and the child is less prevalent today than in times past.

If it could be guaranteed the child would never discover that he or she was adopted, everyone involved might be better served by keeping that fact a secret. But since there can be no such guarantees, parents must ask themselves: "Why risk ruining a happy home by being dishonest with a child?" Most agree the best time to inform a child is when the child is first able to appreciate what has been done for him in the home; generally between the ages of three and five.

In cases where the natural parent is deceased, the adoption gives the child the parent he or she has been missing. The adopted child usually will react to the situation positively, and will be even more appreciative of the parent's willingness to provide a home. Telling him or her about the adoption will have little consequence.

When a child has been adopted and goes in search of the natural parent it usually is done more out of curiosity than because of any feeling of concern. The adoptive parent should try to be relaxed if this interest develops and ask: "What would I do in the same situation?"

Whatever decision is reached about adoption, it should be made after serious consideration of all the parties involved; the children, the natural parent, and the stepparent. Adoption is not like step relations that cease to exist when the marriage dissolves. Adoption is everlasting.

CHAPTER 23

Grandparents in the Stepfamily

Grandparents may not be part of the immediate household, but they are important members of the overall stepfamily. They generally are looked upon by children as being very special people, especially during hard times. At the time of divorce the grandparent can have a direct influence on everyone involved, the grandchildren and the parents of the grandchildren. Yet too often they are unsure of what to do or how to react, not because they are not concerned but more because the circumstances are new to them.

Just as grandparents are looked upon for support at the time of divorce, they can unintentionally be impediments to the new marriage. One stepfather complained about his wife saying, "All her mother has to do is call and she jumps to her every command. I'm not good enough with the kids, I'm not their real father and shouldn't be telling them what to do, or we don't come to visit them enough. When my wife hangs up the phone she complains to me about her mother, then does everything the woman asked."

Grandparents also can become injured parties in a divorce and remarriage. People can become so involved with their own problems that sometimes they do not realize what effect they are having on the people they love. Many grandparents try too hard to persuade the couple not to divorce. After it happens, the son or daughter tend to shy away, afraid of being criticized, "If you had tried harder you wouldn't be in this situation."

If a third party had an influence on the divorce, the grandparents' remarks could be very direct and hurtful. Even if the new spouse had no influence on the divorce, it is easier to blame an outsider for the break-up of the home than it is a loving son or daughter.

In-laws often considered their son- or daughter-in-law in the first marriage a disappointment because they expected so much more for their child. Parents generally tend to idealize their children, seeing them as smarter, cuter, and better than other people see them. This unrealistic evaluation may be helpful in the growing-up years, when the child needs his or her self-esteem boosted. But when the child contemplates marriage, there is only one kind of person suitable in the eyes of his or her parents—another perfect person. Usually, whomever the son or daughter brings home is not quite good enough, "But if it's who you want, you have our blessing." The second time around the reaction is much different.

The stepparent, the new member of the stepfamily, moves into an existing set of circumstances. He or she becomes a parent to the children overnight parent, without having had the time to get to know them. The situation is similar with the children's grandparents. They have been the grandparents for years, and have their own rules and expectations. The stepparent is the new member, and all the grandparents can see is that he or she is going to have some effect—probably not a good one—on their relationships with the grandchildren.

After the divorce, financial reasons might have forced a son or daughter to return to the security of a parent's home, especially if he or she has custody of the children. When the parent goes to work it's better for the children to be in the care of grandparents. As familiar figures, they can serve as excellent parental substitutes, especially where the grandfather can function as a replacement male figure. Grandparents will almost always love the children more deeply than a housekeeper would and they sometimes will be more aware of their welfare.

These benefits are positive and appreciated after the divorce and before the new marriage. However, during this time, grandparents can become so attached to the children in surrogate parental roles that they will not want to relinquish their authority to an unknown replacement.

The grandparents might take this time to question the children about the new stepparent, trying to uncover any undesirable traits. When this happens, action should be taken immediately. Children can exaggerate a situation, giving the grandparents an unfairly negative picture of the stepparent. Also, the children will learn they have substantial power over the stepparent. "I'll tell Grandma." Seeking the children's love and approval becomes a competition between stepparent and grandparent, with only the children winning.

"Honey, we only care about you." They are legitimately concerned about their child, but they also are concerned about what their friends and other relatives think about the divorce and remarriage. "My mom and dad never came to visit during my first marriage. And in the time after my divorce, when I really needed them, they came only on occasion," exclaimed Rachel. "Since I've married Phil, who is a much better husband to me and father to my boys, they visit constantly, and never cease to criticize everything he does." With all their good intentions, grandparents sometimes create only tension and confusion.

The relationship between stepparent and his stepchildren's grandparents can be touchy. But just as the stepparent has to establish his or her position with the spouse and stepchildren, it sometimes becomes necessary to do the same with grandparents. "I want a good relationship with you and I need your support and understanding. But with or without it, this is now my home and I want to fulfill my obligations as I see fit." There is nothing wrong with standing up for one's rights. Sometimes it is a necessary first step to building a relationship.

THE OTHER SET OF GRANDPARENTS

At the time of a divorce, grandparents are often caught innocently in the middle of a complex set of problems. They must decide where to continue giving their support and trust, at the same time trying not to impact their relationship with the grandchildren. Even with contemporary "No fault" divorce laws, there still is much conflict and bitterness in divorce. The only natural thing for parents to do is stand behind their child. The son-in-law or daughter-in-law who once was loved and accepted as part of the family, now becomes the evil person solely responsible for all the misery and heartache.

The two sets of grandparents, who at one time were very close, frequently become enemies during a divorce. Instead of being helpful, they only add to the tension and confusion the grandchildren are suffering. The parent and stepparent need to point out that just going through the divorce is hard enough on the kids. When they are subjected to the animosity and bitterness between the grandparents, the people who often are the children's anchor during a storm, they feel there is no friendly direction in which they can turn.

No matter what circumstances surrounded the divorce, neither set of grandparents divorced themselves from the grandchildren. The divorce was between the two parents. The last burdens a new stepfamily needs are additional problems created by former in-laws. Although a parent or stepparent cannot be directly responsible for the behavior of grandparents, he or she can influence their conduct.

OPEN THE DOOR

Open the door for a good relationship with the spouse's former in-laws, the children's other set of grandparents. Typically they do not know what to do or how to react to their situation. The divorce has separated them from their grandchildren and they are wondering when they will get to see them again. Their rights are limited and they usually are not included in any visitation unless the son or daughter chooses to share that valuable time with them.

The early days of the new marriage will imprint the deepest marks on these grandparents. For reasons that are not entirely clear, it is not always as easy for older people to forgive and forget. If time can be taken to explain—not necessarily asking them to understand, but just to accept the situation—most of them will be willing to cooperate and try to be helpful. Grandparents who continue to be meddlesome and unnecessarily antagonistic must be counseled, gently but firmly.

Recommend to the spouse that a simple contact be made. Offering a weekend or even some time in the summer can renew relationships between the children and their grandparents. These grandparents also can turn out to be some of the best baby sitters a person could find, as long as they are not taken for granted. Don't call them only for favors, but keep them informed about the children and involved in their lives and often they will gladly volunteer their services. But first you must open the door.

NOW THERE IS A THIRD SET

Divorce and remarriage almost always produce more problems than anticipated. None of them are minor, and no one of them will "work itself out." The traditional family produced "our" kids and two fine sets of grandparents. The new stepfamily provides "his" kids, "my" kids, and sometimes "our" kids. Not only are there the two sets of traditional grandparents, there is now a third set—the new spouse's parents, better known as the stepgrandparents. Though they are not blood-related to the grandchildren, they are very much a part of the new stepfamily.

Grandparents often find themselves in the middle of complex situations, with their natural grandchildren sometimes unavailable to them. Janet's two girls live in the home with their mother and Clifford's, their stepfather, while Clifford's three children live with his ex-wife. Clifford's parents get to see very little of their grandchildren since visitation is so limited, but now that he has remarried, Janet's girls are always there when the stepgrandparents come to visit.

There often are several ways to respond to this dilemma. Some stepgrandparents give their new stepgrandchildren warm affection, treating them as equals to their own grandchildren. They still try hard to maintain affectionate contact with their natural grandchildren, and everyone is satisfied that the best possible results are being obtained.

Then there are those who resent their circumstances. "We can no longer see our own grandchildren as we would like and we're not going to treat these stepchildren of yours as though they were ours."

Sometimes it is necessary to take grandparents aside and firmly tell them the facts of life as they now exist. "My kids still need you and we're going to do everything to keep you in contact with them. But now I have a new home with additional stepchildren. If we are going to maintain a good relationship, you'll have to accept what I am and what I have, and that includes my stepchildren."

Some adults are much like children. Until they have learned the rules, they are confused. They may not like what is going on but, if they want to maintain family ties, they will have to live with it. The fact some grandparents have a tendency to feel sorry for themselves doesn't help matters. Encourage them to make contact with the ex-spouse for the sake of the children. It's awkward and it can be difficult, but they should not let the divorce stop them from seeing the kids.

The whole concept of step-life is to achieve a family life that will give every member a sense of belonging. Anytime one member feels slighted or unwanted, the struggle for completeness is set back. Ask all relatives to be equal in their involvement with every other member, whether it is a blood relative or a step-relative.

CHAPTER 24

Let Them Be Parents

The intent of this book is to help stepparents live a good life within the framework they have chosen, the stepfamily. However, no matter how hard a stepparent tries, the key to the success of this new unit is in the hands of the natural parent—the stepparent's spouse who lives in the household.

These few pages are written exclusively for those stepparent spouses, the natural parents, and the principal message is: "You married them. Now let them be parents."

We have explored the legal rights of a stepparent in an earlier chapter. While this is a body of law in need of a thorough airing—and subject to much disagreement—the laws presently on the books stand as written and must be obeyed. One "right" a stepparent has that is often refused is his or her right to be a parent in the home.

Stepparenting is described as stepping into a role which has been vacated. A mother or father has been separated from the children by death or divorce and the stepparent has, by marriage, moved into that place. For often unknown reasons, the spouse who is the natural parent, refuses to allow the stepparent the right to fulfill his or her new parental responsibility.

Having responsibility without compensating authority is both confusing and frustrating. A man is expected by his new wife to take over the leadership of the home, but he is not allowed to lead the children who reside within it. A wife who is not allowed to mother her stepchildren cannot perform her role as mother of the home adequately.

"When Donna and I dated," said Mel, "She always talked about how her boys needed a father who would properly discipline them. The year and a half since their father died had been hard on her, and the boys had gotten completely out of control. We have been married two years now and every time I try to make them mind, she gets defensive and says, 'You think I'm not a good mother?' It's not a question of her motherhood, but it's my fatherhood that's hurting. I remind her of what she said about the boys needing a dad, but she won't let me be one."

Children will never learn to respect a parent or a stepparent who

210 ~ STEP-BY STEP-PARENTING

will not discipline them, even if that person wants to but can't because of the spouse's interference.

"Mike's three children only come on alternating weekends and one month during the summer," complained Gloria. "I shouldn't say it, but I'm glad they don't visit more. Mike directs them in everything. If I try to tell them something he interrupts and says I don't understand. He doesn't want to admit that the kids get on his nerves and that I might be of some help. He's trying to be both a father and mother both and he really does not have to."

Parents will find all sorts of excuses to keep the stepparent from fulfilling his or her role. But the parent should understand that by denying a stepparent's right to be an active parent, he or she also is frustrating the stepfamily's opportunity to enjoy the feeling of completeness.

PRIDE STANDS IN THE WAY

Pride, one of the seven deadly sins, often is the principal reason why parents try to stop a new spouse from enjoying parenthood. "I made it three and a half years without a man's help with my three kids and I don't expect you to do it now!" It's not that she doesn't want to burden her spouse with the responsibility of helping to raise the children, she just is too proud to admit she needs help. "My wife is one of the most stubborn people I know," said Jess. "She refuses to admit that the kids are too much for her and that they are driving her crazy."

It is not a matter of asking a stepparent to help. That is the wrong language to use to describe the situation. It's not asking, it is letting the stepparent take an active part in home and family matters. Recognizing the job is too much for one person is not a sign of weakness. Raising children is, by its nature, a two person job. By refusing to allow the stepparent a chance to share in the difficult/rewarding job of raising your children, you are refusing to let them share an important part of your life.

When both she and he have brought children to the stepfamily, it is hard not to compare and complain about the other person's kids. After the husband has complained about the things his wife's youngsters did or did not do, it's difficult for him to admit that his child had not been exactly angelic either. The husband and wife need to unite in parenthood to raise *their* children, no matter who the natural parent is.

HARBORING JEALOUS FEELINGS

Jealousy can cause problems in any relationship. Whenever one person becomes envious or resentful of another, emotions tend to take over. "When I married Hal, my two girls, ages twelve and seven, fell in love with him. He was the ideal husband and stepdad," Cheryl said. "I really wanted him to take over just as though he were their real father. But after a time, I felt they cared more for him than me, their 'real' mother. I tried not to let Hal know my feelings, and the only way I could handle the situation was to take back the responsibility to discipline the girls. I actually have accomplished nothing. Hal resents me for not letting him make the girls behave. The girls have learned that I am not as consistent with discipline and they're getting away with more things than they should."

It is hard to cope with feelings of jealousy. But as long as those feelings stay under control they do not pose a serious problem. But when those feelings get out of control, people tend to act more from their emotions than from a foundation of good common sense.

A spouse harboring jealous feelings should think about the advantages of a good stepparent-stepchild relationship. Instead of pondering on what you "think" you have lost, be thankful for what you have. In most cases a good stepparent-stepchild relationship will draw the entire family more closely together. Everyone will benefit, including you, the parent.

AFRAID TO LET GO

The stepparent's arrival in the new stepfamily is not easy, but it also is a frightening experience for the parent. The parent, mother or father, has been through some trying times. The departure of a spouse by death or divorce has left the remaining parent to raise his or her children alone. Even if the parent was divorced, did not have custody of the children and saw them only on alternate weekends, there was no one to turn to at those awkward times.

The parents had to be both mother and father to the children. With all the responsibilities falling on one pair of shoulders, what transpired during that period may have changed the parent's attitude to parenthood. Now that there is another parent in the home, it is not easy to relinquish any of that unilateral authority to another person. "I have done it by myself for so long, I just can't let go."

It may not be easy, but it is something that has to be done, or the marriage will suffer. It may require releasing some parental authority a little at a time and keeping the mouth shut a lot of the time.

Parental responsibility is a natural job for two people. The traditional family had two parents to share the burden. Why shouldn't it be the same in the stepfamily? The stepparent will never really feel part of the family until he or she is included in everything.

UNQUALIFIED

The fact that a new spouse has never had children is not an excuse to keep him or her from sharing yours. Many men entering a second marriage will choose younger women, many of whom have not experienced motherhood. And it is likely some of them never will, because of the husband's age or for financial reasons.

212 ~ STEP-BY STEP-PARENTING

A new wife's willingness should be enough to qualify her for the job. She will not have experienced the earlier stages of the child's life, but she should not be considered unqualified for the job until she has been given a fair chance.

STUBBORN AND BULLHEADED

When a parent uses phrases like "You don't know" or "You don't understand" he or she usually is really saying "We're going to do it my way no matter what!" There are going to be times when the stepparent is not aware of what the child has been through or the pressures which lie ahead. But that is not fair reason to exclude them. If the stepparent does not understand a particular situation, a good explanation should bring them up to speed.

A combination of feelings of guilt and stubbornness can cause many parents to be lenient in the administration of discipline. When a stepparent attempts to instruct the child, the parent's guilt feelings lead her to interfere, frustrating the stepparent's efforts to build a good relationship with the child. Then the parent eases her guilt feelings by relaxing normal disciplinary limits. "You don't understand what that child has been through," she says. Whatever the stepparent tries to do, it is not right, or it not good enough.

The parent must work through his or her guilt feelings and focus on the needs of a stable home. The hopes and dreams of many second marriages are dashed by failed attempts at relationships between stepchild and stepparent. Parents who deny the stepparent his or her chance to be an equal partner in the family clearly jeopardize the success of their marriages.

Many people look upon the second marriage stepfamily as a continuation of an existing family, with the addition of one new member, the stepparent. That is wrong thinking. Even though most members of the original family are still present, the second marriage constitutes a new beginning. The stepfamily is a new family which needs a fresh new start.

CHAPTER 25

Older Stepchildren

Sometimes the stepparent feels the challenge is to survive in the marriage until the stepchildren grow up and leave the home. But one question remains: What about the older children who already have left the nest? "What about us? We have our lives to live and they have theirs." That is true, but building a good relationship with older stepchildren is still important to the marriage and the stepfamily.

In previous years, most of the individuals fifty years old or older who remarried were those who had lost a spouse due to death. But now that the divorce laws have eased, it seems as though there are no age limits or restraints on divorce and remarriage. It is not uncommon for a man over fifty who has been married for twenty years or more to divorce and marry a woman many years younger.

It is not the intent of this book to analyze the reasons for those divorces. The fact is, they are happening. What happens to the grown children?

No matter what their ages, stepchildren will put a strain on the marriage relationship. "I just don't love his kids the same way I do mine." The stepparent is burdened with guilt because of his or her lack of concern for the child—really the young adult.

Obstacles still can exist in relationships with older stepchildren who have left the nest and are out on their own, but in most cases stepparents find less pressure here than with a stepchild living in the household. Though problems do exist with both young and older stepchildren, they tend to be less complex with the older ones. Most expert observers believe the age of the stepparent usually will determine what type of relationship can be built.

YOUNG ADULT STEPDAUGHTER

A young woman who marries a man with older children can expect any number of reactions. A great deal of what she will experience will depend upon the surrounding circumstances. Did the father leave his wife for the younger woman? Did the mother initiate the divorce? Or, is the father a widower? If the father divorced with the intent of marrying the younger woman, the children are likely to resent their new stepmother. Those feelings are likely to continue, particularly if the natural mother keeps adding fuel to the flames of anger.

Once the fire has died down the resentment soon dies with it, friendly relationships can be established. The hope is that will happen quickly. The stepmother and father can do very little to hurry the process.

Where the mother initiated the divorce and the father then married a younger woman, the age difference is more a shock than resentment and is easier to handle. Most young adults are satisfied if they are told ahead of time of such important decisions. Feelings of jealousy may develop when the stepmother is attractive and close in age to the stepdaughter. Once the shock wears off, however, and it should not take long, a good relationship should be attainable.

A young stepmother would be wise to avoid any attempts to mother her older stepdaughter. When the stepdaughter asks for advice, it usually is within the context of friendship. Respond as a friend.

If the father is a widower, his daughter usually wants someone close to her mother's age for her father. If the father marries a younger woman without consulting her, her feelings will be hurt, but she is not likely to express her feelings openly. As long as the stepmother—no matter what her age—does not try to fill her mother's shoes, a good relationship can be created.

When a father has left his wife and children for a younger woman, the children's sympathies stay with their mother. Even though the children still want to stay close to their natural father, the relationship is strained because of their feelings of abandonment. If his new, younger wife has children, the older stepfather can move into a fatherly role quickly. His natural daughter may still need "older male" involvement in her life; someone to fix her car, for example, or give her financial advice. If the natural father's new home is close by he should have opportunities for good relationships with both daughter and stepchildren.

If mother initiated the divorce and remarries soon thereafter, her daughter—the new stepdaughter—may resent her new husband. But if he plays has part cautiously, he should be able to gain her respect fairly quickly. How cautiously? Do not criticize her father. Do not move too quickly into her father's role, and respect her feelings about her father and the entire divorce-remarriage situation. The new stepdaughter soon should be a friend.

There is no uncertainty about a daughter's feelings when her father dies. She loved him and no one can take his place. But she should not expect her mother to live the remainder of her life alone. The young adult daughter knows this. A good mother and daughter talk before the wedding will pave the way for any decent stepfather, and the three should soon become a "real" family.

WHEN THEY ARE FRIENDS

The circumstances are very different when the father marries a friend of his daughter. "I may have to see you when I visit my father, but don't think I'm here for any kind of relationship with you!"

Allen, a handsome physician of 47, became attracted to Michelle shortly after his first wife's death. Since Allen's daughter Sharon and Michelle were roommates at college it wasn't unusual for Michelle to spend her weekends in their home. She would even join Sharon and her father for dinner on special occasions. Since she was a biology major in college, she found it interesting to talk with him. One thing led to another and one evening Allen telephoned Michelle for a date. The rest is history ... until they broke the news to Sharon.

The shock of finding out your father just married your best friend can be devastating to a young woman. She has difficulty coping with the feelings that she was used by her friend and by her father. The hurt and betrayal that she feels cannot be alleviated by a few kind words. When this happens, the father usually starts his little talk with "Honey I want you to understand." But how can she? She thinks that both her father and best friend made a fool out of her.

The young stepmother has to ask herself how she would feel if it happened to her. The father and stepmother can only hope that time and thoughtful efforts to rebuild the relationships will heal the hurt. Often they will.

STEPPARENT AND OLDER STEPSON

A young stepmother's relationship to her older stepson can include its share of mixed feelings. A young man who already has left the nest does not want to give the impression that what happens in the family affects him one way or the other. His reaction to his new stepmother often will reflect the relationship he has with his father. Even if his father initiated the divorce, if it is close and personal the son will not be as rebellious toward his new stepmother, as long as she tries to co-operate.

A too-friendly approach by a young stepmother might lead to a stepson's infatuation. Later he may be so embarrassed by his actions he will withdraw from the relationship. A wise stepmother will work at maintaining a friendly relationship, at the same time making her intentions clear. The father, son, and stepmother can become a compatible trio.

When a stepson harbors resentment toward his stepmother and re-fuses to reach out to her, there is little she can do no matter what her age. An older stepson's feeling of independence frees him from any need to lean on a stepmother for parental guidance. He may desire her friendship, but he'll pass when it comes to asking her advice. A sensible step-son would appreciate what his stepmother can do for him, even if he lives out of the home, but no one can do his thinking for him.

Stepfathers who marry after his new wife's son has left home have practically no influence on a relationship. But good feelings between mother and son can promote togetherness between stepfather and stepson. A son's main concern is for the safety and happiness of his mother. Even when she is the one who initiated the divorce, it usually will not effect his feelings toward his stepfather.

MARRIED STEPCHILDREN

Married stepchildren have a tendency to think more sensibly than younger children. They have certain basic concerns about their parent's new marriage. Is he or she a good person? Will he or she be good to my younger brothers and sisters who are still at home? And, what about his or her financial status?

Older children are more prone to be protective, wanting to keep their parents from further hurt. Some children will go as far as having the future stepparent's background investigated. One question every person contemplating remarriage should consider is this: "Will he or she damage my reputation?" In most cases, the person in love—even an older person—is too involved emotionally to think straight. Some-one else must do it for them.

The younger person has the parents to serve as protectors. But when the parent is getting married, an older child generally is the one who tries to be protective. A child will seldom change a parent's mind about marriage. However, if the person will listen to anyone it is most apt to be a child who is married.

Concern for younger siblings still in the home is common for the married stepchild. Some of these children have kids of their own and parental instincts are beginning to manifest themselves. And if a young-ster moves out of the home prematurely, where is he or she apt to go? Usually to an older brother or sister's house. A problem solved ahead of time often can prevent a larger problem from occurring later.

Usually their financial status will change anytime two people mar-ry. Sometimes it is for the better, and other times it is not. Whichever situation exists, the adult stepchild might be giving this some serious thought. If his or her father worked hard to provide for the well-being of his family, these kids do not want some stranger taking it from them and their mother. Or, it might be the opposite situation; a father has wealth and his children do not want it shared with a stepmother.

If the married stepchildren care seriously about their natural par-ents, it should not be difficult for a stepparent to establish positive re-lationships with them. Often a good person to person talk can express the stepparent's genuine interest in their mother or father. If the new spouse really cares, a little extra time spent making friends with the stepchildren can do wonders for the marriage?

IT LOOKS HELPLESS

Sometimes, no matter how much stepparents give or how hard they work to make others accept them, it just doesn't work. The adult children are completely intractable. That's the time when the couple must sit down and share their true feelings with each other. If the wedding has not taken place, they may decide the children simply are too much of an obstacle to overcome. Or they may decide to go ahead with the marriage with or without their blessings.

If the children are selfish in their thinking and concerned only with themselves, nothing will help. If they truly are interested in a mother or father's happiness, they will come to accept the situation—especially when they see the happiness in their parent's life.

"I objected to my mother's marriage plans seven years ago," recalled Adam. "And I have regretted it ever since. The man she wanted to marry was very good to her, and I was thinking only of myself when I finally talked her out of it. His work was requiring him to relocate and I didn't want to have my mother move away. She has lived alone ever since. Now I have the guilt of depriving her of some happy years."

A smart stepparent will appreciate what his or her stepchildren are doing for their parent and will not consider it interference. If it actually is interference, the stepparent can always set them straight. Once their love and respect has been won they often will care for the stepparent in the same way they do their parent.

That's not a bad deal.

Conclusion

Every person will have situations in life over which he or she has little control. Usually the individual will reap what he has sown. In a stepfamily, most relationships are determined by two factors—the stepparent's actions and the stepchild's responses.

A stepparent might do everything in his or her power to establish a positive relationship with a rebellious stepchild only to have those efforts rejected. There also are times when a stepparent's concern and affection for a hurting child will lead that child to a warm and loving relationship.

The happiness and satisfaction for which most people are searching does not come so much from what they receive out of life as it does from their feeling about themselves. "I have done my best," is all anyone can expect from himself or from other people. When a stepparent looks at what he or she has done in the stepfamily and is satisfied, knowing "I have done my best," that person can live with almost anything that happens. But when a person could have done more, and knows it, an intense feeling of dissatisfaction develops.

Step-parenting is not easy, but in most situations a little extra effort pays off. Do not let just surviving satisfy you. Make the best of the situation.

Index

A complete catalog of Betterway Books is available FREE by writing to the address shown below, or by calling toll-free 1-800-289-0963. To order additional copies of this book, send in retail price of the book plus $3.00 postage and handling for one book, and $1.00 for each additional book. Ohio residents add 5½% sales tax. Allow 30 days for delivery.

Betterway Books
1507 Dana Avenue
Cincinnati, Ohio 45207